AF564676

INDIA AND CHINA IN THE ASIAN CENTURY
Global Economic Power Dynamics

INDIA AND CHINA IN THE ASIAN CENTURY

Global Economic Power Dynamics

Edited by

P. JEGADISH GANDHI
Founder-Director
Vellore Institute of Development Studies (VIDS)
Vellore

DEEP & DEEP PUBLICATIONS PVT. LTD.
F-159, Rajouri Garden, New Delhi - 110 027

INDIA AND CHINA IN THE ASIAN CENTURY
Global Economic Power Dynamics

ISBN 81-7629-985-5

Printed in India at MAYUR ENTERPRISES,
WZ Plot No. 3, Gujjar Market, Tihar Village, New Delhi - 110 018.

Published by DEEP & DEEP PUBLICATIONS PVT. LTD.,
F-159, Rajouri Garden, New Delhi - 110 027 • Phone : 25435369, 25440916
E-mail : deep98@del3.vsnl.net.in • ddpbooks@yahoo.co.in
Showroom :
2/13, Ansari Road, Daryaganj, New Delhi - 110 002 • Telefax : 23245122

Contents

Preface

Today, any news about India and China is daily bread of discussion all over the world. Far from demarcating the territorial "border" lines in the third quarter of the 20th century to dovetailing with the cross-borderless trade development linkages in the first quarter of the 21st century, India and China has come a long way in new geo-political and economic strategies in Asia.

Following are excerpts from the Joint Declaration by the Indian Prime Minister Manmohan Singh and the Chinese President Hu Jintao issued on 21st November, 2006 at New Delhi.

"The leaders of the two countries have noted with satisfaction the all-round progress made over recent years in India-China relations and their regional and multilateral cooperation. They reiterate the shared vision and fundamental principles for the future development of India-China relations, as embodied in the Declaration on Principles for Relations and Comprehensive Cooperation of 23 June, 2003 and the Joint Statement of 11 April, 2005 signed between the Prime Ministers of the two countries.

Both sides agree that the relationship between India and China, the two biggest developing countries in the world, is of global and strategic significance. Both countries are seeking to avail themselves of historic opportunities for development. Each side welcomes and takes a positive view of the development of the other, and considers the development of either side as a positive contribution to peace, stability and prosperity of Asia and the world. Both sides hold the view that there exist bright prospects for their common development, *that they are not rivals or competitors but are partners for mutual benefit* (Italics mine). They agree that there is enough space for them to grow together, achieve a higher scale of development, and play their respective roles in the region and beyond, while remaining sensitive to each other's concerns and aspirations. Strategic partnership between the two countries with a similar worldview is consistent with their roles as two major developing countries. With the growing participation and role of the two countries in all key issues in today's globalising world, their partnership is vital for international efforts to deal with global challenges and threats. As two major countries in the emerging multi-polar global order, the simultaneous development of India and China will have a positive influence on the future international system.

In order to promote the sustainable socio-economic development of India and China, to fully realise the substantial potential for their cooperation in a wide range of areas, to upgrade India-China relations to a qualitatively new level, and to further substantiate and reinforce their Strategic and Cooperative Partnership, the leaders of the two countries have committed themselves to pursuing the following *"ten-pronged strategy"*:

I. Ensuring Comprehensive Development of Bilateral Relations.
II. Strengthening Institutional Linkages and Dialogue Mechanisms.
III. Consolidating Commercial and Economic Exchanges.
IV. Expanding All-Round Mutually Beneficial Cooperation.
V. Instilling Mutual Trust and Confidence through Defence Cooperation.
VI. Seeking Early Settlement of Outstanding Issues.
VII. Promoting Trans-border Connectivity and Cooperation.
VIII. Boosting Cooperation in Science and Technology.
IX. Revitalising Cultural Ties and Nurturing People-to-People Exchanges.
X. Expanding Cooperation on Regional and International Stage.

Both sides believe that comprehensive economic and commercial engagement between India and China is a core component of their Strategic and Cooperative Partnership. They will endeavour to raise the volume of their bilateral trade to US $ 40 billion by 2010. They shall make joint efforts to diversify their trade basket, remove existing impediments, and optimally utilise the present and potential complementarities in their economies, in order to sustain and further strengthen bilateral commercial and economic cooperation. Towards this end, both sides will attach utmost priority to an early implementation of the decisions taken in March 2006 by the Ministerial-level Joint Economic Group, including the recommendations of the Joint Study Group, through mechanisms already created for this purpose. The Joint Task Force set up to study the feasibility and benefits of an India-China Regional Trading Arrangement shall complete its work by October 2007.

Bearing in mind the priority attached by India and China to scientific and technological development and innovation as a cornerstone of their efforts towards sustainable socio-economic development, the two sides shall establish an India-China Partnership in Science and Technology. The two sides welcome the establishment of the Ministerial-level Committee on Science and Technology Cooperation as a positive step in guiding, coordinating and facilitating cooperative activities. They agree to launch joint projects in the areas of (i) earthquake engineering, (ii) climate change and weather forecasting, (iii) nano-technology with focus on advanced materials, and (iv) biotechnology and medicines with focus on bio-nano. The cooperation framework shall include entrepreneurs on both sides, besides the two Governments and their respective institutions.

As two large developing countries with relatively successful developmental experiences, India and China share unique responsibilities to protect and promote the interests of the developing world in the emerging international order and to help them benefit from the positive forces of globalisation.

The two sides agree to strengthen their cooperation in the World Trade Organisation. They support the establishment of an open, fair, equitable, transparent and rule-based multilateral trading system, early resumption of Doha negotiations, and are determined to safeguard the legitimate rights and interests of the developing countries. As founder Members of the G-20 and the G-33, they are determined to strengthen their cooperation and to coordinate with other members of the WTO, especially the developing countries, in order to secure an early resumption of the negotiations on the Doha Work Programme, placing the development dimension at its heart.

Recognising that regional integration is an important feature of the emerging international economic order, the two sides agree to expand their coordination within regional organisations and explore a new architecture for closer regional cooperation in Asia. They positively view each other's participation in Asian inter-regional, regional and sub-regional cooperation process, including in the progress towards the East Asian Community. In this context, the two sides agree to cooperate closely in the East Asia Summit. The Indian side welcomes China's attainment of observer status in the South Asian Association for Regional Cooperation. The Chinese side welcomes India's membership of the Asia-Europe Meeting. The two sides agree to expand their cooperation on issues on common interest under the Shanghai Cooperation Organisation.

They also agree that this Joint Statement provides a valuable blueprint for enduring development and diversification of the relations between India and China and sustained enrichment of their strategic partnership."

The joint declaration issued by New Delhi and Beijing during the visit by the Chinese President, Mr. Hu Jintao, provides one more proof of Beijing's keenness on pursuing the line of a 'strategic partnership' with India instead of a policy of 'great power rivalry', which marked bilateral relations since the late 1950s till around the mid-1990s. Beijing has its reasons for such a change in policy but for New Delhi the present should provide an opportunity for engaging in closer cooperation with a compatriot Asian 'economic powerhouse' for maximum economic gains.

(Editorial: *The Hindu-Business Line*, November 24, 2006).

II

Vellore Institute of Development Studies (VIDS) was started in September 1996 as a registered organization to synthesize divergences and convergences in societal transformation with a Mission statement "Empowered to empower the 'least' in the society i.e., the true service to humanity and Almighty."

In the past ten years (1996-2006), VIDS has, through its three strategic Aces—Awareness, Advocacy and Alliance empowered socially suppressed sections, especially the bonded labourers and child labourers, enabled people to formalise opinions and viewpoints on contemporary public issues, impacted the policy-makers on contextual socio-economic concerns, networked with the Asian, National and local NGOs on mutual areas of social concern and programmes and enriched the academic and church communities with periodical debates, discussions and dialogues on the latest social concern initiatives and alternatives.

The most notable events conducted include: the first Workshop on "The Role of Elected Sathuvachari Panchayat Leaders" (1996), 84th Annual Conference of the Indian Economic Association (2001), an Afro-Asian Interfaith Meet (2002), Symposium on Child Labour with the Japanese Labour Union Leaders (2005), Orientation Lecturers on Indian Socio-economy to the visiting Japanese Teams, Abolition of Bonded Labour Awareness Seminars in Vellore, Thiruvannamalai and Thiruvallur districts in Tamil Nadu and successful advocacy of alliance-strategies to eradication of child labour system.

VIDS has contributed significantly to the public bus transport performance evaluation studies and pricing policies as an Expert member in the formulation of Ninth (1997-2002) and Tenth (2002-2007) Five Year Plans of the State Planning Commission, Government of Tamil Nadu and with Academic Council membership impacted the educational programmes of Vellore Institute of Technology (Deemed University) and Thiruvalluvar University, Vellore and special lecturers in honour of great Indian economists, Malcolm Adiseshiah, P.R. Brahmananda and the Nobel Laureate, Amartya Sen.

VIDS has published 30 books on various facets of Asian and National level socio-economic concerns and perspectives. The contextual most outstanding publication is *The Socio-Economic Thoughts of A.P.J. Abdul Kalam (2004),*—President of India and its Tamil and Telugu versions. Two more books are also added—*Dr. Kalam's PURA Model and Societal Transformation*

(2005) and *Dr. Abdul Kalam's Futuristic India* (2006). P. Jegadish Gandhi, Founder-Director VIDS and his wife had the privilege of meeting with the President of India on 27th June 2005 at Rashtrapati Bhavan, New Delhi.

VIDS is networking with Association of Christian Institutes for Social Concern in Asia (ACISCA, Japan), Anti-Slavery International (London), Informal Service Centre (Nepal), Association for the Rural Poor (ARP—Chennai), Tamil Nadu Forum for Eradication of Bonded Labour System (Trichy), *Udhavum Ullangal* (Helping Hearts, Vellore), Centre for Education and Communication (CEC—New Delhi) and Ecumenical Christian Centre (ECC—Bangalore).

III

In recognition of its decadal services, the VIDS has been admitted as the first mofussil member-centre in the Association of Christian Institutes for Social Concern in Asia (ACISCA) at the 10th General Assembly of the ACISCA held at Chiangmai, Thailand during October 8-12, 2006.

To mark the decennial celebrations, VIDS has proposed to bring out two Commemorative volumes—*Disaster Mitigation and Management: Post-Tsunami Perspectives* and *India and China in the Asian Century: Global Economic Power Dynamics.*

VIDS is committed to identify the young talents and empower them through the "thrown-up" challenges. I would like to proclaim that G. Narasimha Raghavan, Research Fellow and Ph.D. Research Scholar, Department of Economics, PSG Arts College of Arts and Science, Coimbatore signifies the presence of great many highly talented young academics and devoted researchers in our local colleges. I record my deep appreciation and thanks to Raghavan who has ably undertaken the tedious task of browsing the lengthy materials and of preparing a highly commendable comprehensive "Introduction" to this commemorative volume on "India and China."

I record my thanks to Professors: A. Ranga Reddy (SV University Tirupati), Md. Abdus Salam (Aligarh Muslim University), M.S. Kallur (Gulbarga University) and S. Iyyampillai (Bharathidasan University) and, the Research scholars, P. Balamurugan and G. Narasimha Raghavan for their invited papers.

Apart from academics, I have drawn heavily on the published materials in leading newspapers and journals in India and abroad on the super economic power dynamics of India and China. My sincere thanks are due to all of them in a special way.

Friendly thanks are due to Prof. S. Thiagukumar, Voorhees College, Vellore for help in language work of the manuscript and Mr. L. Pradeep Kumar and Ms. S. Sasikala, SLN Xerox, Sathuvachari, Vellore for their diligent computer work.

I personally thank Mr. G.S. Bhatia, Managing Director, Deep and Deep Publications Pvt. Ltd., New Delhi to bring out not only these Special volumes, but also 11 other books published in the past ten years for Vellore Institute of Development Studies.

P. JEGADISH GANDHI
Founder-Director, VIDS

Acknowledgements

Special thanks are due to the Editor of ***Manorama*** for reproducing two cover stories—*India and China: Towards a Cooperative Partnership in the 21st Century for Asian Peace and Prosperity* by C.N. Ranganathan and *India has come of Age* by Ashok Jacob—from the Year Book 2006.

Sincere thanks are due to the Editor of *Outlook—Business* for reproducing two lead articles by Ashish Gupta—*The Asian Century* and *Power of One*—from the Special Issue: India & China (5 June 2006).

Courtesy thanks are due to the Editors of *The Hindu* and *The Hindu Business Line,* Chennai for the reprint of the articles by their freelance journalists.

P. JEGADISH GANDHI

List of Contributors

1. **Dr. Md. Abdus Salam**, Dept. of Economics, Aligarh Muslim University, Aligarh.
2. **Dr. Andy Xie**, Hong Kong-based Economist covering Asia for Morgan Stanley.
3. **Mr. Ajai Chowdhry**, Chairman and CEO of HCL Infosystems Ltd.
4. **Dr. Alok Ray**, Professor of Economics, Indian Institute of Management, Kolkata.
5. **Mr. Ashish Gupta,** Senior Editor, Outlook, New Delhi.
6. **Mr. Ashok Jacob**, Joint Chief Executive Officer, Consolidated Press Holdings Ltd., Australia.
7. **Mr. P. Balamurugan**, Research Scholar, Dept. of Economics, Bharathidasan Unviersity, Tiruchirappalli.
8. **Mr. Batuk Gathani**, Columnist, *The Hindu-Business Line,* Chennai.
9. **Dr. C.P. Chandrasekhar**, Jawaharlal Nehru University, New Delhi.
10. **Dr. Dan Steinbock**, ICT Research Director of the India, China and America (ICA) Institute—a US—based think-tank.
11. **Dr. S. Iyyampillai**, Reader in Economics, Bharathidasan University, Tiruchirappalli.
12. **Dr. Jayati Ghosh**, Jawarharlal Nehru University, New Delhi.
13. **Dr. P. Jegadish Gandhi**, Founder-Director, Vellore Institute of Development Studies, (VIDS), Vellore.

14. **Dr. Jorge Heine**, Ambassador of Chile to India.
15. **Dr. Juan Somavia**, Director-General, International Labour Organisation (ILO)
16. **Dr. M.S. Kallur**, Chairperson and Professor, Dept. of Economics, Gulbarga University, Gulbarga.
17. **Dr. S. Majumder**, Advisor, Japan External Trade Organisation, New Delhi.
18. **Mr. G. Narasimha Raghavan**, Project Fellow and Ph.D. Research Scholar, Dept. of Economics, PSG College of Arts and Science, Coimbatore.
19. **Ms. Pallavi Aiyar**, Columnist, *The Hindu*, Chennai.
20. **Dr. Qiu Yonhui**, Research Professor, The Chinese Academy of Social Sciences.
21. **Dr. Ramgopal Agarwal**, Formerly a Senior Advisor at the World Bank, Senior Advisor, Research and Information System for Developing Countries (RIS), New Delhi.
22. **Dr. A. Ranga Reddy**, Professor of Economics, S.V. University, Tirupati.
23. **Dr. C.V. Ranganathan**, Formerly Ambassador in China & France.
24. **Ms. Rasheeda Bhagat**, Columnist, *The Hindu-Business Line*, Chennai.
25. **Dr. R. Seshasayee**, President, Confederation of Indian Industry (CII).
26. **Mr. S. Sethuraman**, A Former Chief Editor of PTI and a Freelance Journalist.
27. **Mr. G. Srinivasan**, Columnist, *The Hindu-Business Line*, Chennai.
28. **Mr. K. Subramaniam**, A Former Finance Ministry Official.
29. **Dr. Sumit K. Majumdar**, Professor of Technology Strategy, University of Texas at Dallas, U.S.A.
30. **Dr. M.S. Swaminathan**, Renowned Agricultural Scientist and Chairman, National Commission on Farmers.
31. **Dr. S. Venkitaramanan**, Former Governor, Reserve Bank of India.
32. **Dr. A. Vasudevan**, Former Executive Director of the Reserve Bank of India.

Introduction

"It's not India *versus* China in future. It's India and China,"
—*Krishna Palepu*

Perspicacity is a *sine qua non* for every keen observer of global power relations. And it is this magnitude of discernment that has made Nehru to take cognizance of India and China's joint renaissance as a beacon to "symbolize the new spirit of Asia". Deng Xiaoping of China was no less short of Nehru's sanguinity when he stated with blasé attitude, "The 21st century can only be the Asian century if India and China combine to make it so". To put on record statements as heavy as this, in times as shadowy as was then, was nothing in short of a vision a visualization to see the rise of nations that were smothered due to colonial powers and internal dissensions. Incidentally, the way to achieve this vision was not trouble-free. The dreamers have been laid to rest, but nightmares in the form of The Great Leap (1958-60) of China, and the Emergency (1975-77) of India stifled the growth of these nations. Years of inertia and inward-looking policies, by the beginning of 1980s—substantially in China and to a small extent in India—gave way to liberalized policy measures and a scheme to usher in an 'open economy'. Things started to perk-up by the 1990s, with gyrating economic performance and mounting clout in the international showground, reaffirming Lal's avowal that "At long last, the two Asian giants seem to be on the move". It is precisely here that we need to explore what the book's subtitle, *Global Economic Power Dynamics,* connotes and signifies.

The Age of Metaphors and Allegories

It is no longer eclectically expedient to use hackneyed analogies like 'China and India: Making of a Next Japan'. This epoch has been marked by limiting analogies and systems of equivalence. Rather, the observance of comparing nations, of late, has transcended the literal use of words and metamorphed into in figurative phrases. An apparent example is the not-so-odd metaphorical allusions made to nations comparing them with animals—tiger, dragon, and elephant. As a matter of fact, it was not unusual of scholars to contrast a Chinese (crouching) tiger economy with an Indian (lumbering) elephant economy. Let us not forget, however, that the equations have changed, and eventually have the metaphors. The age-old recognition of Dragon with China has reincarnated as the powerful symbol of Chinese historical capability. Tiger, the folkloric arch rival of the mythical Dragon, cannot but be identification for the neighbour of the People's Republic of China, viz., India. On a lighter note, recent symptoms of such representations have come to mean 'prosperity' for the dragonised Chinese, and 'strong' for the tigerised Indians.

Going still further, such totemic significance does not end with just exciting forms of comparative analysis of India and China; they, more than ever, reflect the métier of the neighbours. To see the figurative crypts as mere ceremonial naming of nations, is to be parochial. It is essential to see the relationships as allegories—to read, not just between the lines, but to see the story behind the word. These allusions help one to look at the broader definitions of associative representations, and aid in one's understanding of the allegory built into the accounts of India's and China's growth and development.

Invisible China and the Need for Comparison

In the scholarly tome, *Asian Drama* (1968) by the Nobel Laureate Gunnar Myrdal, China is, amazingly, not one of the *dramatis personae*. Even the Washington-based Brooklings Institute published a book, "Asia's New Giant" (1976), and the honour went to Japan. So, where was China all these years?

There was an unwavering mind-set among the development economists of that period to obliterate China from any deliberation on national development and escalation, far from 1949 onwards, the "communist rule in China [had] produced a united, totalitarian state in the mainland". Communism was redundant, they agreed, and was anti-human. China's exclusion from the comity of nations in Asia, was to a very large extent, accentuated by the fact that despite being a communist state, it was "success[ful] in generating prosperity and well-being". This was downrightly annoying and challenging to the Western advocates of humanitarian values, ethical standards and democratic ideals. This was all till China's resurrection and reappearance in the international political scene after the 1979 reforms of Deng Xiaoping.

The *raison d'etre* behind the evocative, and sometimes perfunctory, comparison of India with China, a recent phenomenon albeit, is 'to judge India's success and failures in comparative terms', the trend having become a staple concern of global observers. But why with China, will be the rejoinder. What other nation is as big in size and population and culturally as interesting as China? A note of caution, however: the trajectory of the reformist zeal of these two nations, especially China, is interspersed with significant statistical problems. The differences that get manifested in the exercise of comparative statistical scrutiny, will have to be taken with a pinch of salt, there still being doubts on the 'certainty' of Red China's statistics, even on basic areas like population and size, leave alone the methodological variations in calculating vital economic indicators.

Historical Relations between India and China

Leaving alone existing anomalies in comparing the two nations, it is of immense import to understand the past relation of the two neighbours, which has promoted the continuation of understanding this relationship through the core target of this book, which is to suggest the future of 'India and China in the Asian Century'. The eminent historian Eric Hobsbawm posited that "What makes a nation is the past; what justifies one nation against others is the past". China and India, the two largest countries of Asia, oddly enough, find themselves as countries representing both the old and the new. Adam Smith's statement will throw light on the earlier position of the countries: "The retinue of a grandee in China or Indostan [sic] accordingly is, by all accounts, much more numerous and splendid than that of the richest subjects in Europe...". The renowned Austrian-based Sinologist Mohan Malik considers India and China among the ancient, but enduring, civilizations, "each with the quality of resilience", which has tolerated their continued existence against all impediments over time. Amartya Sen argues that there was uninhibited "intellectual links China and India, stretching much of the first millennium", and it is this sharing of experiences and thoughts, that have been important for the nations. Any at rate, be it India or the Western worlds, the appeal with China as a commercial centre began with a product that symbolizes the relationship—silk, and hence the trade links through the legendary Silk Route. However, this geographical contiguity got stultified with imperial, colonial and ideological superimpositions of both nations, and history took a different turn in each of the nations.

Differing Development Paths

Of the three countries that define Asia—Japan, India and China—the latter two have taken differing directions after their independence. China's overwhelmingly agro-based economy saw in the Revolution of 1949, the need for a 'highly closed' economic development strategy. That was till the year 1979, when the then Chinese communist leader, Deng Xiaoping, called for a "move away from an earlier system of centralized planning to a more market-oriented system of production." Many saw the shift as a transgression of the sacrosanct revolutionary inspirations, instigating Xiaoping to remark with characteristic simplicity: "Black cat, white cat, all that matters is that it catches mice"—a straightforward manner of stating that what China need was jobs and income. From then on, there was no looking back, and China's 'Walking with Two Legs' stratagem of statist and market-oriented commerce began to create a new social and economic order.

Though India became free from colonial hegemonic powers in 1947, the development plan was not all that disposed towards free market regime. The aims were to effect structural transformation of rural and backward areas, and reduce inequality of income and asset distribution in the society. This developed into the well-known 'mixed economy' model, to be worked within a framework of political democracy. India was not propitious to demolish state intervention in many areas like its Mandarin neighbour, and put with the licence-raj system till the beginning of the last decade of last millennium. By July 1991, India was placed in a precarious external trade payments position, and had to enter the era of what Jegadish Gandhi termed, "Globalistic New Economic Reforms", as opposed to the socialistic pattern followed previously.

Contemporary Concerns

Not everything has been good once both the nations opened their economies. A definite stymieing of state's and the private sector's roles have become apparent in China, coupled with the rising inequality in incomes, unbalanced regional development and burgeoning rural-urban divide. Critics articulate that a wider space has to be provided for private players in the market—policy-wise and institution-wise. The majority mindset has moved to preferring less interference of the state and a decisive move towards 'Market Taoism'. In India's case, the possibility of co-existence of state and free market is no longer debated, save for establishing a supportive public intervention programme along with market mechanism. Furthermore, *a la* China, India must construct additional channels for social and economic opportunities, like social security and old age pension.

II

India and China as Global Players

"The comparison to the old world is something to get excited about" said Michel Powell, underlining the fact that everything worthy of comparison opens up a new path of discovery and realization. In the exercise of comparison, a thorough scrutiny of the character of the qualities of the comparing things is carried, not just with the purpose of ascertaining their resemblances and difference, but also, at a higher level, regard them with discriminating action.

Against this backdrop, 35 essays by prominent journalists, eminent diplomats, academicians and scholars, in the Compendium, "India and China in the Asian Century: Global Economic Power Dynamics" find a significant place. And, the areas of interest covered by the book spans from understanding the present position of the protagonists of modern Asian drama, delineating their problems and opportunities to charting a future course of action for Indo-China trade links. The book has been classified into four broad areas of discussions: *Dialects and Dynamics of the "Asian Century", China: The "Dragon's" Development Dimensions, The "Tiger's" Development Strides and "The Asian Giants" Global Economic Power Dynamics.*

The Century of the Asians

The phrase 'Asian Century' came to pass in the late 1980s, during a 1988 meeting with People's Republic of China (PRC) leader Deng Xiaoping and Indian Prime Minister Rajiv Gandhi. The term is used to illustrate the conviction that, if certain demographic and economic trends persist, the 21st century will be dominated by Asian politics and culture, and the main players considered in this region are China and India.

A communist state getting itself transformed into a high performing manufacturing hub of the world is nothing short of a miracle according to **Ashish Gupta**. However, the Asian century is more than ready to accommodate one more miracle-in-the-happening, viz., India's knowledge revolution. Maintaining the *status quo* would take the nations no where, and hence these nations could do with faster and closer integration with the global economy. Cheap and efficient labour is one aspect of this growth, while a growing middle class is another. What is worth taking note of in the Chinese Miracle story is the effort taken by Chinese companies to be truly world-class, in terms of quality and presence—an apt example would be the Chinese consumer durable company Haier having 16 R & D units and 13 manufacturing units the world over. Agreed, China and India do have a widening rural-urban divide, but efforts to reduce them are envisioned. It is the people who ultimately will make it an "Asian Century", for as the Chinese maxim goes: *if you want 100 years of prosperity grow people.*

That China has problems in reporting numbers to the world is known, but as a relief, China's effort to revise its estimates of GDP raises important issues for future of the nation, declared **A. Vasudevan**. For one, China's upward revision has surpassed the GDP level of Italy—sixth largest economy in the world. To take into account the underreporting by private firms in China is to place China among the most industrialized and developed of nations, namely the G8. The author is of the opinion that China will well neigh become a member of the G8, and will make it G9 soon. It is higher productivity (citing Paul Krugman), rather than large investments that have effected China's high growth rate. One more important upshot of the upward revision is its effect on the interest rate elasticity, signaling greater scope for "financial sector diversification and deepening of financial markets." Three important lessons are there for India to learn from China, if India needs a place in the 'Asian Century': revisiting the methodology of compiling macro data; focus on productivity, not on the magnitude of investments; and, China is a large market waiting to be exploited. To be read along with this recent development is the effort to bring alive the SAFTA, a free trade intra-regional system for Asia. By 2008, given SAFTA's effectiveness, the volume of trade could be $14 billion, provided the member nations keep their prices competitive. This would also widen the scope for financial services and technical collaborations, including knowledge management, educational and information technology, ultimately paving an avenue for the establishment of a South Asia Economic Union that would act as a springboard to making the century truly 'Asian'.

The usefulness of India's growing population will reap a 'demographic dividend', pronounced **Sumit K. Majumdar**. This will help India, which has proved the Malthusian contingency wrong, in two important ways: India's 500 million people are in the median age of 24 years, and India's market is yet to be fully tapped. In contrast to this, China's median age is 34 years. In the case of the US, a population of 90 million with median age of 37 years will less attractive to business persons, and so will Europe be, with a median age of 40 years, and negative growing rate of populace. On the qualitative side, Sumit Majumdar has reasoned that a youthful population means that Markets +

Minds = Motivation, and adding motivation, it will be Markets + Minds + Motivation = Money. The time has come for India to take notice of how the "animal spirits" of entrepreneurship has developed. The most important fortune that India can have is its youthful and educated populations, for it is they who would propel the world's innovations, and would be, in turn, one of the largest markets for products and services.

Taking a China-centric view, **Alok Ray** has argued that China's growth will soon outpace that of the US', and will replace the present super power as the global growth engine of the 21st century. The abundant labour supply of China will drive down wage rates in developed countries, as MNCs, which shift their base to China, would reap from cheap labour. It is unparalleled in history to find a communist nation like China, 'open' up its economy to a far greater extend that most capitalist nations like Japan. On the down side, China's low wage rate has led to "impoverishing the working class and fattening the capitalists in the industrialized nations." Alok Ray has cited the prognostication of analysts who believe China will hold in control the global wage rate, inflation rate and the interest rate for well over two decades. The lesson for India from this 'China's growth story' is: upgrade the skill levels and the productivity of workers, engage in the efficient model of public-private economic partnerships, and foster a globally attractive investment climate.

Keeping in view the need for cooperative partnership between India and China, **C.V. Ranganathan** asserted the need for the two nations to broaden their mutual understanding at the highest political levels in the changing contemporary global and regional situation in Asia. Deng Xiaoping cautioned that "if India and China fail to develop, it cannot be called an Asian century." Hence the need for confidence building measures (CBM) at the defence level. This has been demonstrated the way in which international terrorism was handled. In the Mapping the Global Future report of 2004, it was stated that "most forecasts indicate that by 2020 China's Gross National Product (GNP) will exceed that of individual western economic powers except for the United States. India's GNP will have over-taken or be in the threshold of overtaking European economies." Peace and stability in relations with geographical contiguous nations in Asia was necessary for exploiting the energy resources of the region.

The present era is one where the euphoria of Americanization has died down, and is characterized by international cooperation, and not by unilateralist actions. India's clout has however, was on a rise, for the US has taken cognizance of the strategic importance of India, and would like to work together with her. One of the strengths of China's relations with the US is that both of them hold permanent seat in the United Nations. This nevertheless reflects some aspects of the strained Sino-US relations. Given such a situation, it would not be long to see the triumvirate's (US-China-India) role in international political and economic spheres.

On the issue of prospects for India's membership into the UN's Security Council, the author has stated that only by bringing in a consensus among the five veto power nations that India would be in a position to secure the coveted place. And for that, good relations with those nations become mandatory. In the area of regional cooperation, a slew of organisations (ASEAN, APEC, SCO) in 'the arc of advantage'—India, China, Japan, Korea and the ASEAN—have come up, that aim to promote mutual growth. Additionally, China's 15 year struggle to join the WTO too has borne fruit, and its importance has to be well considered. Thus, for multiple reasons India needs to take deep interest in a part of the Asian landmass where these new regional cooperation organisations' stability and prosperity have a beneficial impact on India. What India must learn to do is to take advantage of the present turn of major diplomatic events, so that the prospects of a bigger role in international affairs are not affected.

The current obsession of the international community with China and India is yet one more sign of the rising global imbalances, stated **Batuk Gathani**. Besides, the burden of tilting the balance was with the US, whose trade deficit has been ever widening. More to the point, the American economy would be badly affected if the Asian investors were to withdraw their investments in the country, giving them no room for cheap credit. In the case of the European nations, the high level of unemployment could be exacerbated, if the MNCs shifted their bases to the cheap labour havens of China and India. These threats apart, the Asian "awakening economic giants", are also on a global move, with 80 companies of China looking out for prospects in the Western world. India, however, needs to improve its competitive edge in the international arena, emulating the much acclaimed Chinese "pragmatism".

A casual perusal of the economic supremacy and dominance among continents and countries reveal Europe dominance in the 19th century and America's rise in the 20th. In the 21st century, India and China are touted to be the most powerful nations. Thus, globalization can no longer be equated with Americanisation, asserted **Jegadish Gandhi**. According to him, the super powers that be would have a dynamic economic structure that would ensure sustainable long-term economic growth, broaden bilateral relations, increase the degree of intra-regional integration, and lead to greater global assimilation. This would increase cross border trade and investments. A case in point is the ability of India and China to identify new products and diversify the trade basket to attain the planned target of $ 30 billion in bilateral trade by 2009.

The rise of communist China has been considered by many to be a miracle and a mystery. It is here that Gandhi demystified the growth of China to its continued evolution of economic policies in the areas of the allocation of capital, labour mobility, urbanization and the creation of an improved framework for the development of the private sector to ensure that this development momentum was sustained. Despite this advantage, India stood to gain because of the robust financial markets in the country. In the social sphere, India's overall literacy rate of nearly 60% was well behind China's 88% as it had a "very well developed system of higher education that takes advantage of what the rest of the world sees as a genetic predisposition towards science and engineering."

Citing President Kalam, the author has categorized Asia to be the area of future business. One spot of concern in such a scenario was the requirement for adequate energy supplies, and a need to look for newer forms of energy. With India's share of 7.2 per cent of the global GDP and China's 15.7 per cent, it is of great import for both nations to strike "synergies in trade and business", with a view to give shape to a new economic world order—a truly Asian 21st Century.

In the essay on Knowledge and the Asian Challenge by **C.P. Chandrasekhar and Jayati Ghosh**, it was stated that exports were an important source of dynamism in India and China and that "knowledge capital" would play a crucial role in their export dynamism. While it was the manufactured good that catapulted China into the international market, it was services that worked wonders for India. It is the contention of the authors that larger exports and/or a higher rate of expansion of exports can stimulate growth because of positive net exports or a trade surplus that would serve as the demand stimulus and inducement to invest for an individual country. And it would be doubly useful if knowledge based exports like software services, identified as hi-tech-services, account for a significant share of exports, as in the case of India. There is a need, though, to differentiate between knowledge in the production of goods and services, and knowledge for the production of goods and services—the former being knowledge in application in production and the latter being Research and Development. It is promising to note that India and China can become a part of the 'internationalization of R&D', as more than half of the world's top R&D spenders conduct R&D activities in developing countries. Evidently, China and India have become important bases for knowledge-based production of exportable goods and services, given their skilled and youthful manpower.

In what said to be a comparison of the Asian giants with Latin American nations, the essay by **Jorge Heine** focused on India and China's active participation in the Latin American Countires (LACs). While China's presence in the LACs has been for more than 15 years, India's, on the other hand, has barely crossed 2 years. Citing World Bank and United Nations' publications, the author has attempted to dispel a number of myths about the supposed displacement of jobs across the region caused by "unfair" competition from China and India. Alternatively, the LACs have benefited from the rise of China and India. The South American markets are ready to provide a readymade outlet for Chinese and Indian manufactured goods, as well as for services and IT products. One nation that has been affected much because of China's entry is Mexico, which has replaced it as the main exporting country to the United States. To reach the $10 billion in Indo-LAC trade that some have identified as a goal for 2008 would be a reasonable target, and can be achieved if India and LACs remove extant trade barriers and facilitate the flow of goods and services, along with private joint ventures with Latin American corporations.

With over 4 billion people in Asia, underemployment, insecurity, poor working conditions, and a shortage of marketable skills remain widespread, rued **Juan Somavia** of the ILO. To cite an example of the "decent work challenge", in 2005, some 84 per cent of workers in South Asia, 58 per cent in South-East Asia, 47 per cent in East Asia, and 36 per cent in the Arab states did not earn enough to lift themselves and their families above the $2 a day poverty line. The real challenge, then was to effect a reduction in decent work deficits through (a) promoting economic growth that translates into the creation of decent jobs, (b) respect, promote, and realize fundamental principles and rights at work, (c) extend social protection for workers in agriculture and the informal economy, and (d) support institutions and systems that strengthen labour market governance. It is the contention of the author that the next ten years will be critical ones in Asia, for improving the lives of the people in this region, was also an exercise in global policy leadership.

The Dragon and Development

The last year of the second millennium was the year of Metal Dragon, the most strong-willed of dragons in Chinese astrology. As can be noticed, China too became combative and made its presence felt, by joining the World Trade Organisation (WTO) in 2001. Essays relating to such issues would be dealt with here.

Highlighting the shift of China's Communism to socialistic democratic model, **A. Ranga Reddy** analyzed the reason for the swing from an ideology of Socialism and Marxism. Initially, Agriculture was the area of reform after the formation of PRC in 1949. What the Chinese learnt long ago was that every nation-wide experiment must be suited to local conditions and pragmatism must play instead of dogmas. They also realized the importance of the rule of law in ensuring a gradual reformation of the economy and society. The second phase of reforms (1994 onwards), was towards building a rule-based market system and Western style institutions and practices but again with distinct Chinese characteristics. Such matter-of-factness approach has made Red China prophesize about reaching 10 per cent of the global trade. Two factors have made China look at the international trade scenario with hope: faster flow of Foreign Direct Investment, and the entry in to the WTO. The author is not just concerned with the decline in poverty, but also with the increasing corruption and alarming rate of environmental degradation. Paying encomiums to the great visionary Deng Xiaoping, the author has brought to light the fact that it is he who argued vociferously that privatisation can be reconciled with socialism. Regrettably, the author noted, India still observed China as a non-market economy.

If at all anything worried **Jayati Ghosh** when writing in her essay Macro-economic Policy in China's Economic Growth, it was the sporadic bouts of deflation and overheating of Chinese RMB. All this pointed to the form and variety of capital formation in China. While the budgetary appropriations and foreign investment accounted for very small shares of less than 7 per cent of total fixed assets, the other avenues for borrowing of capital by investing units from banks and non-bank financial institutions, investing units from central government ministries, local governments, enterprises and institutions, and by raising capital through issuing bonds by enterprises or financial institutions. What is worrying is the fact that such "off-budget" sources of capital are increasingly used for consumption rather than for capital formation. As a result, administrative measures, including the use of central "commands" have become obligatory in China.

The most exciting thing about China is that unlike India where caste and birth determined status, the Chinese imperial examination system remained theoretically open to all, so that through study, even peasants could aspire to join the bureaucracy, pointed out **Pallavi Aiyar**. With semi-privatisation of education in China, institutions have to raise funds from outside to ensure their survival. This got reflected in demanding high fees from students. When it comes to pay, the students of Chinese institutions were able to secure jobs that paid a salary almost equal to a 'blue-collar worker'. This has engendered a revamping of the education system, throwing emphasis on ensuring quality education and highly qualified teachers from the Western part of the globe. It is a self deluded idea that India's IITs and IIMs are world-class. This can be understood from the well-regarded Shanghai Jiaoton University (SJTU) Academic Ranking of World Universities in which China has two universities in the top 300, while India has none. China would soon have world-class universities, but as is often mentioned, there is still too much governmental control, with cumbersome permissions and procedures.

Intellectual Property (IP) will be touted as the next architect of corporate affluence submitted **G. Narasimha Raghavan**. Intellectual Property Rights were for creations of the mind, such as inventions, industrial designs, literary and artistic works, symbols, and names and images. Intellectual Property protection in China is to be understood through the traditional relationship schema called *Guanxi*. That China is a haven for counterfeits and pirated products can be deciphered from the information that counterfeiting alone is estimated to be in the tune of US $ 16 billion, with counterfeits accounting for 15-20 per cent of all branded goods made in China. *Guanxi* simply means building a rapport with a person, based on mutual trust and respect. This relationship could be with one's suppliers, buyers, and/or with the government officials. It is only through *Guanxi* that the right kind of relationship with the government can be struck—a move that would in the long-run articulate the importance of protecting IP for the nation as a whole.

S. Venkitaramanan stated that the reason that China has gone ahead with initiating divestment of its shares in public sector banks was with a view to improving their management and performance. FDI was just an incidental benefit. The route chosen for disinvestment was through IPOs—for 2006, it was the Shanghai Investment and Trust Bank Investor (Temasek of Singapore likely investor) and Bank of Beijing Investor (where ING Group of Netherlands is a likely investor), among others. Contrast this with the discordant line adopted by our Indian Leftist brigade against the divestment of a 10 per cent stake in BHEL. This method of restructuring of the Chinese economy, especially in banking, has many lessons for India: their courageous and pragmatic decision to invite private investors, to help speed up the reform process. As against this, India is still fighting shy of such an open invitation to multinational bankers.

There are two forms of growth that can be witnessed in China: growing economic rate, and growing income inequality rate, according to **C.P. Chandrasekhar and Jayati Ghosh**, who have presented their views in another article entitled Rising Inequality in China. From the mid-1970s to the mid-1980s, there was a perceptible decline in the inequality of China, only to increase during the late 1980s, and more strikingly during the 1990s, when the economy was opened to a considerable extent. In addition to intrarural and rural-urban differences in income, from 1990s onwards, the difference between inland and coastal China increased. With respect to employment, a steady decline of workers in agriculture was detected, with total rural employment growing sluggishly during 1990-2002. The perpetrator of inequality was the wage rate differentials, between rural and urban, between agriculture and service. Part of this accusation was borne by high levels of FDI in the coastal areas, vis-à-vis the interior lands. Discernible obliteration of agricultural reforms along with stringent conditions on migration from rural to urban centres has heightened the increases in income and wealth inequality.

With a 2.3 trillion dollar economy, and a 1.3 billion populace, China seems to be awake to the reality of the growing income inequality—regionally and sectorally. And that is why, **S. Sethuraman** contended that its Eleventh five-year plan (2006-2010) has made a departure from the earlier few plans, and gave equal importance to modernization of agriculture, with a special focus on building rural infrastructure, attempting to erect a "a new Socialist countryside". Accordingly, China's eleventh plan has envisaged spending more on health and education of the people. This would, to a large extend, redress, if not ameliorate, the imbalances in the social and economic spheres. A reform worth noting is the doing away of the age-old agricultural tax. China's stunning growth performance in the last two decades averaged more than 9 per cent. On reworking the statistics, the National Bureau of Statistics of China found that by 2004, China was the sixth largest economy in the world. By 2006, it was the fourth largest, next only to the US, Japan and Germany. A highly discernible change in China's economy was the growing importance of consumer spending, a clear sign that the economy benefited from the domestic as well as the export markets. From a social point, the twin targets for the year 2010 were: doubling the per capita income of 2000 and reducing energy consumption by 20 per cent. A case was made to look for alternative modes of fuel like wind, nuclear or even solar. In all, every nation's growth would be seen from the standpoint of consumption of earth's resources and conservation of environment.

Juxtaposing the communist state China and the commercial venture Wal-Mart, in order to spell out the lessons to be learnt from China, was what **K. Subramaniam** has done. And both impact global trade. The unique business philosophy of Wal-Mart was to sell at low price, but in large quantities. Soon, its reach extended, and about 4300 stores in ten countries, only to become "the largest toy seller and grocer". Once the need for continuous supply of products at cheap prices were understood by China, it became, through a chain of 10,000 suppliers one of the most reliable of the American super store's merchants. If Wal-Mart was a country, it would be China's eighth largest trading partner. After WTO inducted China into its circle, the Middle Kingdom had to permit foreign retailers to enter as fully-owned subsidiaries subsequent to 2002. Wal-Mart's relation with the Chinese was such that the fifth largest sea port in the world, Shenzhen, was built to suit the interest of Wal-Mart. There is no gainsaying that Wal-Mart may suddenly cut its relation with China, which has become so much dependent on a corporate entity. However, such an incident is only a probability and not an eventuality, as it made out in India. This argument is used caution India's acceptance of FDI in the retail sector.

The Tiger and Development

Symbolizing India to be a 'Tiger' is an imagery for the nation's single-minded focus of becoming a 'Developed Nation', as envisioned by India's President Abdul Kalam. And to achieve this, it is necessary that it becomes a leaping, and not a crouching, tiger. This section will spotlight on what India could learn from the Mainland, and how to carry on the learning.

Ashok Jacob has two very significant questions, whose answers he has given in the essay on India's progress and future. The questions were: Where does the rest of the world see India today?, and can India, like China, translate free market reform into economic prosperity? China is considered to be a star performer among the developing nations, and its hallmark has been the sustaining rates of growth over the last two decades. The author has marked out eight trends which aid in creating self-sustaining market dynamics across the developing world, and christened them "the Eight Catalysts of Ultimate Contagion." These eight factors need to be incorporated into a developing nation to help it achieve a healthy economy. Of the eight criteria, the ones on deregulation and Foreign Direct Investment, along with wider distribution of wealth, hold special significance to a nation like India, given its typical inability to garner external funds, and the observable rural-urban divide. Moreover, the areas of technological innovation and institutionalized property right—in both tangibles and intangibles—are vital to establishing a strong techno-legal environment. Recent performance of India would compare well with China, principally on the industrial and the IT fronts. Still being a larger agro-based economy, India would augur well to emulate China in many aspects. The present 'privatization spree' of the Indian government is one such instance.

Sanguine forecasts of the author, with regard to India related to the improved access to credit for the up-and-coming middle class, and pragmatic geopolitical stance taken by the nation by resuming talks with Pakistan and China. Where India has really overtaken China was in the regions of law—property rights—and information technology. And the region where India was knocked down was the fiscal impropriety of the government, besides excess state control on the IT industry. In all, India's positives would overshadow and offset its negatives. This, then, would subtly holler to the world that at last, "India has come of age."

The essay on India's positives by **Ajai Chowdhry** is one among the most optimistic of essays on India's "inherent strength." The author lists a number of India's achievements post liberalization: Indian economy's excellent performance, the improving communications and commuting infrastructure, and the soaring Information Technology sector. This has turned the table and India techies in the US have come back to India in quest of better action and remuneration. It is not mistakable to state that India's new found greatness has made the Western world fidgety. India's services and IT prowess can categorically be said to have boosted India's entry into the West's horizons. No doubt exists on realizing India's potential in the field of hardware too. All these, along with a proud and educated youth population, would prompt India's confident stride into the 21st century.

India's population during independence was 350 million, while at the turn of the 20th century, it crossed the one billion mark, pointed out **M.S. Swaminathan**. Yet, according to UNICEF report, India has the largest number of malnourished children in the world, nearly 57 million out of a total world figure of 146 million. A light of ray was the inauguration of The Year of Agricultural Renewal, better referred to as the Year of the Farmer, from June, 1, 2006 [by defining "farmer" to include fisher men and women, dairy, sheep, poultry and other farmers, as well as those rural and tribal families engaged in a wide variety of farming related occupations such as sericulture, vermiculture, production of biofertilizers and biopesticides, and agro-processing]. An Indian enigma worth pondering over is the relatively better growth of other sectors of economy, with agriculture pushed to the periphery. This form of marginalization has resulted in spread of agrarian distress and rural discontent, and spread of the Naxalite movement, besides the expansion of urban slums. So, the question what can be done was countered by the author through a five-point programme: undertake soil health enhancement, promote water harvesting, conservation, and its efficient and equitable use, speed up credit reforms coupled with credit and insurance literacy, bridge the growing gap between scientific know-how and field level do-how, and lastly, establish village knowledge centers. The strategy was to better the prospects of on-farm and non-farm livelihoods. What came through as a major transformation was that the National Commission on Farmers has suggested the mainstreaming of the human dimension in all agricultural programmes and policies.

Based on a study by the World Bank, titled *Inclusive Growth and Service Delivery: Building on India's Success,* **G. Srinivasan** drew attention to the disturbing actuality of the growing fissure in economic progress and service delivery. The author has spotlighted startling findings like: The headcount poverty rate in rural Orissa (43 per cent) and rural Bihar (41 per cent) is higher than similarly measured poverty rates of African countries such as Malawi or Ghana. Along with the report, Planning Commission Deputy Chairman Mr. Montek Singh Ahluwalia's estimations are also appended. Temporally, the 1970s therefore saw a raft of targeted anti-poverty programmes, while the Green Revolution raised farm production. In the 1980s policy change aimed at accelerating growth were formulated and applied. The last three years have seen 8 per cent GDP growth while the Eleventh Plan growth target could be even higher and close to 9 per cent. Inter-regionally the states in India did not have a uniform growth rate—Gujarat, and Tamil Nadu, did well, while Madhya Pradesh and Orissa performed badly. These were rendered more blatantly in the case of poverty figures. However, in the case of the nation as a whole, the poverty rates have been on a downward trend, something like reduction of 0.8 percentage points every year. While the knowledge economy offered a bouquet of opportunities, it was for us to make use of them. Understandably, the emphasis was on providing quality education, especially at the primary level itself.

Citing the Global Competitiveness Index, 2006 of the World Economic Forum, **S. Majumdar** made the point that China was ranked 54 and India 43 in the ascending order, meaning that India was more economically competitive than China. Would this, then, decide where FDI will go?, will be a natural question to raise. Justifiably, the differences in the index of competitiveness can be attributed to the diametrically opposite growth strategies of the two nations. Moreover, India has a well-developed corporate sector, technology, and has even gone in for Public-Private partnership in infrastructure development programmes. In China's case, the slow privatization of national enterprises, even after reforms, has resulted in a big gulf between home-grown and FDI-based industries, and an eventual decline in national competitiveness.

Another area of caution for the Chinese is the preponderance on investment—led growth. This can lead to accumulation of bad loans. So, China has to change this strategy of getting foreign funds, without developing its local industries.

China's modernization programme during the mid-1970s has led to two most interesting developments: from import substitution to export; and China becoming not just a destination for Foreign Direct Investment (FDI), but a home for Asia's new multinationals, indicated **Dan Steinbock**. During the 1980s, China saw the replacement of low-tech services and manufacturing units by natural resource development projects that brought in more foreign funds. The 1990s was the era of entry of Foreign-Invested Enterprises (FIEs), and the the small- and medium-size enterprises gave way to multinational companies. So, why was China still a challenge to all developing nations, can be answered when an understanding of China's lessons can be assured: Construct SEZs, Internal economic reform must precede external changes, and attract FDI. As straight as can be, the lessons for India in particular are two-fold—take advantage of the expertise and enterprise of Indian expatriates, and the economy must be opened to foreign investment capital.

The Asian Giants as Super Economic Powers

Max Weber regarded power as the ability to make use of every opportunity/possibility existing within a social relationship. When we talk about super powers in economic and social fields, the usual qualification is its unilateral use and the belligerent attitude that goes with it. In Asia's case, the super power status will be but an enabling tool to rise in the comity of nations.

Have there been cases of unbalanced reportage about China's and India's capabilities, questioned **Qiu Yonhui**. Economic miracles they may be, but more than there was more to China and India that needed to be told to the public through the media, print media in particular. Interesting topics, however, are covered relating to civilization, food, architecture, popular culture, among others. The usual manner of reading newspaper was to see whether there were causalities, and then the trend changes to trade talk and border issues. As such, no real effort was made to portray the depth and breadth of the neighbouring nations. Knowing about each other has become essential for survival in the other's county. And this can also lead to change in the attitude towards each other. At the most vital stage, knowing more about a nation can elicit educated opinion among the readers, rather than variegated and biased judgments.

That Both China and India undergoing a period of economic transitions during the last many years, can be gauged by their economic activities, pointed out **Md. Abdus Salam**. There were several episodes of reforms in the India economy since the 1970s, but the major reform gained momentum only during the 1990s. Also knows as the Structural Adjustment Policy, its major aims were to substantially reduce controls on capacity creation, production and prices and to allow international competition. In the specific field of industrial policy, the three most significant changes undertaken related to delicencing, dilution of provisions of the MRTP Act and liberalisation of foreign investment regulation. Eventually, India's overall performance began to radiate in the form of surplus food production, significant expansion in the production of durable consumer goods, growth in telecom and information technology and provisioning of better services like airlines, banks and construction. The uncrossable hurdle was the growing revenue deficits and overall fiscal deficit. For China, it had introduced market-oriented reforms in 1980 that is a decade earlier than India. Industrial and agricultural output in China grew by an average 10 percent per year after the 1980 reform process. It became a low-cost producer in fields from textiles to telecommunications, auto parts and attracted large-scale investment from foreign companies.

On comparison, it was evident that over the last 20 years, China's GDP has grown at about 10% a year, compared with India's 6% growth rate, and that China's trade in goods and services as a percentage of GDP grew from 35% in 1991 to 49% in 2000, while during the same period, India's percentage rose from 18% to 30%. If India has to close the gap between China, reforms must aim to raise the productivity of Indian labour and improve the work culture, besides eliminating poverty and improving the quality of life of the people.

Despite the encouraging prognostication that by 2020, China and India would have a middle-class consumer base of one billion people, it was very disappointing for **Rasheeda Bhagat** to find that there was almost negligible interest among the journalists to gather information on India. At least, not as much as China mattered! Going by the definition of a "middle-class" person (as given by Dr. Yuwa Hedrik-Wong), as one with an annual income of or above $ 5,000, by 2020, China would have 650 million "middle class" people and India some 350 million. While there was genuine interest in China as a surging economy has changed the economic equations in the entire region, India's annihilation was not justified despite the fact that it was to emerge a leader in economic growth. It was imperative for corporates to leverage China's growth, its huge domestic market and its lower manufacturing costs, by building-up a partnership with Chinese firms. A remarkable result that came from contrasting India with China was India's new role as a "key supplier in the service dimension of manufacturing." The advantage of manufacturing for China and services for India will be a powerful but a positive shock to Asia, and no one would be able to escape from this impact. The China-India template can graduate into an Asia Free Trade zone provided state intervention remained at naught. This alone would translate into a win-win situation for the two Asian biggies.

What was lacking in China was consumption-led growth, while at the same time, in India it was manufacturing—led growth, examined **Andy Xie**. Concentrating on growth *per se* was a dangerous trend; the emphasis, rather, must be on income distribution. It was still the in-thing among scholars that it was the manufacturing sector that would sustain employment growth, and so India must also develop manufacturing infrastructure. China's export-led growth and the already available capital—intensive infrastructure were its advantages, no doubt. But, China's single-minded pursuit of growth has led to side stepping of many social issues. The next area of concern for China was that of their currency appreciating in the short-term, along with the scope of China's trade surpluses. Asia's renaissance in the world economy would be visible only when India shifted to a manufacturing led growth strategy, and China stopped relying more on its exports. Both India and China were dependent on the US economy—more for China than India—and its collapse would affect both the Asian nations. They would, nevertheless, come back to normalcy, given their robust and resilient economic performance.

As economic success stories, China and India have broken from ideologically stultified external policies, observed **M.S. Kallur**. And it is this aspect that has transformed these two predominantly agricultural economies into an industrialized and a service economy respectively. Achieving food sufficiency was China's objective, while in India, agriculture was the very backbone of the economy. Regardless of the fact that both nations wanted to reform their agricultural sector, China was prudent enough to encourage farmers to diversify production, once food sufficiency was accomplished. India lost out on this dearly due to rising minimum support prices that artificially boosted production of major cereals, thus discouraging diversification of production towards non-grain commodities. Another feather in the hat of China was the creation of a whole new economic sector that became the most dynamic feature of the economy, namely, the rural non-farm sector, consisting of the small-scale food-processing units. In the mean time, the Indian government spending was on irrigation, dominated by creation of large surface irrigation schemes. These yielded smaller marginal returns, in terms of both growth and poverty reduction. Lack of development of rural infrastructure was one more area that cost India gravely in agriculture, unlike China.

India's early entry in to the WTO has helped it in more than one way. For instance, India has been exporting horticultural products to many Western nations, post-WTO. This has also led to a major shift in farm production toward non-food activities such as livestock and aquaculture. The demand from EU for organic food products can be met by both India and China. Membership in the WTO has benefited both the nations in the field of agriculture. The requirement is to leverage on this prospect by investing science and new technologies to harness energy and water, optimize their economic structures for allocative efficiency, in addition to better banking, and insurance systems.

The target for the mobile industry was to surpass the 3 billion mark by the end of this decade, informed **Dan Steinbock**, on the essay on Mobile Industry in India and China. The intention of mobile service providers and manufacturers was to exploit the most populous, but a growing nation like India and China in Asia-Pacific, just as Mexico and Brazil in Latin America. Even South Africa, Morocco and Egypt were among the must-win markets for mobile companies. According to the mobile industry, a three pronged strategy to identify big markets were evolved: large population, rising per capita income and relatively low penetration. Accordingly, China and India cannot remain out of their ken. Mobile penetration was 21 per cent in China, and India's was still just 2.5 per cent. In 2004, the total number of mobile customers stood at 1.6 billion and by 2006, it was expected to be close to 2.6 billion. True to form, emerging markets were unmistakably in China and India. When looking at developing markets like these in Asia, the strategy followed was one of innovation with diffusion. For it was in these nations that larger profits awaited the mobile industry.

The very continuation of the Made in India Fair in Beijing for the fourth consecutive year was reason enough for the booming bilateral trade, reasoned **Pallavi Aiyar** in the essay, India-China Trade: A Long Road Ahead. In 2002 the total volume of bilateral trade was a paltry $ 5 billion, while the first seven months of 2006 recorded trade to a tune of $ 13.6 billion. Was this a signal for the "veritable economic renaissance of the emergence of an economic colossus, 'Chindia,' that bring together the might of two of the world's fastest growing economies," questioned the author. However, rather than getting enamored by such chimerical concepts, much had to be done for Sino-Indian economic relationship to sustain and grow. Not everything, then, was striking. India's exports to China were still overwhelmingly dominated by low-value, primary products with a huge reliance on iron ore. There were still hurdles for Chinese investments in Indian infrastructure projects due to "security" concerns. The third factor is the lackluster Chinese investments in India. What ever said and done, there was still an increasing willingness to engage, on the part of China, with India Inc. Will this forge a formidable partnership, dubbed 'Chindia', soon?

A superpower was a state with the first rank in the international system and the ability to influence events and project power on a world-wide scale, defined **S. Iyyampillai and P. Balamurugan**, in their joint paper on India and China as superpowers. Further, the authors have identified three criteria for a nation to be termed 'superpower': a sound economy, military invulnerability and have a wide land under its control. In this essay, the authors have pegged the present superpower USA as the centre of their argument on whether China and India can become a superpower, and more so, should they? India as the second most populous nation still had considerable influence of agriculture in the economy. China, alternatively, was more of a manufacturing hub. On comparing India and China with the USA, the Asian nations' improving social indicators came to light, and so did the deteriorating crime levels of the Americans.

The first issue taken up was with respect to the ability of China and India to don on the garb of superpowers. Due to the two oriental nations' internal policies and external difficulties, it was quite evident that they would not outshine America's economy in the 21st century. Rather, a quadrilateral power system would emerge with US, China, India and the EU. The second and more important issue taken-up by the authors was a normative question relating to China and India's justification to become a superpower. Power does not always come with compassion, and every powerful nation would perpetrate inhuman activities. The USA was the most prominent of such nations. Given the two nations' internal weaknesses and needs, it was better for these nations to remain outside the purview of 'superpowers' and "aim to attain economic development with human face consisting of socio-economic, ecological equality and balance and friendly diplomatic relations with the rest of the world." If at all, India and China wanted to become superpowers, they ought to address the two challenging tasks of reducing population growth, and increasing per capita income, *inter alia*.

By the logic of the 'gravity theory of trade', which said that shorter the distance between two nations, larger would be their trade, India and China, by virtue of being neighbours, should have been one of the biggest trade blocks in the world. And yet they are not, pointed out **Ashish Gupta**. Nonetheless, it would be too simplistic to just ward odd such a combination in the near future. One of FICCI's predictions for the Indo-China trade was pegged at $ 10 billion for 2007. Notwithstanding the low value composition of India's trade basket to China, there was huge potential for collaboration in various sectors like information technology, IT-enabled services, biotechnology, education, financial services, healthcare, tourism and energy. However, strong resistance on the part of India to enter into bilateral trade ties was prevalent, with China soon to achieve the full-fledged market status. An ideal win-win situation for both the nations would be "Chinese manufacturing plus Indian services and Chinese hardware plus Indian software". Another area of prospect for the Asian giants was for cooperation in energy security. In all, the USP of Sino-India trade would be to "offset each one's weaknesses with the other's strong points." Then alone will there be victors on both sides.

Sustaining growth over quarter of a century, and also impacting positively majority of the 1.3 billion people who make-up China was an economic feat in no small terms, discovered **Ramgopal Agarwal**. The greatest stumbling block for Indo-China relationship was the strong undercurrent of suspicion in their economic relations. It is this attitude that has prevented the Asian entities to leave behind the US' market. For both India and China, the struggle for economic activity was bursting with many opportunities, especially for the Indian side in areas such as pharmaceuticals, auto and auto parts and engineering goods. To come out of this struggle in a successful manner, India must, at the first instance, recognize China as a market economy. This would be an emblematic approach by India to open up the Chinese bureaucracy for trade and investment negotiations. The next step would be to decode this amiable situation into economic partnership agreements. One more complementary step would be to ease the logistical routes between India and China. At long last, there would be a need for a vision of a shared economic struggle.

Peppered with impressive statistics relating to China and India, the essay by **R. Seshasayee** estimated that by 2010, the combined exports of the two Asian 'tigers' would rise to 20 per cent of the world exports and by 2030, the figure would be higher at 30 per cent. Hence, a need has arisen to coalesce, and work as trading partners, which would also result in, besides external expansion, inclusive growth. The nature of India's exports to China was in the form of high labour intensive and low capital intensive products. This trend has to change, and more value added items like optical and medical instruments, inorganic chemicals, rubber, etc., must be given greater emphasis. On the contrary, China's export of electrical machinery (a high value product) to India constituted a major portion of its export share. It is universally acknowledged that India has a comparative advantage in services and knowledge trade. Potential areas of trade between the two nations then must be on more knowledge-based industries like IT, ITES, biotechnology, tourism, among others. The author has advocated two key recommendations: allow greater market access, by removing all non-tariff barriers between China and India; build a platform for exchange of technologies and innovation in manufacturing. After all, what has to be apprehended is that the markets in both the countries are yet to be fully tapped, and potential existed in abundance.

The Rhetoric of 'Chindia'

India and China are non-alike conjoined clones, joined at the Himalayas. Together, they account for one-third of the human population and have been named as countries with a highest potential for growth in the coming decades. Efforts are on the way to integrate the economies of the two countries, with a view to create the commanding *Chindia*—a portmanteau neologism, that considers the strengths of the two economies as complementary and matching. Leaving alone all the contrasting features of the two economies, it would still be doubtful if synergetic relations in commercial transactions can be effected. Say in foreign relations though, it is plausibly convincing. It is never to be understood as a race between two giants. What has to be an unspoken statement is that *Chindia* has to be a 'mental force' of a collective character, and not be rhetoric for a united temperament.

As T.N. Srinivasan says, China and India will be forces to reckon with in the globalised world: *Whether or not India overtake China in the next two decades, it is clear that both countries will be economic powerhouses in the medium-term. Undoubtedly, their growth will have significant impacts on the world economy.*

G. NARASIMHA RAGHAVAN

Part I

Dialects and Dynamics of the "Asian Century"

The Asian Century

Ashish Gupta

Dialects and Dynamics of the "Asian Century"

INTRODUCTION

Let China Sleep, for when she awakens she
world. When the great French conqueror Napol
made that remark, he may not have realized the
his statement. But two centuries hence, there is little
The Middle Kingdom has stirred and the world
but to take note of the great "China Miracle." A mi
transformed much of the Chinese countryside
cities that—with their skyscrapers, wide roads,
rails, Volkswagens and Harley-Davidsons—can ch
York and Paris in size and style. A miracle that
metamorphosed a poor, Third World country in
manufacturing hub with China-made stuff filling
floors of Wal-Marts, Tescos and even your
supermarkets. A miracle that has made a commu
the dream destination for the all the capitalists in

The Asian Century

Ashish Gupta

INTRODUCTION

Let China Sleep, for when she awakens she will shake the world. When the great French conqueror Napoleon Bonaparte made that remark, he may not have realized the true import of his statement. But two centuries hence, there is little confusion. The Middle Kingdom has stirred and the world has no choice but to take note of the great "China Miracle." A miracle that has transformed much of the Chinese countryside into sprawling cities that—with their skyscrapers, wide roads, flyovers, metro rails, Volkswagens and Harley-Davidsons—can challenge New York and Paris in size and style. A miracle that has metamorphosed a poor, Third World country into the world's manufacturing hub with China-made stuff filling up the shop floors of Wal-Marts, Tescos and even your neighbourhood supermarkets. A miracle that has made a communist country the dream destination for the all the capitalists in the world.

The world, to a lesser extent, is also taking note of another rising Tiger that escaped Napoleon's attention: India. The "Indian Miracle" is not so much on the surface though. The streets are still narrow, the countryside is still barren and most of the slums are still there. But India has a knowledge industry that's charming the world's business leaders. If China is the factory of the world, then India is the world's laboratory. Its rapid growth in information technology, IT-enabled services and business process outsourcing has made India the service hub of the world.

Dynamics of Global Players

For every success story in the manufacturing sector of China, there's a parallel in the Indian knowledge industry. If Haier turned itself from a near bankrupt refrigerator unit two decades back into China's largest—and the world's fifth largest—household appliances maker with global revenue of $ 12,8 billion (in 2005) and presence in more than 20 countries, Infosys did equally well, growing from virtually nothing in 1981 when it was set up to a $ 2-billion company in 2006 with a global presence. If China accounts for two-thirds of all the shoes produced in the world, two-fifth of personal computers and 85% of the world's toys, then India boasts of a 60% share in the global offshore industry and 40% of the BPO market. If Shanghai-with its space-age skyline, sprawling industrial zones and bullet train—is the second home of the world's manufacturing giants like General Motors, ABB and Agilent Technologies, Bangalore—with its innumerable R&D centers and excellent IT infrastructure—is the new innovation hub of the likes of Google, Hewlett-Packard and Motorola.

Both China and India are still relatively poor. But the blistering growth of the two—home to two-fifth of the humanity—is being closely watched with awe and trepidation. While economic commentators from across the world are busy prophesizing the ascendance of the next "super powers", the world media is chasing every move of the "Asian giants." For good reasons too. Over the last five years, China has grown at an annual rate of 9.7% to become the world's fourth largest economy today with a gross domestic product (GDP) of $ 2.3

trillion in 2005, overtaking the United Kingdom, France and Italy. India, which joined the race much later than China, has picked-up pace of late, growing at an average of 8% a year for the last three years to log a GDP of $ 700 billion in 2005-06. "For global players, the question is no longer, 'India or China?' You have to be in both," says Meera Shankar, Indian Ambassador to Germany.

Drivers of Growth

But the big question the whole world asks is, Will China and India expand their influence and become the real drivers of growth in the 21st Century? Paul Rawkins, Senior Director at Fitch Ratings, believes that China has already proved that it can be the driver of global growth. "China's robust growth helped the world escape recession after America's stock market bubble burst in 2000-01," Aneesh Tripathi, Knowledge Head, KPMG, a global consultancy major, points out that while India and China constitute around 6% of the global GDP, their contribution is nearly 13% if the incremental growth in GDP, for 2004 is seen. "And this incremental growth is likely to increase in the coming years," pointing to the demographic profile of the two countries. "Remember, by 2020, India will be the youngest country in the world with around 547 million people below the age of 25, although China will have a much higher ageing population due to its strict one-child norm." What this means is that India will have a much larger, more flexible and innovative labour force than the rest of the world.

Efficient Production and Productivity

China's integration with the global economy will be the biggest driver of global growth, according to Nagesh Kumar, Director-General, Research and Information System for Developing Countries (RIS), a New Delhi-based think-tank. "The reason is simple: Economies become truly richer through increased productivity growth either from technological advances or from more efficient production, thanks to international trade. The same cannot be said of all the wealth produced by stock market or asset bubbles, which is happening more in the western world."

Vast Pool of Cheap Labour

One obvious advantage China and India enjoy is their vast pool of cheap labour. With unemployment still a major problem in the two countries, there's no sign just yet of any pressure on this supply chain. Stephan Green, China-based Senior Economist at Standard Chartered Bank, believes that the large surplus of underemployed people in the Chinese countryside will continue to provide an incessant source of cheap labour for its various factories and industries. This will help China's urbanization, already at 46%, continue to rise by 1-2% every year.

Bulging Middle-Class

Another key factor in the China-India story is their rapidly bulging middle class-currently there are around 150 million Chinese, and some 50 million Indian households fall in the category. This will lead to a consumption-led growth in the two countries, which, in turn, will also be the new driver of global growth. "India and China share the advantages of scale," says Farida Khambata, Vice-President, International Finance Corporation. "Both countries have large, productive workforces and are benefiting from the virtuous cycle of rapid growth, creating a large domestic market which fosters further growth," "For a growing number of products and services from aircraft to mobile phones to compact cars and two wheelers to cement and steel, India and China are already the largest markets in the world," says Nagesh Kumar of RIS.

Chindia, Anyone?

And what if the two countries join hands?" Cooperation is just like two pagodas, one hardware and one software," Chinese Prime Minister Wen Jiabao had said during his visit to India last year. "Combined, we can take the leadership position in the world. When the particular day comes, it will signify the coming of the Asian century of the IT industry," he told a packed crowd of IT professionals in Bangalore. Although the two countries have not yet made any serious effort on that front-what with China harbouring the dream to build-up a world-class software industry on its own and India looking to make serious inroads into hi-tech hardware manufacturing—the fact remains that

China and India complement each other's strengths. China will remain dominant in mass manufacturing, India is a champion in software, design and services. "Chinese manufacturing plus Indian services will create an ideal win-win situation," says Wang Jinzhen, Assistant Chairman, China Council for Promotion of International Trade.

There are other areas of mutual interest where China and India can come together. In fact, after running into each other a number of times in the race for oil equity abroad, India's Oil and Natural Gas Corporation (ONGC) and China National Overseas Oil Corporation (CNOOC) have come together to jointly bid for third-country oil assets. "We soon realized that the competition between us only worked to the advantage of the sellers, with asset prices going up dramatically," explains ONGC Chairman and Managing Director, Subir Raha, who believes India and China should also explore the possibility of swaps to minimize freight and insurance costs in transporting crude. Another area identified for mutual cooperation is multilateral trade negotiations. "If the two Asian giants take a joint stand in global forums like World Trade Organisation, International Monetary Fund and the United Nations then their voice will be heard," says Manoj Pant, Professor, School of International Studies, Jawaharlal Nehru University. But despite the obvious advantages, the clashing political and economical interests have so far prevented the two countries from moving towards what is known in academic circles as 'Chindia'. The two governments are, however, playing a proactive role in their economic development.

EYE ON THE FUTURE

Inviting Chinese Hospitality

Back in 2002, Girija Pande, Asia Pacific Head, Tata Consultancy Services (TCS), used to fly down to Hangzhou province in China from his Singapore office every weekend. He had to find a site for the company's third development centre in the mainland after Shanghai and Beijing. Every time he visited the province, he was welcomed by the mayor. During one of their casual exchanges, Pande remarked that the lack of a good vegetarian restaurant would disappoint the mostly South Indian project managers of TCS. When he visited the province for the fourth time, the mayor took him to a spanking new vegetarian restaurant promoted by the state government. There you are! There's no limit to Chinese hospitality towards foreign investors. Tax sops, flexible labour laws and no red tape—it can't get better. "Starting a business in China is as easy as walking into a rented house. No licences, no clearances, no permissions, just rent a shed and begin work," says Venugopal Dhoot, Managing Director, Videocon.

Attracting Indian Incentives

Not to be left behind, India too is hard-selling itself to global investors. Despite strong political opposition, the country is opening-up more and more industries. And there's competition among states in offering tax holidays and other incentives to attract FDI. For instance, when Ford wanted to set up its manufacturing plant in India in 1995, Tamil Nadu, Gujarat, Haryana and Maharashtra were all vying to woo the US car major. What helped Tamil Nadu clinch the deal was the "customized package of incentives" it offered to the company.

Special Economic Zones

And both India and China have their eyes set on the future. India is leaving no stones unturned in ensuring that it keeps its lead in IT offshore and BPO segments. In fact, the country's knowledge industry is pushing hard to go up the value chain. India has already established a strong 65% market share in the booming Knowledge Process Outsourcing (KPO) which is expected to become a $ 17-billion industry by 2010. India is also going all out on the physical infrastructure front, the country's weak point. Major highway projects like the Golden Quadrilateral and the North-East, South-West corridors are expected to be completed in December 2006 and December 2009, respectively. Also, a number of special economic zones (SEZs)—the same animal that takes most of the credit for China's runway success in the last three decades—and industrial townships are slated to come-up in different parts of the country. The government has already given nod to 160 SEZs that are expected to attract investments of Rs. 1 lakh crore in the next three years and create nearly five lakh jobs.

Enhancing Value-added Chain

Chinese government, meanwhile, is aggressively pushing its low-cost, mass-producing industry to move into higher value-added goods by encouraging R&D in domestic companies and luring foreign firms to move-up the value chain by giving them tax incentives. "Thus, in the next 10 years, while the low-cost, mass produced goods will move to the hinterlands, the coastal areas will move into high-value added industries like telecommunications, information technology and pharmaceutical research," says Green of Standard Chartered. Already, according to the Organization for Economic Cooperation and Development (OECD), China has overtaken the United States to become the world's largest exporter of information communication technology goods. What next? A Chinese Sony? Well, the country clearly doesn't want to remain just an assembler of someone else's knowhow. A slew of Chinese companies, such as Haier, see themselves as serious players with global ambitions. "We don't talk about our country of origin because Haier is a global player, having 16 R&D centers and 13 manufacturing units across the world," says T.K. Banerjee, President and Chief Executive of Haier Appliances (India)

NO CAKE WALK

Challenge to Broad-base Growth

It is not to say the two countries have an easy ride ahead. Their first challenge is to broad-base growth. Of the total 2.3 billion people in the two countries, nearly 1.5 billion earn less than $ 2 a day, according to World Bank data. Add to that the problems of illiteracy (35.2% in India in 2004 and 24% in China in 2003) and unemployment (9.9% in 2005 and 4.2% in 2004). And you know tomorrow's superpowers are still a long way away from prosperity.

Over-investment in China

Then there are economic factors. Some commentators like Surjit Bhalla, Managing Director, Oxus Research and Investments, believe that China's inefficient use of investment will drag down its growth rate in the future. Its incremental capital output ratio-increase in annual investment divided by the increase in GDP—has risen in recent years. This suggests that the country is having to spend more money to generate the same amount of growth. Again, they say, there has been over-investment in some sectors such as cars, steel and property and that some of the projects will prove unprofitable. Add to that China's fragile banking system burdened with non-performing loans (some says it's close to 50% of China's GDP). Also, many global economists believe that China will become old before it becomes rich. "By 2027, 14% of its population will be more than 65 years of age, but the per capita income will be around $ 12,000 a year," says Green of Stan Chart.

Infrastructure Constraints

India's ills include poor infrastructure, rigid labour laws, corruption, red-tapism, high fiscal deficit, rural poverty and poor governance. Both China and India are still to take the benefits of reforms to the rural areas even though most of their labour force remains in agriculture.

Worst Business Environment

Ironically, the two countries that together attract 12.5% of the world's FDI, are among the worst when it comes to business environment. According to the World Bank, to start a business requires 71 days in India and 48 days in China (compared to 6 days in Singapore); enforcing debt contracts requires 425 days in India and 241 days in China (69 days in Singapore).

More "Pluses"

But then, clearly the pluses outweigh the minuses. According to an IMF report, China just has to continue its reforms (especially those of banking and its loss-making public sector units) to enjoy faster growth than America ever achieved and within a decade become the biggest exporter and importer of items in the world. India is rated a better environment for investment than China, thanks to its higher returns on capital-achieving a GDP growth of 7-8% on an investment rate of 29% against a 9.5% growth on an investment rate of 45% by China. Other attractions include India's legal and regulatory environment and democratic institutions. "India will be a power to reckon with because of its demographics and high rate of growth," says Kamal Nath, Minister of Commerce and Industry. He believes the world will woo India because it is a counterbalance to China and the US.

Optimistic Outlook

Most global banks and investment firms have optimistic outlook for both India and China. The now-famous Goldman Sachs report, *Dreaming with BRIC* (Brazil, Russia, India, China), of 2003, has predicted that in dollar terms China could overtake Germany in the next four years and the US by 2039. India's economy could be the third largest after China and the US in the next 30 years. It said India will continue to grow at more than 5% in the next 30 years if the reforms continue. A recent report by Price Water House Cooper, *The World in 2050'*, states that India has the potential to become the fastest growing large economy in the world by the year 2050. A Deutsche Bank Research report, 'The largest economies 2020 according to Formel-G'. says India will be the third largest economy by 2020.

So, make no mistake, we're at the beginning of the Asian Century. And it proves an old Chinese proverb right: "*If you want one year of prosperity, grow grain. If you want 10 years of prosperity, grow trees. If you want 100 years of prosperity, grow people.*"

A Place for India in 'Asian' Century

A. VASUDEVAN

INTRODUCTION

Two interesting developments await India Inc. to seize opportunities to grow to be a part of the dream of making this an Asian Century. The present official thinking is favourable for the Indian business to get its act together. We shall at the outset deal with the developments and then discuss the implications thereof for India.

First is the news, dated December 20, 2005, concerning China's upward revision of its estimates of Gross Domestic Product (GDP) for 2004. The upward revision places the GDP to be higher over the earlier estimate by about 17 per cent, driven largely by the growth of the services sector whose share in GDP has moved-up to about 41 per cent.

News reports also suggest that China has not made revisions of GDP for the preceding years but would gradually bring out revisions beginning 1993. The revisions are based on the new methodology, presumably corresponding closely to what was suggested by the UN System of National Accounts, 1993. But the revision effected for 2004 does not mean that it is the same as the growth rate. In view of the lack of revised data for 2003, one would presume that the growth rate during the year has not changed.

Ahead of Italy

The implications of the revision and the timing of the announcement immediately after the Hong Kong meet on trade negotiations are of relevance for India. The revision places China ahead of Italy—the sixth largest in the world in terms of economy size.

Some academics in China, however, believe that the latest revision of GDP for 2004 doest not capture fully the reality. In their view, the values of transactions of the private sector are sharply under-reported. If this view is correct, China could well edge out or equal the UK or France in terms of economy size. Industrialised countries can no longer afford to ignore China and will have to seriously consider giving it a place in their elite club. The summit of the Group of Eight countries (G-8) that normally takes place around May/June could well see a new member in China. This could mean that either the member now occupying the eighth position would have to be left out or the G-8 would have to be extended to become G-9. The concept of symmetry of treatment that plays a critical role in international finance can, however, be ignored by the summiteers if China does not come out with its national account statistics for some of the years preceding 2004. One should not be surprised if data for at least 2003 are released in the next few months. What does the GDP revision mean in US dollar terms? As the exchange rate is given, China's GDP in US dollar terms would be higher than what was believed to be the case before the data revision. Could this be interpreted as China's way of saying that its currency is not overvalued, given the inherent strength of the economy?

Product of Technology

Another significant implication is that China's high growth rates are secured not by large investments, implying wastage of capital resources as Paul Krugman had argued some years ago, but by higher productivity. Since this productivity would be regarded mainly as a product of technology shock (what economists call the total factor productivity) rather than of labour productivity growth, one should consider China as being positioned at the new frontiers of science and technology. But reality suggests otherwise—China is not a technology leader but an emulator. The gap between China and the US in the fields of science and technology is still very large. Once the technology shock is discounted, a curious question arises as to why productivity should be so high in China and not in other countries. Is it because workers' productivity is high due to sound work ethics and factory discipline? Or, is there an incentive system unnoticed by outsiders?

The upward revision of GDP would also imply a high income velocity of money, given its stock. In other words, the demand for money in China would have been low. Real money demand in China would have been less positively responsive to income and negatively related with short-term interest rates. The yield curve should have been higher than what was the position before data revision. From the policy view-point, interest elasticity of demand for money would signal scope for further financial sector diversification and deepening of financial markets. China's financial reforms and practices so far have been not as transparent as they should be with the result that questions of financial vulnerability are often aired.

Relevance for India

The above discussion has relevance for India in more ways than one. First is the need to re-look at India's national income statistics. India has adopted the UN system of national income and made revisions in relevant data some years ago. But as these revisions have not been marked in India, it would be useful to revisit the methodology, particularly in respect of compilation of data of the contribution of the services sector and of the unorganized sector within the commodity-producing vector, as also the price deflators that are deployed.

Second, the case for accelerating investment rate in order to post higher growth would be less relevant than the case for enhancing productivity. It would be necessary to work out strategies for improving work ethics, labour contract laws, and incentives for application of new or innovative technologies.

Third, with only 41 per cent services sector share in GDP, China could post higher growth rates than India with 52 per cent services sector share in GDP. It is difficult to know as to what should be the right share of the services sector to optimize the overall growth but it is becoming increasingly clear that securing a better balance between the growth in the services sector and commodity-producing activities would be necessary for India to address the problem of large-scale unemployment.

Finally, the large market size of China should be exploited for the trading opportunities it affords. To make inroads into the markets of China, Indian goods (and services) would have to be price competitive with those that export goods to China, besides being qualitatively as good with sound after-sale servicing and other business practices. Will India take up the challenge?

SAFTA is Real

The second development relates to setting in place the South Asia Free Trade Agreement (SAFTA) from January 1, 2006. Enormous useful work has been carried out on the operational procedures by the Committee of Experts of the seven nations forming the SAARC—Bangladesh, Bhutan, India, Maldives, Nepal, Pakistan and Sri Lanka. SAFTA envisages reduction of tariffs for intra-regional trade among the seven countries along with concessions covering tariffs, para-tariffs and non-tariffs for the least developed countries of the region. While some issues like the negative lists in respect of high value goods for purposes of trade have to be still sorted out, it is necessary to use the opportunity thrown up by the Agreement to make large-scale investments in the region as also to improve the volume of trade. The Prime Minister's suggested estimate that the volume of trade could increase from the present level of $ 6 billion to $ 14 billion in two years from January 1, 2006 should be within reach provided the Indian business community and exporters of the rest of the countries of SAARC ensure that intra-regional trade is price competitive. It is also possible to extend financial services and technical collaborations including knowledge management, educational and information technology services rendering it possible to ultimately realize a full-fledged South Asia Economic Union as a stepping stone to making the century truly Asian.

Towards the Indian Century : Some Reflections

Sumit K. Majumdar

INTRODUCTION

India has, historically, had an issue with its population. In many parts of the country, because of intrinsic fertility and fecundity, the population density has been very high and India has always had one of the largest populations of the world. It is this precise characteristic that gave India the reputation of being the ultimate Malthusian test case some decades ago. With population seen as outstripping food supplies, in the early 1960s, many observers thought that a demographic disaster, of the kind that hit China in the 1950s when several millions perished of famine, was in the making. How times have changed! India has not only successfully warded off the Malthusian contingency, given the huge success of the Green Revolution, but it has a population that will generate demographic dividends for the world.

Median Age

India's population has a median age of 24 (half of its population is under 24). The median age of the Chinese population is 34. It is this statistic that makes the Indian economy much more important than China's. With half its population under 24, while half of China's population is over 34, India has the edge in its ability towards driving the world's growth. With over a billion people, of whom more than 500 million are under the age of 24, the vast pool of youth in India will provide the critical market for growth to take place. In comparison, the comparable market size of those under 24 for China is much smaller. Also, if there are saturation and satiation points for market demand, they will be reached much later in India than in China.

Declining US Market?

A reasonable question is what about the US market? In the years to come, that market may simply not matter to global trade. The population size of 300 million is clearly overshadowed by the combined two-billion-plus markets of India and China. Each country overshadows the population of the US considerably. Yet, it is not the absolute market size that matters. It is the distribution of the population within a country. The median population age in the US is 37 years. By that token, it is a considerably older country than India and marginally older than China. Is a GDP growth rate of three per cent in an ageing country, with a median age of 37, more attractive to a businessman than a GDP growth rate of 10 per cent in a youthful country, where the median age is 24?

India also has 550 million individuals under 24, while the US might have a population of 90 million such persons. Clearly, in the not so distant future, the market attractiveness of the US will dim substantially.

Europe, A Rapidly Ageing Society

If such analysis is conducted for the European countries collectively their median age of 40 makes them a rapidly ageing society where the dynamism that fuels growth will quickly be extinguished. In country after country across Central, Eastern and Western Europe, the high median age, coupled with a net population replacement rate that is negative—there are more deaths than births—means the population is being laid threadbare. This means that the seriousness with which one might have viewed the European markets has diminished, if not evaporated.

Qualitative Dimensions

India's population, which till quite recently was seen as a potential liability, is, in fact, its greatest asset. The benefits are clearly quantitative, propelling global growth. Yet the more, important characteristics are behavioural and qualitative. Very simply, a youthful population means that Markets + Minds = Motivation. Carrying this line of reasoning further, Markets + Minds + Motivation = Money. With a hungry population, hundreds of million strong, all waiting to become economically emancipated and relatively well off as rapidly as possible, the market for projects of various sorts, in sector after sector, is truly gigantic. But it is the hunger and the drive for progress in its youthful population that signal key qualitative shifts in expectations for the Indian economy as a whole.

Index of Expectations

Today, on a scale of one to 10, with 10 being the highest level of expectations, the feel-good factor in India is possibly eight while a decade ago it may have been six. Certainly, a generation ago it was a four. It is fair to state that currently for China the index value is also probably eight, while for the US it might be a six of seven and for Europe as a whole four-five.

Simply put, India, followed by China, holds the motivational high ground in the world's economic pantheon. In less than a generation, the "animal spirits" that the late Lord Keynes so evocatively described as the ultimate generator of entrepreneurship and economic activity have come to the fore in India. The drive for the consumption of products, services and ideas, the drive for the betterment of one's life, the drive to improve the physical accoutrements and constituents of a slightly shabby society, and the drive to just succeed, in general, are all palpable in the Indian firmament.

Drivers of Innovation

All macro-economic phenomena are ultimately driven by ground-level micro-economic, behavioural and psychological factors. Thus, what does the presence of a motivated market, the size of which has never before been experienced by any country in the history of human civilization, mean for India and the world?

Very simply, markets drive innovation. It is both market size and scope that drive the actual design of the functionalities that a customer might want and the diffusion of the ultimate products or services over time. Customers also have a direct role in dictating the contours of innovation, and the adage 'if you build it they will come,' while applying to infrastructure such as roads and bridges, does not apply to the consumer and industrial products and services that make up most of GDP.

Given India's large and youthful population, India is going to be the laboratory from where the major innovations of the world are likely to develop. Consequently, company after global company is planning on developing products and services in India, with a view to testing them here, before their national and global diffusion takes place. Thus, India's customer base is going to define what appropriate customer functionality is, and, by that token, the Indian consumer is going to be defining the logic of world markets.

India is likely to become, therefore, one of the most important economic powers on earth. First, much of the world's new innovations is going to be propelled by India's youthful population because their constituency is simply too critical and powerful to not take into account. Second, the sheer size of the Indian market means that in volume terms too it becomes the largest market on earth.

World Economy : Made in China?

ALOK RAY

INTRODUCTION

Today India's imports from China exceed those from the United States. It is estimated that, at the current rates of growth of exports from India, China will soon overtake the US as the top destination. This is another reminder to the world that China is replacing the US as the global growth engine. In fact, the 21st century may very well be China's, as the last was Japan's. The importance of China for the global economy is reflected in many different spheres. That "wages in the US are being set in Beijing" is one reason why. China, as the leading supplier of an increasing variety of consumer goods at low prices, is forcing the wage rates in competing countries to come down. Like China in the manufactures goods sector, India is being viewed as the emerging leader in the supply of services. This, in turn, is threatening wage rates of service workers (specially in software and IT-enabled services) and those in Research and Development in the developed world.

Abundant Labour Supply

An American student, in his feedback form following the end of the course that this author taught at a US university, wrote: "After outsourcing jobs to India, our universities have started importing 'cheap' professors from India. This must stop in the interest of protecting our job." This is not an isolated outburst. Many American students are concerned about losing high-paying jobs to Indians, just as factory workers are of losing manufacturing jobs to China. According to Mr. Richard Freeman, a Harvard professor, the entry of China, India and Russia into the global economy has effectively doubled the global labour supply. The consequent increase in the global labour-capital ratio is bound to reduce the global wage rate while raising the returns to capital (or the rate of profit) throughout the world economy. So, it is natural that the real wage rate in the developed countries will come down, while the rate of profits of MNCs (that are shifting their factories to low-wage countries such as China and India) hit all-time highs.

An Army of Cheap Labour

Further, the entry of China in the 1980s is qualitatively different from that of Japan's in the 1950s. China combines an army of cheap labour with an economy which is much more open than Japan. Currently, the sum of exports and imports of China as a ratio of its GDP is around 75 per cent. That of Japan (also for India) falls in the 25-30 per cent range. So, the impact of China's entry into the global market is unparalleled. Naturally, the increase in global resources is raising the global growth rate. But the distribution of income is going against labour and in favour of capital in the First World. According to *The Economist*, in most developed countries, the share of wages in national income (which over a long period in history had remained fairly stable) is now close to their lowest level in decades. For the same reason, the share of profits in the US, Europe and Japan is at the highest level in 25 years. The entry of Communist China into the global economy is impoverishing the working class and fattening the capitalists in the industrialized nations! It has also contributed to keeping the global inflation rate low, despite surging prices of commodities, such as oil and steel. Both the rise in the global commodity prices and the low inflation are primarily due to the China factor.

Global Impact

The return to profitability of many steel and cement companies is largely attributed to the construction boom in China. The rapid rise in the use of cars in the newly affluent China (and India) is often held responsible for the recent surge in oil prices. The scope for further rise in the demand for cars and oil is enormous in China. In the US, there is an average of one car per two individuals, the corresponding figure in China is one per 70. Thus, the future profit of the major global car manufacturers is inextricably tied-up with the growth in the Chinese market. Yet, the global inflation rate remains low because of the continuous fall in the prices of a bewildering range of consumer goods exported from China. If China eventually revalues the yuan by 23-30 per cent, as the US is demanding, the inflation rate in the US, Europe and Japan would go up significantly. Even the global interest rate is being determined by China and a few other Asia countries. China's huge foreign exchange reserves (more than $ 700 billion) are largely invested in US government securities. This is keeping the US interest rate low, thus enabling American consumers to maintain their artificially high standard of living with cheap credit. The real-estate boom in the US in also built with cheap money. If China changes its global investment policy, the US interest rate will go up, much to the peril of America's prosperity. For how long will China maintain its hold over the global inflation rate, the wage rate, the profit rate, the interest rate and commodity prices? Some analysts believe that it will take at least two decades for China to absorb its surplus labour into the industrial sector. Till then, China rules.

Best Growth Story

It is being viewed by many foreign investors as the next best growth story in the world. As the Chinese Prime Minister put it. China is becoming the global factory while India is poised to become the global office. Many well-known multinationals are in the process of shifting at least a part of their R&D centres to India. In fact, some analysts (including the much quoted BRIC Report by Goldman Sachs) believe that India has one advantage over China—the percentage of population in the working age group will remain above China's in the coming decades.

But, unfortunately, that by itself is no guarantee of superior economic performance unless India upgrades its skill levels and the productivity of workers. Whether we will accomplish that will largely depend on the reach and quality of the education system and the level of efficiency in the public-private economic partnership that can foster a globally attractive investment climate.

> Despite the gains, imbalanced growth remains China's Achilles' heel. Chinese growth is heavily dependent on FDI flows largely concentrated in the costal regions and account for 50 per cent of exports and 60 per cent of imports. Without these FDI flows, Chinese growth rates could well have slowed down by 3.5 percentage points, to Indian levels. With FDI to China set to plateau and that of India on a roll, there is increasing nervousness in China. India is, in fact, set to give China a run for its money with total factor productivity growth picking up to match that of China.
>
> *Source*: Pyaralal Raghavan: "India-China Growth Race", *The New Indian Express*, November 27, 2006.

India and China : Towards a Cooperative Partnership

C.V. RANGANATHAN

INTRODUCTION

In 1988, the former Prime Minister of India, Rajiv Gandhi, visited China. That visit by India's head of government to China came after a gap of 34 years since his grandfather, Jawaharlal Nehru's visit in 1955. This undesirable hiatus in the millennial old India. China's relationship was a reflection of much that had gone sour in bilateral relations from the late fifties of the last century. The prevalence of three cold wars, between the Americans and the former Soviet Union, between the Americans and the Chinese and between the Chinese and the Soviets also had a baneful influence on India-China relations during most of those years.

An Asian Century

During his 1988 visit, Rajiv Gandhi had a meeting with the late Deng Xiaoping, the father of China's social, political and economic reforms post the Mao Zedong era. At that meeting Deng said, "in recent years there has been comment about the next century being the Asia-Pacific century. I do not agree with this viewpoint. The combined population of the two countries is 1.80 billion. If India and China fail to develop, it cannot be called an Asian century."

Within two decades of that statement, its prophetic importance is beginning to be realized by the Indians, Chinese and the world at large even as India and China have significantly deepened their constructive engagement straddling many diverse fields. This includes a broadening of mutual understanding at the highest political levels over where India and China are placed vis-à-vis each other and with respect to the rapidly changing contemporary global and regional situation in Asia which impact on both countries. The implementation of Confidence Building Measures (CBM's) in the military fields to ensure the maintenance of peace and tranquillity along the long border, albeit disputed, and an intensification of exchanges at different levels between the armed forces are other welcome developments. A remarkable growth in the two-way trade between India and China has resulted in China and Hong Kong becoming a top ranking economic partner of India. There is a palpable and growing interest on the part of Indian and Chinese entrepreneurs to partner in mutually profitable joint ventures and investments in manufacturing and other service areas. Well-known Indian companies have invested in China in fields as diverse as information technology, telecommunications, energy, pharmaceuticals, chemicals, packaging, automotive, tourism and hospitality. Improved communication through direct flights between the two countries has led to increasing numbers of exchanges in cultural tourism. The growing spending power of vast sections in each country is an impetus for deep mutual exploration of the myriad 'soft' sectors such as information technology enabled services, human resource development, entertainment, food, fashions, and similar areas. Exchanges between academic scholars and non-governmental civil society organizations either on a bilateral basis or under the aegis of international bodies are burgeoning.

Interactions with China

Thus India is in the process of having a density of interactions with China, which the latter has enjoyed for some years with developed and developing countries. One can discern a palpable self-confidence in India at various levels to strengthen relations. Robust and steady growth of its economy, the rapid adaptation by its industrialists and business entrepreneurs to the challenges of globalization and to competition from China in areas where India was traditionally strong, add to India's self perception that India can 'rise' in the global economic order. The capacity of the Indian political system to absorb and represent multiple, at many times opposing views, on the directions of economic and social policies through democratic institutions is a phenomenon, which is the pride of Indians and admired universally. The professionalism of India's armed forces, backed by a minimum nuclear deterrent which India will never be the first to use, ensures respect for India's territorial integrity and capacity to undertake voluntary international responsibilities in the cause of peace and stability.

Both India and China, each with its distinctive history, culture, political system and social organization remain among the very few major developing countries, which have emerged stronger by rapid adaptation from the past to suit the present. They have broken from ideologically stultified external policies, which marked their existence for previous decades. They have demonstrated their capability in handling international terrorism which threatened parts of their countries and are significant partners in the world-wide struggle against terrorism. Lastly, they are with some success structuring their economic policies so as to benefit from globalisation. They are able to reposition themselves to engage and contribute to the emerging international order. In India there is a large middle ground of political consensus and support to the ruling government of the day in the pursuit of its domestic and external polices. The *raison d'etre* for the ruling Chinese Communist Party is to demonstrate that it is capable of making China strong, prosperous and raise the living standards of its millions. Respect for its legitimate interests in its neighbourhood and by the major Powers has been ensured by its strong economic growth and the consequent enhancement of its military strength.

Deng Xiaoping's statement to Rajiv Gandhi is also prophetic in the sense that the sequential rise of China first and then India is not a matter for China and India alone. A noteworthy feature of the early years of this century has been a gradual shift from the almost unilinear focus on China to India. The report of the National Intelligence Council of the U.S.A. released in December 2004, titled "Mapping the Global Future" says in its executive summary "in the same way that commentators refer to the 1900's as the 'American Century' the 21st Century may be seen as the time when Asia, led by China and India, comes into its own. A combination of sustained high economic growth, expanding military capabilities, and large population will be at the root of the expected rapid rise in economic and political power for both countries." Further, "most forecasts indicate that by 2020 China's gross national product (GNP) will exceed that of individual western economic powers except for the United States. India's GNP will have over-taken or be in the threshold of overtaking European economies."

Comparisons between India and China highlighting the strengths and weaknesses of each have almost assumed industry proportions in India, in China and the West. The global impact of the growth in recent years of the political economies of both are the much discussed topics at major gatherings, such at Davos and at the Summit Level meetings of the Group of 8 advanced countries where Presidents, Prime Minsiters and industrial and business leaders take part. The point to emphasize in all this is that there has been a shift in the centre of geo-political gravity away from the occident and it is now well-recognized that India and China are the drivers of the Asian and international political economies. Other major powers and regional groups in Asia such as Japan and the Association of South East Asian Nations (ASEAN) have recognized this and have strengthened their engagements with India and China.

International Developments

International developments since the demise of the former Soviet Union have highlighted anew what nature, geography and man's ingenuity had promoted in ancient and pre-modern historic times. Namely, the spread of the intellectual influence and commerce of the two large civilizational states, India and China, over a wide swathe of continental and maritime Asia. In contemporary times it is more than ever evident that Indian and Chinese interests intersect over a very wide area extending from West Asia through Central Asia and South Asia to South East and East Asia. India and China either share immediate borders with countries of this vast region or are near neighbours to them, not separated by big distances. China is an immediate neighbour of India's northern neighbours and India and China share a long mountainous border. Within this arc from the West of Asia to its East is contained the source of raw materials, particularly energy required by both. As it is also the source of problems caused by unstable governments, unresolved conflicts and violent extremism, which impact on regional peace and stability which in turn could affect both countries.

No More Americanization!

In a continuum from World War II, it is inevitable that the U.S.A. is expected to play a responsible leadership role, as the world's richest and strongest power. However, globalisation can no longer be equated with Americanization in view of the emergence of Asian powers, particularly, India and China. For Washington, dealing with Asia is seen as the "most challenging of all its regional relationships", according to the Report of the National Intelligence Council, 2020 Project. The traditional role of the U.S.A. in Asia and elsewhere has been as some sort of regional balancer in an era where its predominant military power, political and economic influence were unchallenged. By the turn of this century, as events have shown, there is so much that falls outside the power and capabilities of even the strongest. The unilateralist action in Iraq, while exposing the weaknesses of the international peace and security-maintaining institutions, has starkly proved that use of military means alone throws-up more problems than solutions. Threats posed by extremists, of the ideological or religious kind, who resort to violence destroying innocent lives almost everywhere have perhaps worsened. The unevenness of the spread of the benefits of globalization which need to be addressed by trade and financial systems, the indiscriminate destruction caused by natural disasters, disease, famine and deteriorating environments, all point to the seamless interdependence between the strongest and the weakest. Unilateralist actions as a response to situations is seen as harmful; international cooperation on the basis of consensus of the many and effective multilateralism provide stable foundations for seeking solutions to regional and international issues.

There are now signs that the second Bush Presidency is realizing that U.S.A.'s foreign policy cannot be based on a sense of exceptionalism about American interests. On the other hand, these interests are best served by showing greater sensitivity and regard for the interests of the majority of the international community and other states seen as major players on the world stage. India has benefited from this apparent change. Henry Kissinger, while addressing a forum of Indo-Americans is quoted as saying, "the geopolitical objectives of India, which they are pursuing in a hard-headed way are quite paralled to ours (Americans)." Other prominent Americans who have dealt with India have listed some of these shared objectives and issues : anti-international terrorism, prevention of the spread of weapons of mass destruction, energy issues, the direction of the global economy, and belief in the democratic way of life and all the values that this implies.

Towards Indianisation

The July 2005 visit of Prime Minister Manmohan Singh to the U.S.A. resulted in a resounding reaffirmation of these common objectives. There was, in addition, the removal of a major irritant in Indo-U.S. relations surrounding India's fission and fusion explosions on the path of developing nuclear weapons in 1974 and 1998. Unreasonable technology sanctions were imposed, which have hampered India's development of nuclear and space applications for peaceful purposes such as electricity production by the U.S.A., the main up-holder of the

Non-Proliferation Treaty (NPT). Under the Indo-U.S. nuclear cooperation agreement, India is neither limited nor inhibited from pursuing its nuclear weapon programme as per its autonomous judgement of the security situation. As India has invested in a three-stage nuclear programme comprising heavy water, fast breeder and thorium reactions for power production, the agreement opens the way to access the much needed fuel and other technologies from various outside sources to supplement indigenous efforts. In the long run a diversification of energy resources, with less dependence on fossil fuels is in India's interests and meet to some extent greenhouse gas emissions. Apart from this agreement a new phase of cooperation in knowledge-based industries, services, promotion of India as a destination for U.S. investments, initiatives in agricultural production and joint research in space exploration and other areas has been opened-up. On the whole, the series of Indo-U.S. agreements reached during the PM's visit bodes well for the realization of the deep potential in the relationship which has the strong moral backing of business, academic and social circles. Such support is perhaps not as evident in India's relations with other countries. It goes without saying that the implementation in details would need U.S. Congressional and Indian Parliamentary and public opinion support. At every stage a strong expression of political will would be required on both sides to manage the different constituencies who oppose deviations from the impractical norms set in earlier decades.

Strategic Significance of US

Ever since their relations were normalized in the seventies of the last century, China attaches the maximum strategic significance to U.S.A. The density and wide range of relations in many areas of human endeavour which China and U.S.A. enjoy cannot be matched for a long time to come between India and U.S.A. Close and growing economic relations between them has resulted in considerable reliance of the U.S. economy on China's stability and steady growth. All major businesses in U.S.A. have developed deep stakes in China. While think tanks in the U.S.A. and China, such as the Pentagon and its counterpart in China, view the long-term intention of the other with suspicions over accruing military capabilities, the fact remains that each requires the close and confidential understanding of the other over several strategic issues where largely their interests coincide. These include for instance, the denuclearization of the of the Korean Peninsula, peace in the Taiwan Straits, prevention of the spread of weapons of mass destruction and non-proliferation, stability in West Asia and on other issues which are brought before the U.N. Security Council, where China and U.S.A. are permanent members. Sino-U.S. difference over a host of issues covering trade, human rights situation in China, legal, economic and others are well publicized, but the larger compulsions forced by interdependence have taught the two countries to manage their differences, while forging their further cooperation in diverse areas.

Complementing its visible economic, scientific and technological achievements, the pursuit of its external relations in a realistic, rational and pragmatic manner has poised India in a happy strategic situation, the best since its Independence. India's relations with each of the major powers, U.S.A. European Union, Russia, China, Japan, ASEAN, Iran and other countries of Africa and Latin America, are not zero sum games. Nor is the reinforcement of each compartment of these separate relationships meant or directed against another. The totality of these separate relationships go to strengthening the age-old wisdom of India which is grounded in respect for diversity, pluralism, independence and autonomy of decision-making. In the context of the triangle of India-U.S.A.-China, the conduct and management of India's relations with the two must be freed of the fanciful rhetoric prevalent in the U.S.A., China or India of the possibilities of partnering one or the other against the third.

The UNSC seat for India

All this does not mean that differing or ever opposing view points on issues of important interest to India have been resolved. The case of India's entry into the select group of Permanent Members of the U.N. Security council is a case in point. While hardly any major power denies India's eligibility to be a Permanent Member of the Council, various considerations are at play in this particular theatre. It has always been the seat of real politik rather than representative of the principles of universality, realism and fairness. Various considerations extraneous to the merit of India's candidature weigh on USA and China. A good majority of Africans, Latin Americans and Europeans too have their own views on reforms of the U.N. system of which revision of the membership of the Security Council is seen as only one of the connected issues. Enshrined privileges, as we know in India, are difficult to uproot. Eventually only a consensus of views without any veto (by the Five Permanent Members) which is universally accepted by the membership of the U.N. would be viable in keeping with the workings of the world's only Parliament. This entire issue needs to be seen in perspective by Indians as a reflection of the fact that not in all areas has the burden of history or old thinking been removed in matters that concern high politics or commerce.

If effective multilateralism in the U.N. awaits various reforms and the amendment of the U.N. Charter, the multilateral cooperation necessary to make regional organizations effective is something that both India and China have practised in recent times. Good neighbourly diplomacy followed by both has been extended from their immediate neighbourhoods to a policy for multilateral regional regimes in Asia. The South Asian Association for Regional Cooperation (SAARC) had been hampered by poor India-Pakistan relations in the past, unstable neighbouring countries and the perception that as the largest country in the region which had registered impressive economic growth, India would exercise economic hegemony in the sub-region which the Association covers. With India and Pakistan turning away from confrontation to cooperation and dialogue, the mood to implement the important agreements in the economic and other areas has become much better. After the Summit level meeting where the heads of all the seven states of SAARC met in Dhaka in 2005, it is reasonable to expect that the commitments on social and economic cooperation taken in 2004 will be carried forward.

Regional Cooperation

China actively participates in a number of inter-governmental institutions for regional cooperation covering wide space in the Asia-Pacific region. Such participation is as much meant to assuage the fears of the members of these institutions that China's economic growth would be at their cost or that its growing military strength would threaten their security. It also accords with its self-perception that it is fully capable of playing in "responsible" role in regional and global affairs. These institutions include the Association of South East Nations (ASEAN), Asian-European Meeting (ASEM), Asia-Pacific Economic Cooperation (APEC) and the relatively new Shanghai Cooperation Organisation (SCO). Post its membership of the WTO, the signing of a Free Trade Agreement with ASEAN is a step in the direction of intergration of the ASEAN and Chinese economies in a manner where the former can benefit from China's growth.

An Asian Economic Community

India too is a Summit level partner of the ASEAN and has undertaken to sign a Free Trade Area Agreement with the group. With some of its individual partners such as Singapore and Thailand, India has embarked on a comprehensive economic agreement and a Free Trade Area Agreement. Looking further east in Asia, Prime Minister Manmohan Singh has talked about an Asian Economic Community which encompasses India, ASEAN, China, Japan and Korea. Terming this an "arc of advantage" across which there would be a large-scale movement of people, capital, ideas and creativity, the vision is based on the conviction that India has much to offer to Asia, helping to knit the continent together in a manner never seen before. An important principle to be followed in realising this vision is that cooperation within and across regions and their institutions should be open, inclusive and potentially integrative. This would mean paying due regard to the reasonable interests of extra-regional major powers such as USA, European Union, Burma and others. Attempts at exclusion, and India was a victim in the past, of this, would only lead to confrontations, thus militating against the consolidation of interdependence in a globalising world.

In the neighbourhood, India is a contributor to the sub-regional official grouping covering the Bay of Bengal area which includes Bangladesh, Myanmar, Sri Lanka and Thailand (BIMSTEC). The group envisages multisectoral technical and economic cooperation. Supplementing this official institution is a separate academic forum which is exploring trade, transport, tourism, cultural and other links between Bangladesh, China (through the participation of a south-western province, Yunnan), India and Myanmar (BCIM Forum). This is a venture whose time has come. China is investing heavily in this province and in Tibet to remove the enormous disparities in development within China, through big infrastructure projects which could have an impact on India's underdeveloped north-eastern states. Through its active participation in the BCIM forum, Myanmar has shown that it does not view itself as a zone of exclusive Chinese economic development and welcomes India's investment there in projects which would facilitate Myanmar becoming an entrepot to serve the growing economies of India and China. Cooperation between the two in the development of transport infrastructure and connectivity is an area of great promise for India's neighbourhood which would benefit its states in the north-east to link up with South-east Asia. The much talked about "Look East" policy would assume greater credibility if a vast and populated region of India is eventually connected to the rest of Asia.

Shanghai Cooperation Organisation

Composed of Russia, China, Khazakhstan, Krgyzstan, Tajikistan and Uzbekistan, the SCO was initially set up to settle border disputes, enhance military trust and confidence and face the common threat of religious extremism, terrorism and secession. Set up even prior to the September 11 assault on the World Trade Centre in New York, the SCO has put into place inter-governmental institutions to step up regional economic cooperation, mutual trade and investment and implement ambitious energy and transportation projects. Obviously Russia and China play leading roles in the organization, one to recover eroding influence and to promote integration in a large space which belonged to the erstwhile Soviet Union, and the other to expand opportunities for its growing economy. In its last

Summit level meeting of 2005, the SCO called for a definite time limit for the removal of American military presence in Afghanistan, thus emphasizing the common desire that USA's global military presence, which includes a vast area of sensitive importance to both China and Russia post 9/11, should not become entrenched in the long term. Joint military exercises by the member states of SCO and especially involving a bilateral exercise between China and Russia in 2005, are symbols of seeking regional security through the autonomous efforts to the members of the region.

It is a welcome sign that India was invited to participate in the SCO as an observer at its last Summit level meeting in 2005, along with Pakistan, Iran and others who share the extended neighbourhood of Central Asia. Possibilities of working out arrangements for flows of energy and other resources and connecting India overland to countries with whom there are ancient cultural and trade contacts await reinvigouration and renewal in the contemporary context. To the north-west of India, stretching to Central Asia also lie some of the source of India's problems which manifest themselves in extremist violence. Thus, for multiple reasons, India needs to take deep interest in a part of the Asian landmass where there are new countries whose stability and prosperity have a beneficial impact on India. Configuring foreign policy, taking into account the strategic and geopolitical interests of the major players in the region, China and Russia, and fashioning an inclusive and cooperative framework are the requirements for the safe-guarding of Indian interest The official and non-official trialateral academic dialogues between India, China and Russia which have been in existence for the last few years would need to be substantiated by specific programmes of cooperation covering fields of interest to all three countries. They look at the rapidly evolving world with similar perspectives and the time has come for active cooperation in joint projects such as would be appropriate to the three civilizational states.

Two Biggest Growth Economies

Thus it is increasingly evident that India and China are destined to interact over a wide swathe of Asia stretching across its continental and maritime mass. The recognition of this reality and the confidence that currently India and China are the two biggest growth economies has acted as a spur to the governments to broaden the agenda of bilateral cooperation. At the same time pragmatic steps have been taken towards the solution of longstanding problems such as the boundary dispute.

During Chinese Premier Wen Jiabao's visit to India in April 2005, several agreements were signed with the Government of India which would serve to consolidate the trend towards friendly relations first set in motion during the 1988 visit to China of Rajiv Gandhi. In the Joint Statement issued on 11th April and signed by the Prime Minster of India and the Chinese Premier, it was decided to establish an "India-China Strategic Cooperative Partnership for Peace and Prosperity." The partnership is based on the Five principles, mutual respect and sensitivity to each other's concerns and aspirations and equality. Among the various important agreements signed, two related to the political parameters and guiding principles for the settlement of the boundary question and a protocol on modalities for the implementation of confidence building measures in the military field along with the Line of Actual Control in the India-China border areas.

The Agreement and the Protocol sum up the results and understanding following several rounds of discussions between civilian and military officials over a decade and a half and the operational ground experience of the two armies in keeping the peace following two earlier agreements in 1993 and 1996. The Agreement crystallizes in the clearest and mutually acceptable terms the bottom lines which could govern an eventual settlement, which would be based on political (not purely academic) considerations. It closes a yawning gap in public acknowledgement by both parties of a de facto situation which came into being after 1962, but which was never formally accepted as something approximating to a reality which both countries could live with. As such, the Agreement should be of immense help in the education and creation of public opinion in the plural society of India and society in China, which has seen bursts of strident nationalism. A good augury is that the Border Agreement has not been subjected to criticism by the media in India, pointing to the degree of political maturity achieved in the relationship. Viewed in its totality the relationship between India and China has assumed a more wholesome character, where difference are managed imaginatively and where governments act as facilitators for a wide spectrum of activities to be undertaken by diverse sections of the two peoples, within and outside the two governments.

New Opportunities

Post the tragic events of September 11, 2001, from which ironically both China and India have benefited, USA is positioned in a crucial position in the India-Pakistan-China (we could add Afghanistan) equation. Absence of any possibility of a military conflict with potential to escalate into non-conventional areas, strict control over spread of weapons of mass destruction from an area identified with illegal proliferation, prevention of the re-emergence of religious or other fundamentalism with resort to violence against innocent civilians, domestic stability based on moderation and development are the common interests of all four countries. New opportunities are thus present to solve a long-standing disputes and to take forward-looking steps for the benefit of the peoples of South Asia.

To conclude, India is well poised to take advantage of the present turn of major diplomatic events involving it. There is growing international respect for India, that while pursuing its geopolitical, strategic and economic interests, these are by no means exclusive or exceptional, affecting the interests either of neighbours or of the major powers. Partnership and closer relations with India are seen as eminently desirable. For India, the diplomatic challenge is to manage each of its growing compartments of relations with USA, China and Japan in a manner where the underlying frictions between them and China do not affect the prospects of the bigger role in international affairs, which each of them envisages for India.

"China Cannot be contained"

"What will President Hu Jintao's visit be remembered for?"

The visit will be a landmark one. We are already pledged to be cooperative partners. Now we are trying hard to add substance to this partnership—in the political area, economic cooperation, cultural exchanges and even in confidence-building measures in the defence area.

There is a reluctance here to give projects to Chinese companies in certain sectors considered security-sensitive. Does China feel discriminated against?

Our economic relationship is developing fast, Chinese companies have the largest volume among foreign contracts in road, power stations, gas pipelines, telecom. So, Chinese companies are already very active. During (economic) development, problems occur sometimes. We need to overcome these quietly. I was very happy to hear the new foreign minister's remarks that India's policy is to not discriminate against Chinese companies.

—Sun Yuxi, Chinese Ambassador to India.

Source: *Outlook*, November 27, 2006.

India and China : On a 'Global Move'

BATUK GATHANI

INTRODUCTION

Observers of India and China in Western capitals are often perplexed by the current obsession about these two Asian nations' growing share of world trade and expanding economic profiles, which at best are rated as "modest and steady." According to latest estimates, while India has 7.2 per cent share of global GDP, China has 15.7 per cent compared to the US' 26.4 per cent, and the Euro Zone economies' 19.3 per cent. The heart of matter is that economists are worried about the rising global imbalances and suggest that American politicians, business and industry, should stop blaming key Asian economies and monotonously demanding currency revaluation, especially China's.

US Spillover Effect

Asia observers point out that market forces regulate currency appreciations or depreciations and "artificial" moves by the authorities concerned would have a less desirable impact. Obviously, Asians and Europeans are both concerned and worried over the ever widening and seemingly unbridgeable divide in the US balance of trade deficit and its insatiable capacity of borrowing more and living off low interest credits. Now, the US current account deficit stands at $ 529,000 million, Euro Zone's at $ 64,100 million compared to surpluses reported by Russia and West Asia's $ 160 billion, newly industrialized Asian economies's $ 124 billion, Japan's $ 75 billion, Latin America's $ 72 billion, China's $ 35 billion and India's $ 5 billion. Asians have also argued that any artificial revaluation of their currencies would trigger deflation. Economist Mr. Avinash Persaud, who is also one of the authors of the report, said that even if it was true that high saving rates in Asia were the root cause of growing global imbalances, the US had become addicted to cheap credits supplied by foreigners and withdrawal of the same would hurt the American economy. The report states that, so far, low inflation, low interest rates and steady yield rates have created a smooth financial environment for the financing of US current account deficit, but there are always question marks about its permanence and even credibility when the US is addicted to cheap borrowing and rising current account deficit. A sudden rise in oil prices could push inflation or the global economy could face prospects of a "natural and unpredicted" catastrophe. For example, scientists are warning about fast-warming tropical seas and the double rate of hurricanes. The global community has yet to "positively respond" to this challenge and the issue is still academic. Hence, it is often argued in the west that western economies are "better prepared" to withstand such economic or natural surprises.

Awakening Economic Giants

The west European nations are spending a substantial portion of their revenue on financing welfare states and obviously this has triggered higher taxation. It is often stated that the welfare State system has also initiated wild abuse of the system and many remain permanently unemployed or become unemployable and addicted to living off welfare State handouts. In the European Union, some 20 million are unemployed or underemployed—almost 9 to 10 per cent of the workforce compared to less that 5 per cent in the US. According to European observers, the two "awakening economic giants" of Asia—China and India—pose a serous threat to European manufacturing and job prospects, with their rising share of global trade and exports. China, in recent years, has drastically improved its productivity and Chinese manufacturers have also become more innovative. There is an overall quest to modernize manufacturing and Chinese companies are fast moving into foreign markets by buying "sick" European and American companies.

According to informed observers, some 80 Chinese companies are on a "global move" and could make inroads into key Western markets. With over 10 per cent economic growth per annum, Chinese companies will not be restricted to trading and manufacturing in the Far East. China and India are looking to expand their horizons for supply of oil and key metals and China is fast emerging as a major buyer of iron ore and other minerals. India is also intensifying its search for oil and promoting the use of alternative fuels, as high prices threaten the country's energy security and economic growth. Both India and China are fast modernizing their civilian nuclear programmes to boost their economies and reduce dependence on foreign oil supplies.

Three of China's companies are biding for stakes in overseas—American, and European—energy companies, while India still has only one—ONGC Videsh. Rio Tinto Zinc is the world's leading metal and iron ore trading company and, currently, China accounts for 15 per cent of its turnover. According to an Indian observer, both India and China should have their own Rio Tinto-size metal companies backed by a more determined search for key metals from domestic resources. As an analyst put it: "It is all there, perhaps in abundance but it has to be located, identified and brought into commercial production, and unless this happens both India and China will have a modest global economic profile." Chinese pragmatism is rated the key motivating factor and India companies have yet to "drastically improve" their competitive edge in the global market place and some fear that the Indian IT technology hegemony may not last for ever.

Learning from the Dragon

Compared to China, India's growth path has lots of speed breakers due to the sophisticated democratic process. But China grows much faster without consensus. Will China face upheaval in the future?

Answer: It's hard to say. China's growth can be stopped by US. But at the same time, China's growth is balanced and they are more focused on more sectors. Whenever a rule is passed by the government in China, it does not take long time to implement it. China is growing fast but India has not used its entire potential. When I was driving from Red Fort to New Delhi, the thing that struck my mind was that the capital Delhi compares to a Tier-3 city in China. I think Indian government should have such infrastructure in all cities. And also I feel, India has some specific big enterprises that govern the entire economy. Then there are lots of middle level enterprises and small companies whose growth is not good.

What can India learn from China's economic growth model?

Answer: China has a more planned way of doing things. India has a few private enterprises that are so big which have destroyed the medium enterprise. In China, the government puts some control. Growth is balanced so that more people are benefited. China has not let one enterprise grow too big, and has also given them enough power to be competitive. I think that inclusive growth is the most important.

—Professor Edison Tse,
The Department of Management Science
& Engineering, Stanford University.

Source: *The New Sunday Express*, November 19, 2006.

Super Economic Power Dynamics of India and China

P. Jegadish Gandhi

EMERGENCE OF NEW ASIA

Over the ages, world history has shown a record of the shifts of economic supremacy and dominance among continents and countries. Europe, with the super economic power of England, Germany and France swayed the global power in the 19th century whereas the American globalised capitalism and the Russian modelled communism impacted most of the developing countries in Third World in the 20th century Globalisation can no longer be equated with Americanization in view of the emergence of Asian powers, particularly, India and China in the beginning of the 21st century. With new formation of economic agglomeration among the Asian countries, under the powerful partnership of resource potentials of India and China, the 21st century will become a truly Asian Century.

The 21st century is widely touted as the one in which China and India will emerge and dominate as global economic powerhouses. The global impact of the growth in recent years of the political economies of both are the much discussed topics at major gatherings, such at Davos and at the Summit Level meetings of the Group of 8 advanced countries where Presidents, Prime Ministers and industrial and business leaders take part. The point to emphasise in all this is that there has been a shift in the centre of geo-political gravity away from the occident and it is now well-recognised that India and China are the drivers of the Asian and international political economies. Other major powers and regional groups in Asia such as Japan and the Association of South East Asian Nations (ASEAN) have recognized this and have strengthened their engagements with India and China.

SUPER ECONOMIC POWER DYNAMICS

Sustainable Growth Trends

China is set to record 8.5 to 9 per cent growth in 2005 and 2006. India's growth estimates are placed at 6.7 and 6.4 per cent for these two years. India's relatively faster growth in 2003-05 averaging 7.5 per cent and its spectacular progress in IT and other technological fields and increasing global competitiveness have earned for it the status of an emerging economic power which could become the world's third largest economy within the next two to three decades. Whereas the revised data for 2004, the census year, showed a 16.8 per cent rise in the size of the economy with GDP growing by 10.1 per cent, a double digit for the third year in succession, to make China the sixth largest economy. With another 9.9 per cent rise in 2005 GDP exceeding 2.2 trillion dollars, China is now the fourth largest economy, having outpaced France and Britain, and behind only to the US, Japan and Germany. China's long-term explosive growth and its emergence as the world' manufacturing hub and third largest trader, and India's catching up as a fast-growing economy with its abundance of skills, are being increasingly seen as a transformation under way of the global economic landscape.

The IMF, through its Asia-Pacific Regional Economic Outlook (REO) Report (May 2006) says Asia's growth has gathered considerable momentum in recent quarters, with the region benefiting from a surge in external demand for electronic products, which has stimulated investment, employment and consumption in most economies. While growth is likely to moderate in China and India, this merely signals "a return to more sustainable—but still very robust levels," adding that real growth year-on-year in India was 7.4 per cent in 2004, 8 per cent in 2005 and a projected 7.3 per cent in 2006 and 7 per cent in 2007. It says growth in the second half of 2005 in China and the Newly Industrializing Economies (NIEs) of East Asia was over 2.25 percentage points higher than expected earlier, with India and Japan providing "positive surprises" as well.

Broadening Bilateral Relations

A remarkable growth in the two-way trade between India and China has resulted in China and Hong Kong becoming a top ranking economic partner of India. There is a palpable and growing interest on the part of Indian and Chinese entrepreneurs to partner in mutually profitable joint ventures and investments in manufacturing and other service areas. Well-known Indian companies have invested in China in fields as diverse as information technology, telecommunications, energy, pharmaceuticals, chemicals, packaging, automotive, tourism and hospitality. Improved communication through direct flights between the two countries has led to increasing numbers of exchanges in cultural, tourism. The growing spending power of vast sections in each country is an impetus for deep mutual exploration of the myriad 'soft' sectors such as information technology enabled services, human resource development, entertainment, food, fashions, and similar areas. Exchanges between academic scholars and non-governmental civil society organizations either on a bilateral basis or under the aegis of international bodies are burgeoning.

Cross-border Investments

Trade between India and China in the early 1990s was only US $ 100 million a year. It is now over US $ 9 billion. China has benefited from India's expertise on the IT side, while India has benefited from Chinese manufactured goods. As relations between the two countries improve, the potential for cross-border investments likewise will improve. These include India's need to improve its overall social system. China could well emerge as India's largest trading partner, surpassing the US, in a year or two if the current trend of 35-40 per cent growth in bilateral trade between India and China is maintained. India would easily achieve a $ 20-billion bilateral trade by 2007. India's bilateral trade with China in 2000-01 was barely $ 2 billion. This increased to $ 12 billion in 2004-05 and is expected to reach a level of $ 15 billion in 2005-06. Both India and China should identify new products and diversify the trade basket if the bilateral trade is to attain the planned target of $ 30 billion by 2009.

According to the latest FICCI's analysis, it would be beneficial for India to focus on exporting products such as chemicals, drugs and pharmaceuticals, plastics, electrical equipment and machine, and agricultural products to China. For China, products such as audio/video equipment, electrical machinery, optical and medical instruments and transportation equipment should find a good market in India.

An Asian Integration

China actively participates in a number of inter-governmental multilateral institutions for regional cooperations covering wide spaces in the Asia-Pacific region. Such participation is as much meant to assuage the fears of the members of these institutions that China's economic growth would be at their cost or that its growing military strength would threaten their security. It also accords with its self-perception that it is fully capable of playing a "responsible" role in regional and global affairs. These institutions include the Association of South East Asian Nations (ASEAN), Asian-European Meeting (ASEM), Asia-Pacific Economic Cooperation (APEC) and the relatively new Shanghai Cooperation Organisation (SCO).

India too is a Summit level partner of the ASEAN and has undertaken to sign a Free Trade Area Agreement with the group. With some of its individual partners such as Singapore and Thailand, India has embarked on a comprehensive economic agreement and a Free Trade Area Agreement. In the neighbourhood, India is a contributor to the sub-regional official grouping covering the Bay of Bengal area which includes Bangladesh, Myanmar, Srilanka and Thailand (BIMSTEC). The group envisages multisectoral technical and economic cooperation.

Having concluded free trade agreements with SAARC, Singapore and Thailand, India is pursuing similar arrangements with several other Asian countries. "This web of engagements may herald an eventual free trade area in Asia covering all major Asian economies and possibly extending to Australia and New Zealand. This Pan-Asian FTA could be the future of Asia and will open up new growth avenues of Indian economy." (*Prime Minister Manmohan Singh,* May 6, 2006)

Global Integration

It is well-known that the rapid integration of China into the world economy has largely been the result of foreign companies establishing a manufacturing base in China. The momentum towards a freer economy has continued into this decade with membership of the World Trade Organisation (WTO) resulting in the standardization of a large number of its laws and regulations and the prospect of further tariff cuts. As the growing clout of the private sector in bolstering the economy makes it all the more crucial to further modernize the legal framework for business, the Chinese government is preparing legislation in three vital areas: Bankruptcy law, company law and the implementation of the constitutional amendment on property rights.

The density and wide range of relations in many areas of human endeavour which China and U.S.A. enjoy cannot be matched for a long time to come between India and U.S.A. Close and growing economic relations between them has resulted in considerable reliance of the U.S. economy on China's stability and steady growth. India's relations with each of the major powers, U.S.A., European Union, Russia, China, Japan, ASEAN, Iran and other countries of Africa and Latin America are not zero sum games. Besides the growing stature of China and India in the global economic system, a remarkable feature in more recent years has been the transformation of developing countries from dependence on external flows to finance their payment deficits till mid-1990s to becoming net exporters of capital.

STRONG AND WEAK SIGNALS

Free Play of Market Forces

In its first country survey of China, OECD says that China, the Middle Kingdom's economic impact on the world has been accentuated by its rapidly increasing openness to trade. Free play of market forces, opening up more and more sectors to foreign investments and readiness to change laws, including on property rights, have helped China's rapid global integration. The fact remains that India is obsessed with how the Chinese have converted their quest for progress into a conquest of constraints. If manufacturing excellence and massive infrastructure are keys to success, India is way behind—currently it is the services sector alone that is powering India, though agriculture and manufacturing are its traditional activities. "China is clearly at least ten years ahead of us in infrastructure and manufacturing. They are growing at a furious pace. We are growing at a satisfactory pace. If we don't do more, and that too in double quick time, the gap between China and India will increase." This is the stark reality of the difference between the economic performance of India and China (*Finance Minister P. Chidambaram,* May 6, 2006). There is little mystery about China's success. Its continued evolution of economic policies in the areas of the allocation of capital, labour mobility, urbanization and the creation of an improved framework for the development of the private sector should ensure that this development momentum is sustained.

Trade Dynamics

Stating that the pace of economic change in China has been extremely rapid since the start of economic reforms just over 25 years ago, the OECD report says China's impact on the world economy has been accentuated by a high and rapidly increasing degree of openness to trade, with the average of imports and exports signifying 35 per cent of GDP in 2004. With such a high degree of openness, OECD's medium-term baseline for the evolution of the world economy suggests that exports from

China would overtake those from Germany in 2008 and by the beginning of the next decade, push ahead of the US and might represent 10 per cent of world trade in goods and services at that point. Contrast China's feverish trade growth with India's goal of achieving one per cent share of the world trade by 2007, and one can see the miles India needs to traverse, despite the much –acclaimed superiority in the knowledge economy and information technology.

Spread Effect of Informatics

Although India's Foreign Direct Investment of US $ 3.5 billion is less than 10% of China's and overall exports of US $ 50 billion are less than 20% of China's, India does have some particular advantages. For instance, it has carved out a stronger position in IT services and pharmaceutical industries, and that is really owing to the predominance of engineering and science graduates and widespread proficiency in the English language. India also has an established system of property rights that places it well ahead of China in this regard. It has a large pool of exceptionally well educated individuals and benefits from an increasingly open society. It is possible that India's focus on service has created an overall wealth disadvantage compared to the Chinese, where over 100 million people work in manufacturing industries, many times the number of Indians working in IT services.

Aptech and NIIT are making it big in China, accounting for over 25 per cent of the Chinese IT training market in 2005. Since having entered the Chinese market in 2000, Aptech has established more than 200 training schools in 57 different Chinese cities and trained some 2,00,000 students in total. NIIT currently has 126 centers in 23 different provinces and is currently teaching an additional 50,000. But China has a long way to go before it can compete with India in terms of the skill levels of its IT professionals.

But India's growth in IT is likely to spread to manufacturing to promote a rising standard of living. Furthermore, it is likely that these two countries will be able to feed off each other's growth. The catalysts for India's coming prosperity are almost all in place. India will, like China, translate free market reform into economic prosperity.

Dominant Financial Markets

We are in a period in which India and China are poised to become dominant markets; whether they will become the dominant financial markets is open to question. This century you are going to see a race between the two from a financial markets perspective. India has an advantage with its financial markets right now and part of it comes from what China thinks is its advantage—stable government and predictable policies. That strength is going to become a weakness for China from a financial markets perspective. What makes China strong from an economic standpoint—its predictable policies—will also make it impossible for its financial markets to be trustworthy. India has an advantage in that it has a legal system, which with all its weakness still has some teeth to it. That is going to be a big factor going forward.

Growth-Speed Side Effects

Despite the over all high trend rate of growth, discussions on the need to manage bouts of deflation or 'overheating' recur periodically in Chinese economic discussions. Thus, the Chinese economy is seen to have experienced a long period of deflation from 1997 to 2001, and recovered from that only in the second half of 2002 (*Jayati Ghosh,* leading Indian Economic Analyst). Surging credit growth, a widening trade surplus and double-digit economic expansion amount to "close to a perfect storm of problematic trends" in China (*Jonathan Andersan*, Chief Asian Economist).

Macro Social Indicators

India's population is young with a segment that is very well educated and well suited for science and engineering. Citizens aged 14 and under comprise 32% of the population as opposed to 23% of China's. The median age of India's population is only 24 years, while it is 31 is China. Now, while India's overall literacy rate of nearly 60% lags well behind China's 88% it has a very well developed system of higher education that takes advantage of what the rest of the world sees as a genetic predisposition towards science and engineering. India has also made strong improvements in literacy in the last decade.

Compared to China, India's most compelling growth remains unreaslied. The differences in electricity and oil consumption, telephone use, GDP and poverty level all indicate considerably more up side for India. Consider that India's estimated population of 1.05 billion is only 19% below China's 1.29 billion. Yet its daily oil consumption is less than one half of China's. Its electricity consumption is less than 40% of China's. An estimated 25% of the Indian population is still below the poverty line versus only 10% of the Chinese population.

Asia : An Area for Future Business

President Abdul Kalam in his address at the joint session of the Philippine Congress (February 6, 2006) said that the "future of business" would be Asia. "There are two reasons for this. One is, the tremendous market that this region possesses with an economic ascend (ancy) phase. The second is, the availability of knowledge-based human capital in this region. With the Western markets getting saturated, this region provides a huge opportunity to businesses to expand their market share," India with its core competence in information and communication technology, space technology, large human capital and heritage can be a partner to this ASEAN e-business network," According to Goh Chok Tong, former Prime of Minister of Singapore: "We are seeing the renaissance of Asia led by China and by India. Both are stirring. At this stage, China is faster than India, but India is also moving, reforming and performing." (*The Hindu*, January 16, 2006)

China and India may finance LDC (Less Developed Countries) development, "to protect their long-term economic interests and to gather international support." Looking at the ratio of total available savings (s) in terms of GDP, 'the main conditioning variable for rapid growth', India with 23 per cent (in 2002) is at a significant disadvantage in comparison to China's 43.7 per cent. India should increase its ratio to at least 30 per cent, but that has to happen despite low incentives to financial savings and high decibel consumption drivers. (*Rita Dulci Rahman and Jose Miguel Andreu*). The President of Asian Development Bank at Hyderabad, (May 6, 2006) said that the Indian economy is currently on the verge of an accelerated growth trajectory and the country could leapfrog into the orbit of developed nations much before expected.

Leading Global Players by 2020

State of the World Report 2006 indicates that world has to welcome both China and India as leading global players. The agenda comprises four-fold steps: One, by making China a member of the OECD (Organisation for Economic Cooperation and Development), and offering India a permanent seat on the UN Security Council. Two, "China, India and the US should act collectively to ensure adequate energy supplies for all, even as they work together to move away from fossil fuels." Three, "commit to developing a new model for agriculture" in the place of "the current mixed system of commodity price subsidies and partially opened food markets." Lastly, countries around the world should embrace China and India more fully by helping their citizens better understand the people and cultures of these two important nations. China's future lies "on a delicate equilibrium between rapid growth, redistribution of incomes, and unavoidable democratization."

The new strategy embodied in China's Eleventh five-year plan (2006-2010) makes a major departure from the traditional focus on higher growth through its exceptionally high rates of savings and investment to achieving a more "balanced growth" for building a "prosperous, harmonious society." They have, therefore, decided to lay greater emphasis, without giving up the centrality of relatively high and sustained growth, on bringing about a leap forward in modernization of agriculture, improving the welfare of farmers, building rural infrastructure to urban levels and laying the foundation for building "a new Socialist countryside."

In case the world economy slows down, India is likely to be less vulnerable since its growth story is driven by domestic demand in contrast to other fast growing Asian economies, which are mainly driven by external demand. The role of India in perpetuating the global imbalance was minimal, not only in the present circumstances but also in near future. Going by the current indication and the projections of the Tenth Five Year Plan (2002-2007), India's current account position was likely to remain in the deficit in near future.

Awakened Asian "Tiger" and "Dragon"

Both India and China, each with its distinctive history, culture, political system and social organization remain among the very few major developing countries, which have emerged stronger by rapid adaptation from the past to suit the present. They have broken from ideologically stultified external policies, which marked their existence for previous decades. They have demonstrated their capability in handling international terrorism which threatened parts of their countries and are significant partners in the world-wide struggle against terrorism. They are with some success structuring their economic policies so as to benefit from globalisation. They are able to reposition themselves to engage and contribute to the emerging international order. Robust and steady growth of its economy, the rapid adaptation by its industrialists and business entrepreneurs to the challenges of globalisation and to competition from China in areas where India was traditionally strong, add to India's self perception that India can 'rise' in the global economic order.

According to latest estimates, while India has 7.2 per cent share of global GDP, China has 15.7 per cent compared to the US' 26.4 per cent, and the Euro Zone economies' 19.3 per cent. If we combine the rates of growth of India and China, it touches a level of 23% which exceeds the rate of growth of the Euro Zone economies and records 3.3% less than that of the US economy. Observers of India and China in Western capitals are often perplexed by the current obsession about these two Asian nations growing share of world trade and expanding economic profiles, which at best are rated as "modest and steady."

According to European observers, the two "awakening economic giants" of Asia—China and India—pose a serous threat to European manufacturing and job prospects, with their rising share of global trade and exports. It is to be noted that some 80 Chinese companies are on a "global move" and could make inroads into key Western markets. With over 10 per cent economic growth per annum Chinese companies will not be restricted to trading and manufacturing in the Far East.

The importance of China for the global economy is reflected in many different spheres. That "wages in the US are being set in Beijing" is one reason why. Even the global interest rate is being determined by China and a few other Asian countries. China is becoming the global factory while India is poised to become the global office. Many well-known multinationals are in the process of shifting at least a part of their R & D centers to India. In fact, some analysts (including the much quoted BRIC Report by Goldman Sachs) believe that India has one advantage over China—the percentage of population in the working age group will remain above China's in the coming decades.

End Message

India and China stood to gain significantly by striking synergies in trade and business. The growing competition at home was making Chinese companies seek markets abroad and develop global brands. By coming together and drawing on their advantages, India and China could not only make a strong regional impact but also make a mark in the world. Many Chinese conglomerates were looking keenly at the Indian market as part of their "go-out" strategy and planning to enter it. "One plus one will be more than two" in the event of the two countries, whose economies were rapidly growing, strengthening their economic cooperation, (*Li Ke,* Secretary-General of Asia Capital Forum at Chennai May 12, 2006), giving shape to a new economic world order thereby making the 21st century a truly Asian century.

References

Abdul Kalam, A.P.J.: "Asia will be the Future of Business," An Address at the Philippine Congress, February 6, 2006. *The Hindu,* February 7, 2006.

Alok Ray : "World Economy : Made in China", *The Hindu-Business Line,* September 21, 2005.

Ashok Jacob: "India has come of Age", *Manorama Year Book* 2006, pp. 40-48.

Aswathi Damodaram: "Investing in China is viewed as an option," *The Hindu-Business Line,* March 12, 2006.

Batuk Gathani: "India and China on 'Global Move'," *The Hindu–Business Line,* September 21, 2005.

Jayati Ghosh : "Macroeconomic Policy in China's Economic Growth", *Deccan Chronicle,* July 4, 2005.

Jegadish Gandhi, P.: "Debt-Free Asia: Vision 2020," *Debt Management in the Globalised Asia: Challenges and Options* (Eds.) P. Jegadish Gandhi & M.J. Joseph, Deep & Deep Publications Pvt. Ltd., New Delhi, 2006.

Kamal Nath: "China could be India's largest trading partner," The India-China Joint Business Forum, New Delhi, *The Hindu Business Line*, March 17, 2006.

Nerys Avery: "A Coolant for the Chinese Economy" *The Hindu Business Line*, May 7, 2006.

Pallavi Aiyar: "China to Focus on Narrowing Urban-rural divide," *The Hindu*, March 6, 2006.

———, China turns to nuclear power to fuel Growth," *The Hindu*, March 18, 2006.

———, "China—reaching out to the world," *The Hindu*, May 6, 2006.

———, "Changing lives in China", *The Hindu*, May 7, 2006.

Ranganathan, C.V: "India and China: Towards a Cooperative Partnership in the 21st Century for Asia Peace and Prosperity," *Manorama Year Book 2006*, pp. 27-38.

Sethuraman, S.: "World Economy: An Integration Under Way," *Manorama Year Book 2006*, pp. 463-470.

———, "Winds of Change in China's Growth Strategy," *The Hindu- Business Line*, February 17, 2006.

Srinivasan, G.: "OECD's Survey of China: Lessons from the Middle Kingdom," *The Hindu-Business Line*, October 25, 2005.

IT Confidence Survey 2005, Eurocom World Wide, "India, China to edge out Europe," *Deccan Chronicle*, March 24, 2006.

State of the World: 2006 *Special Focus on China and India*, The World Watch Institute. Washington.

Asia—Pacific Regional Economic Outlook (REO), IMF, 2005 "Year of the Asian Zoom", *The Hindu—Business Line*, May 3, 2006.

Business meeting with the Chinese Delegation, FICCI: "Chinese team keen to develop Bilateral Trade," Chennai, May 12, 2006.

8

Knowledge and the Asian Challenge

C.P. CHANDRASEKHAR AND JAYATI GHOSH

INTRODUCTION

According to official statistics, China continued to grow at a scorching 10.2 per cent during the first quarter of 2006 vis-à-vis the corresponding period of the previous year, India closely followed China's performance, with GDP growing at an estimated 8.4 per cent during financial year 2005-06. These figures, while concealing much in terms of the distribution of that growth, keep alive the fears of the threat from these two Asian giants to growth in the rest of the world, including the developed countries. The threat is seen as particularly serious because of indications that exports are an important source of dynamism in these countries and that "knowledge capital" has come to play a crucial role in their export dynamism. In both countries the ratio of exports of goods and services to GDP has risen quite sharply in recent years.

Export-GDP Ratio

In 1978, when China's reform began, that ratio was more or less the same in India and China, at around 6.5 per cent. Since then the figure has risen sharply in China, to touch 34 per cent in 2004, and much more slowly in India to just above19 per cent. While much of the expansion in exports in the Chinese case has been on account of exports of manufactured goods, that in the case of India has been principally on account of services.

Between 1985 and 1995, the ratio of goods exports to GDP rose from around 8 per cent to 18 per cent in the case of China, and from 4 per cent to 9 per cent in the case of India. But after that, while the figure for China shot up to 26.7 per cent in 2003, it remained short of 10 per cent in the case of India. Relative to GDP, it is the growth in services exports that explains India's more moderate trade success. Add to this the important role of private transfers, or remittances from non-resident Indians, and the relative resilience of the current account of India's balance of payments in the context of a rising oil import bill is explained.

Effect of Larger Exports

Larger exports and/or a higher rate of expansion of exports can stimulate growth because of positive net exports or a trade surplus that serves as the demand stimulus and inducement to invest for an individual country. Even if not recording a large trade surplus, successful engagement in trade allows a country to dissociate the structure of domestic supplies from domestic production. This permits using the possibilities of transformation through trade to ensure availability of adequate quantities of commodities crucial to growth. Export revenues may be crucial in financing imports of specific commodities that are essential for consumption without running into balance of payments difficulties. Typical examples of such commodities are food, machinery and oil.

At the aggregate level, of course, it is only China that appears truly mercantilist, exporting more than it imports and accumulating wealth in the form of foreign reserves. In the year to March 2006, China recorded a trade balance of $ 108 billion and a current account balance of $ 161 billion, taking its gold and foreign reserves to a record $ 875 billion. On the other hand, India recorded a trade deficit of close to $ 40 billion and a current account deficit of $ 13.3 billion. However, capital flows, especially portfolio capital flows into India's debt and equity markets helped it keep reserves at $ 145 billion. In sum, the role of net exports as a trigger for growth appears to be true for China, but not so for India. But if current transfers into India, consisting largely of remittance from Indian workers abroad are treated as a form of services income, then the deficit on India's balance of trade reduces substantially.

The rapid expansion of exports has been accompanied by high rates of GDP growth, improving the presence of these two countries in the global economy. Measured in terms of prices prevailing in 2000, China's share of world exports of goods and services was 5.8 per cent in 2003 (up from 1.4 per cent in 1978), and though India's share was just 1 per cent it was up from 0.4 per cent in 1978. In terms of constant price GDP, China accounted for 4.6 per cent of global GDP in 2003 and India for 1.6 per cent, both up from 0.9 per cent in 1978.

A point of relevance here is the relative size of GDP in these countries, measured in terms of Purchasing Power Parity (PPP) dollars, which is an indicator of the buying power of the Indian and Chinese populations. Measured in those terms, China accounts for 13 per cent of global GDP in 2003 and India for 6 per cent. This compares with 2.9 and 3.6 per cent respectively in 1978. Thus the rest of the world is benefiting from a growing market in these countries. The role of trade in facilitating growth in the countries, explains in large part the perception that they threaten global growth, including that in the OECD countries. To boot, while China seems to be emerging as the manufacturing hub of the world, India is proving to be the global services hub. And eye of these countries has an eye on the terrain occupied by the other. In the circumstance, evidence such as China's large trade surplus with the US only strengthens perceptions of a major economic threat.

Exploiting Opportunities

In addition, there are reasons to believe that the success of these countries stems from their ability to exploit the opportunities created by the new knowledge economy. Manufacturing areas that the World Bank defines as hi-tech account for a significant share of China's exports. Hi-tech-exports from China exceed those from all countries except the US, including Germany and Japan. Similarly in the case of India, software services, identified as hi-tech-services account for a significant share of services exports. IT services exports are estimated at around $ 16 billion currently. What is more, in terms of indicators of technological competitiveness reported by the National Science Foundation of the US, China and India rank well when compared to some European countries and many developing countries.

However, it is necessary to differentiate between knowledge in the production of goods and services and knowledge for the production of goods and services. While knowledge is being applied in production in these countries, the US still monopolises the control over knowledge. This comes through from evidence of various kinds. To start with, even relative to their own GDP, China and India lag far behind the developed countries in terms of R&D expenditure. While the figure is close to 3 per cent in the case of Japan and the US, and between 2 and 2.5 per cent in France and Germany, it stands at 1 per cent or lower in China and India.

According to the UNCTAD's *World Investment Report 2005*, individual firms such as Ford, Pfizer, Dailmer Chrysler, Siemens, Toyota and General Motors each spent more than $ 5 billion on R&D in 2003. In comparison, among the developing economies, total R&D spending exceeded $ 5 billion only in Brazil, China, the Republic of Korea and Taiwan Province of China. Licensing the use of this knowledge ensures significant revenues to firms from the US, far exceeding that received by other countries, What is noteworthy is that both receipts and payments of royalties in the case of the US are in transactions with affiliated firms. That is, the US is reaping the benefits of its control over knowledge through transactions conducted with affiliates abroad.

Foreign-funded Enterprises

It is for this reason that we need to examine the role of foreign firms in the export performance of India and China. According to George Gilboy (Foreign Affairs, July/August 2004), foreign-funded enterprises (FFEs) accounted for 55 per cent of China's exports in 2003. This dominance increases in the case of hi-tech exports. The share of FFEs in exports of industrial machinery, which stood at $ 83 billion in 2003, increased from 35 per cent to 79 per cent over a decade. While exports of computer equipment rose from $ 716 million in 1993 to $ 41 billion in 2003, the FFEs' share rose from 74 per cent to 92 per cent. Similarly, the share of FFEs in China's electronics and telecom exports ($ 89 billion in 2003), rose from 45 per cent to 74 per cent.

The situation appears to be similar in the case of IT services exports from India. According to Nasscom, offshore operations of global IT majors accounted for 10-15 per cent of IT services and BPO exports and captive BPO units accounted for 50 per cent of BPO exports. Further, MNC-owned captive units have been scaling up their operations steadily with the headcount forecast to grow by at least 30 per cent this year. Thus, foreign firms with control over knowledge appear to be exploiting the availability of skilled and educated labour in these countries. What is more, there is evidence that the best talent is being used to strengthen control over knowledge. According to the National Science Foundation, of the approximately 280,000 foreign graduate students enrolled in US universities, 63,013 were from India and 50,796 from China. Further, of the 37,608 non-US citizen who received doctoral degrees in 2002-03, 10,089 were from China and 3,238 from India. Two-thirds of these students had definite plans to stay back in the US and another 20-25 per cent was considering the possibility of staying back. The US has become a destination for some of the best talent from these two countries.

Internationalisation of R&D

Finally, even to the extent that talent remains in the developing countries, there are signs that through a process of internationalisation of R&D operations, transnational firms are exploiting that talent to retain control over knowledge, According to the UNCTAD's *World Investment Report 2005*, Transnational Corporations (TNCs) account for at least 70 per cent of global business R&D. In 2002, the top 700 R&D spenders reported R&D expenditures of more than $ 300 billion. A rising share of these companies' R&D expenditures are undertaken in developing countries. Between 1994 and 2002, the developing country share of all overseas R&D by US TNCs increased from 7.5 per cent to 13 per cent. As of now, more than half of the world's top R&D spenders conduct R&D activities in developing countries.

In India, leading firms such as Intel, Microsoft and Adobe have R&D operations within the country. In China too, the tread is clearly visible. According to the Wall Street Journal, almost all the global giants in the automobile, telecommunications technology, computer, software, machinery, electronics biotechnology, pharmaceuticals and other major industries have made R&D investments in China. These companies include General Electric (GE), General Motors, P&G, Unilever, Microsoft, Intel, IBM, Motorla, Siemens, Ericsson, Nortel, AT&T, Lucent Bell and Samsung.

All these development suggest that even while China and India are important bases for knowledge-based production of exportable goods and sources, important beneficiaries of this development are transnational from development countries, even if not the mass of the workers in these countries who fear job losses. This implies that as yet countries such as Indian and China are locations that serve as instruments of battle for transnational firms. The war among the latter result in strategies that may be threatening extant or future employment in the developed countries But when faced with that prospect it is not Indian and China that need to be feared by developed country citizens, but their own home-grown transnationals who have taken wing.

India and China Relative to the World

(% *share*)

	1978	*1985*	*1995*	*2000*	*2003*
Exports of goods and services (Constant 2000 US $)					
China	1.4	1.9	2.6	3.5	5.8
India	0.4	0.4	0.7	0.8	1
GDP (Constant 2000 US$)					
China	0.9	1.5	2.9	3.8	4.6
India	0.9	1	1.3	1.4	1.6
GDP, PPP (Constant 200 international $)					
China	2.9	4.5	8.8	11	12.9
India	3.6	3.8	4.9	5.4	5.9

PPP: Purchasing Power Parity.

The Asian Giants and Latin America

JORGE HEINE

INTRODUCTION

The recent visit by Prime Minister Manmohan Singh to Brazil has brought Indo-Latin American relations into focus. The visit was the first to South America by a Indian Prime Minister in 38 years. Mr. Singh took along the largest business delegation to accompany a Prime Minister on a visit abroad. In turn, the impact of the rise of the two Asian giants, China and India, on Latin America and the Caribbean (LAC) is becoming increasingly relevant for the region's growth and development. This, of course, is hardly limited to the LAC region. In the United States, concern over the considerable trade deficit with China ($ 200 billion in 2005, double the amount it was in 2002) has been an issue, as has, albeit much less so, the matter of job out-sourcing to India. And although China has been extremely active in Latin America over the past 15 years or so, it is only over the past couple of years that India has started to seriously engage the region. Indian business which, in the past focused almost exclusively on the domestic market and on North America and Western Europe, is only now coming to realize the opportunities it has been missing out on. That Chinese trade with LAC reached $ 40 billion in 2005, whereas India's trade was only $ 6 billion (although growing fast) speaks for itself. In LAC, on the other hand, some have expressed concern about the effect on local jobs and industry of greater trade with the giants.

No displacement of Jobs

Two recent studies address the issue head on: "Latin America and the Caribbean's Response to the Growth of China and India" by the World Bank, and "China and India and its Trade Relations with Latin America and the Caribbean: Opportunities and Challenges," by the U.N.'s Economic Commission for Latin America and the Caribbean.

They make for fascinating reading, among other things, because they dispel a number of myths about the supposed displacement of jobs across the region caused by "unfair" competition from China and India. There is little doubt China and India are emerging as forces to reckon with: Their merchandise exports reached 8.2 per cent of total world exports in 2005, almost double the 4.5 per cent in 2000. As the World Bank study points out, "today China and India's share of world exports is 50 per cent larger than LAC's share, whereas in 1990 the reverse was true. In the last 1980s, LAC had a trade-to-GDP ratio roughly equal to the trade-to-GDP ratio of China, and two times larger than the trade-to-GDP ratio of India. By 2004, the trade-to-GDP ratio of China was 35 per cent larger than the trade-to-GDP ratio of LAC, and India's trade-to-GDP ratio was only 14 per cent smaller than LAC's." A number of additional indicators in trade in services, FDI, and innovation show a similar upsurge of Chinese and Indian numbers.

Zero-Sum Game as a Win-Win Situation

The real issue, obviously, is whether trade and investment flows should be seen as a zero-sum game, or, under the right conditions, as a win-win situation. The most interesting thing about these studies is their finding that, "since the mid-nineties there has been a rising correlation of business cycles between LAC and the two Asian economies."

Positive Impact

In other words, far from hampering LAC's growth, the rise of China and India had had a largely positive impact on it. The current boom that is taking place in the region, poised for its fourth consecutive year of growth, and with the world's best performing stock markets in 2006—with a 24 per cent yield versus a world-wide average of 12 per cent—is partly related to the upswing in commodity prices. South America is one of the richest regions in the world in terms of natural resources (only the Middle East and North Africa have a higher, largely oil-based, natural resource index—the standard way to measure this comparative advantage—than LAC) and both China and India, one of them "the world's factory," and the other "the world's service centre," are gobbling up mineral and agricultural resources as if there is no tomorrow.

Over the past 15 years their share of the world consumption of may commodities has doubled, reaching 25 per cent in some cases. In 2004 (the figures are higher now), China imported some $ 5 billion in soya, 60 per cent of its total imports, from Argentina and Brazil, $ 3.4 billion in copper, 25 per cent of its world imports, mostly from Chile and Peru, and $ 4 billion, 19 per cent of world imports, in iron from a number of South American countries. For countries such as Chile, Peru, and Argentina, exports to China represent between 10 and 11 per cent of total exports, in some of these cases up from less than one per cent in 1990.

Mexico and Central America, with a some-what different export profile, more oriented towards manufacturing are in a different situation, and here the competition with Chinese and Indian products is quite real. In fact, China recently replaced Mexico as the main exporting country to the United States. On the other hand, Chinese investment in Mexico is huge, reaching $ 28 billion in 2004. Indian companies are also moving into Latin America with great verve. Jindal Steel won the bid for the Bolivian mine E1 Mutun, one of the largest iron ore deposits in the Americas, in May 2006, committing an investment of $ 2.3 billion, in a deal still to be finalized. The Essar Group is building a $ 1.2 billion steel plant in Trinidad and Tobago. Tata Motors has started a joint venture with Marcopolo, Brazil's largest bus manufacturers, and Bajaj Auto has announced the opening of a factory in Argentina.

Complementarity

In short, the complementarity of the Chinese and Indian economies with the South American economies is quite straightforward, with the latter producing many of the commodities and raw materials, the former need to sustain their 8-10 per cent growth rates, and South American markets providing a readymade outlet for Chinese and Indian manufactured goods, as well as for services and IT products. In the case of Mexico and Central America, the challenge is to tap into the FDI and innovation possibilities the two giants offer to supur their own growth.

In both cases, however, the policy implications are quite clear. The steady growth at high rates of the two most populated countries on Earth over the past quarter of a century has given a considerable impetus to the economies of quite a number of LAC countries, especially since 1990, in terms of actual export volumes and international commodity prices.The all-time high price of copper, at more than $ 3 a pound for much of this year (three times what it was a couple of years ago) is only one example of this; China's and India's contribution to the growth in world demand for the "red gold" has been 25 per cent for 1990-2004, and possibly higher now. At the same time, the evidence indicates that we are only scratching the surface in terms of business opportunities.

Thus, whereas China imports a larger share of commodities from LAC than from ASEAN (13.3 per cent versus 9 per cent), the reverse is true for manufactured products based on natural resources imported from ASEAN (15.6 versus 7.8 per cent), which would seem to indicate considerable room for growth for more value-added products from LAC. Interestingly enough, India sources a larger share of its commodities from ASEAN (16.1 per cent) than from LAC (6.8 per cent), and the gap between manufactured products based on natural resources imported from ASEAN (14.5 per cent) and those from LAC (3.9

per cent) is larger than in the case of China. Again this would seem to offer much room for expanded Indo-LAC trade.

The Way Forward

Which is the way forward? To reach the $ 10 billion in Indo-LAC trade that some have identified as a goal for 2008, and which could grow quite beyond that, two things would seem to be paramount.

(1) To continue to deepen and expand trade agreements between India and LAC countries it is critical to remove extant trade barriers and facilitate the flow of goods and services. The ones signed between India and MERCOSUR in 2005 and between India and Chile in 2006 are a first step in that direction (a PTA with Peru is under consideration).

(2) For private firms from all countries involved, the key would seem to lie in getting into the supply chains of production and distribution that cater to the respective markets, thus making the most of their comparative advantage. The move toward organized retail in India, to give only one example, offers enormous opportunities to LAC producers of agro-industrial goods, as do the Special Economic Zones (SEZ) that are coming up, whereas the Spanish—language market for Business Process Outsourcing (BPO) and Knowledge Process Outsourcing (KPO) remains to be tapped by Indian firms that could set up shop in LAC countries. Joint ventures with Latin American pharma companies is another obvious step for the Indian industry to respond to the growing demand for affordable products in LAC.

Dimensions of "Decent Work" in Asia

JUAN SOMAVIA

INTRODUCTION

The 21st century is widely spoken of as the Asian century. Asia's four billion people now live in the region with the most rapid economic growth in the world. Growth has been more than double the global average since 1995 and labour productivity has risen by about 41 per cent, towering over the rest of the world. But this dynamic economic picture is incomplete. Huge growth hasn't been matched by an equivalent growth in the number of jobs. It has not adequately improved working conditions or wages for many of the region's 1.9 billion working women and men. What is more, conventional unemployment is only part of the problem. Underemployment, insecurity, poor working conditions, and a shortage of marketable skills remain widespread. The lack of social protection, especially among workers in agriculture and the urban informal economy, is serious. And despite significant progress in reducing poverty, some one billion people are still "working poor." Last year, in his Foreword to a flagship publication of the Asian Development Bank, President Haruhiko Kuroda warned that if the "policy agenda of the region's economy is not geared to meeting the objectives of full, productive and decent employment, it is easy to conceive a region, say 25 years from now, which despite growth, will still harbour most of the world's poor." All this creates underlying tensions that demand our attention.

Decent Work Challenge

Today, Asia—from the Arab states in West Asia to the Pacific—is facing what I call a "decent work challenge." To understand what this means to ordinary people, consider the following:

- In 2005, some 84 per cent of workers in South Asia, 58 per cent in South-East Asia, 47 per cent in East Asia, and 36 per cent in the Arab states did not earn enough to lift themselves and their families above the $ 2 a day poverty line.
- Informal employment as a share of non-agricultural employment ranges from 83 per cent in India, 78 per cent in Indonesia, and 72 per cent in the Philippines, to 51 per cent in Thailand, and 42 per cent in Syria.
- In 2005 Asia had more than 48 per cent, or 41.6 million, of the world's young people without work. Young people are at least three times more likely that adults to be unemployed. Youth underemployment is also a major concern.
- Some one million workers die annually in Asia due to work-related accidents and diseases.
- Despite progress towards observing key international labour standards, Asia has the lowest level of ratifications of the two ILO Conventions relating to freedom of association and the right to collective bargaining of any region.
- If people cannot find work at home they look elsewhere. Over the past two decades, gross

emigration of labour rose at an annual rate of 6 per cent in Asia-twice the growth rate of the labour forces of the sending countries.

Reduction in Decent Work Deficits

A major reduction in these decent work deficits in this region is possible, as the overall reduction of poverty has shown. It would be a tremendous boost to the quality of life and the security of many individuals, families, and communities. Different countries, given their national realities, cultures and development levels, can strive in different ways to achieve this goal. What are some of the major policy challenges?

First, promote economic growth that translates into the creation of decent jobs and encourages investment and entrepreneurship, skill development, proper labour standards, and sustainable livelihoods. Secondly, respect, promote, and realize fundamental principles and rights at work, namely freedom of association and the effective recognition of the right to organize and bargain collectively, the elimination of all forms of forced and/or compulsory labour, and the effective elimination of child labour and discrimination in respect of employment and occupations, including the promotion of gender equality. Thirdly, extend social protection and increase its effectiveness, particularly for workers in agriculture and the informal economy who are in practice often not covered by labour legislation.

And fourthly, support institutions and systems that strengthen labour market governance, including frameworks that encourage social dialogue and help resolve workplace disputes. Social dialogue, involving strong and independent workers' and employers' organizations, plays a pivotal role in increasing productivity and building cohesive societies. It is the best road towards flexibility and security for both employers and workers. At the ILO we call this the "decent work agenda." This is today an international consensus.

Stable Social Framework

The next ten years will be critical ones in Asia. If the dramatic growth rates it has enjoyed are to continue in a stable social framework, the benefits need to be felt by all through improvements to their lives and livelihoods-in other words, decent work. This is another opportunity for Asia to set a global example. By promoting the decent work agenda it will not only improve the lives of the people in this region, but also exercise global policy leadership and give a tremendous boost to the realization of decent work world-wide.

Part II

China : The "Dragon's" Development Dimensions

China : Towards Marxian Democratic Model

A. Ranga Reddy

INTRODUCTION

The Communist Party of China (CPC) has decided to build a "harmonious Society of Socialism and uphold Marxism as the guiding ideology.[1] The paper highlights China's" paradigm shift of Communism to socialistic democratic model.

1. Stages of Reforms Implementation

Reforms were first introduced in agriculture (1978-93), foreign trade and investment sectors (that too in limited Coastal regions) and later extended to industry. The initial reforms in agriculture brought prosperity to a vast number of poor people, created conditions for the subsequent phenomenal growth in rural industries and built-up a big political support base for more reforms.

The Chinese relied more on introducing competition. The rapid growth of new enterprises mostly Township and Village Enterprises (TVEs) and some private firms created competitive pressure on the State Owned Enterprises (SOEs). The monopoly of the Central State Trading Corporation was replaced by a large number of regional trading Corporations competing with one another.[2]

The Chinese leaders realised the dangers of nation-wide experiments suited to local conditions, gradual reforms, pragmatism instead of dogmas and the importance of the rule of law. China followed dual pricing. In the transition from plan to market, farmers and industrial units were required to buy and sell fixed quantities of inputs and outputs through the planning mechanism at Government controlled prices. The remaining part could be bought and sold at market prices. There were few incentives for farmers and SOEs to improve productivity and profits as these would be expropriated by the government.

Perhaps the most significant difference between the Chinese reforms and those in Russia and east Europe in the 1990s is that China did not destroy old institutions without building new ones. In the period after the catastrophe of the Great Leap Forward China's leadership remained divided about economic strategy. Although self-reliance was a shared aim, one group, that included Zhou Enlai and Deng Xioapang, sought to restore what was in effect, an import substituting strategy that had brought important gains during the 1950s. (Gautam Sen (2000).

In the second stage of reforms (1994 onwards), China has made significant progress towards building a rule-based market system and Western style institutions and practices but again with distinct Chinese characteristics. In certain respects, China has reversed some of the initial policies. China has downsized government bureaucracy, introduced tax reforms with internationally accepted practices, made State—owned banks more commercially-oriented, introduced prudential regulations on the financial system, started privatisation and restructuring of SOEs resulting in big layoffs. It unfixed the exchange rate and introduced current account convertibility, incorporating private property rights and the rule of law explicitly in the Chinese constitution (which is indicative of a big ideological shift for the ruling Communist Party).

China's increasing inequality is largely caused by the rising urban-rural gap and inter-regional disparities. Government policies have contributed to this as 'Social policies favour urban over rural areas and economic policies favour the coast over the interior. State owned enterprises suffer from a few basic problems in all countries, such as soft budget constraint, multiple objectives, multiple control authorities and absence of incentives for managers and workers to improve performance. China is no exception. The Chinese pension system is entirely by the current contribution of employers and employees. The seriousness of the crisis can be guaged from the fact that at the outset of reforms there were 30 workers contributing to the pension system for each retiree, but by 1995 there were fewer than 5.

2. Fast Foreign Direct Investment Flow

China's share in the total World trade went up from 1 per cent to about 4 per cent and is projected to go up to 10 per cent by 2020 to make China the second largest trading nation in the world. Foreign Direct Investment (FDI) flow into China jumped from near zero in 1978 to more than 355 billion yuan in 2003 and China became the second largest recipient of FDI after the US. The 21st Century is widely projected to be China's Century just as the 20th Century was Japan's. The export boom of China was facilitated by the re-location of intensive steps of production from Hong Kong and Taiwan to the Adjacent Special Economic Zones (SEZs) in the Chinese Coastal Provinces. Labour Unions, though officially allowed in China, mostly played a cooperative role with the management, instead of the collective bargaining role practised in non-communist countries. Managers were given the right to hire and fire workers in the export-oriented factories in the SEZs.

The saving rate in China was quite high at 35 per cent of GDP in 1979 whereas in 1994 it was 44 per cent of GDP. It is easier to transform a small country (like Singapore or Vietnam) than a very big, over populated country like China. FDI flows in

1999 have been $ 38.8 billion against the peak level of $ 44.2 billion in 1997. Chinese reform strategy—its contents, timing, sequencing and implementation—was un-conventional in many respects and the reforms initiatives were bottom-up (Crossing river by touching stones—Deng's Celebrated phase).

Most of the FDI inflows to India came from the original neighbourhood (US, UK and Germany). Interestingly, Mauritius is the second largest source of FDI inflows to India in recent times. It is interesting to note that unlike China, the fuel and power sector dominates (about 28 per cent of total investment) in India. The Telecommunications sectors too contributes about 19 per cent of that total investment during the period 1991-2000. India has excelled in the area of Computer software and has evolved as an information technology hub for the world market.

It is now open as to why some economies have attracted large FDI flows and grown fast (for example, east Asia and now China), over the last 40 years and others have not. The Latin American and Caribbean economies are geographically closer to the highly developed economies. Yet, these regions could not take advantage of this physical proximity. Their economies could not become part of the original, intermediate or even extension of the intermediate neighbourhoods. Perhaps due to the fact that most people came from cultures where neighbourhood was too weak.

3. Expansion of Exports

Mao Zedong and Lin Biao were intended upon Semi-autarchy with only very limited engagement with the capitalist world economy. Both groups considered the latter hostile and a dangerous adversary, but important differences of opinion obviously existed. The goal of export promotion was formally adopted in August 1979, by assigning top priority to fulfilling export contract obligation. As far as foreign investment was concerned, investment by overseas Chinese had been regarded by China's communists as somehow genuine, indeed, local in terms of national loyalties. The success of China's export efforts is evident in the rise of its trade GDP ratio. According to one estimate, China's trade/GDP ratio rose from 10 per cent in 1975-79 to 36 per cent in 1990-94. In current US dollars the value of exports had risen from approximately $ 16 billion in 1978 to $ 138.4 billion in 1995. Export volumes, which had doubled between 1970-78, rose more than eight fold between 1978 and 1997.

China's low wage work force has provided the basis for Chinese overseas firms to persist in productive activities in which their own home country had lost comparative advantage. Labour—intensive processes and production have generally moved to China while more capital intensive and knowledge intensive parts of the production process are located elsewhere in the more advanced economies of the region-mainly Hong Kong and some parts of South East Asia.[3]

Basically, overseas Chinese foreign investors are largely in the export sector of China's economy. Hong Kong itself exports 200 per cent of its GDP, most of which originates in China.[4]

Much of the activity of Chinese overseas investors has been concentrating regionally. Twelve coastal provinces and municipalities have absorbed 90 per cent of foreign direct investment. The principal recipients of inward flows are Guandong, Shanghai, Fujian and Jiangsu. The investment was mainly in export activities and real estate and gradually diversified from light industries to electronics, telecommunications and transport.

The noteworthy feature of Overseas Chinese foreign investment in China is the shift from labour-intensive to capital intensive sectors in the 1990s. The Chinese Overseas Community engaged in a profitable economic relationship in China, but one that is also moulded by unique cultural and political factors specific to their relationship with China.

4. Entry into World Trade Organization

China may no longer have the luxury of taking a cautious approach to reform. For instance, with China, set to open up its banking sector to foreign banks by 2007 under World Trade Organization (W.T.O.) accession commitments, foreign competition for domestic banks will soon be an inescapable reality.[5]

Academic research has still not identified which institutions are the key ones for fostering growth. But there is an emerging consensus that a sound legal framework, strong financial sector supervision, good corporate governance, and low levels of corruption are conducive to growth. Having good institutions will help foster the expansion of the private sector, which has accounted for much of China's recent dynamism and the strengthening of the remaining state sector enterprises.

Xenophobia—hence Yeltsins's Russian nationalism defeated Gorbachev's Soviet internationalism, Milosevic's serb nationalism replaced Yugoslow internationalism is no different in China. As the Communist Party decays, the cadres use their political position to support their efforts to make money through managing the (SOEs), starting new local authority business (TVEs) or private enterprise.[6] At the beginning of the 1990s, there were just over 1,00,000 private operations (those employing eight or more workers), employing 1.8 million workers; they now employ 24 million, with possibly 30 million more in units employing less than eight workers. Many of the party cadres are involved in private business, either directly or by using their political position to support private business.

5. Decline of Poverty Level

The headcount indices were 16 per cent and 35 per cent for China and India respectively for a common poverty line of approximately $ 1 per day at purchasing power parity (World Bank Development Indicators, 2003). Chinese economic performance since 1978 is a bigger miracle than the earlier east Asian miracle. In China, massive systematic changes were being brought about in the World's most populated economy while at the same time maintaining a near double-digit growth rate, a huge build up of foreign exchange reserves, a sharp decline in Poverty and a wide participation of different sections of society in the benefits of economic growth, in most of the years over more than two decades. 80 million people are poverty stricken, largely distributed in the 592 poverty stricken counties, which are getting support from the State.[7]

From the beginning, Deng made it clear that they would not follow any particular country's development model nor would they move away from the single party political system maintaining tight control over society. Average life expectancy improved from only 32 in 1950 to 69 years in 1982, which was Maoist era.

By the international poverty line ($ 1 day, using 1985 Purchasing power parity), the percentage of rural poor declined from 60 per cent in 1978 to 11.5 per cent in 1999. Rural per capita real income more than quadrupled while urban per capital real income trebled over the period 1978-'97. The share of agricultural labour in total employment went down from over 70 per cent in 1978 to around 50 per cent in 1996. It took the US 50 years and Japan 60 years to achieve a similar structural transformation (Alok Ray, (2002). Unemployment reached 8 per cent of labour force by the mid 1990s. However, the official Chinese data give the unemployment including furloughs as 7.9 per cent of the labour force for 1998, as against 6.5 per cent in 1997 and 5.6 per cent in 1996. Clearly the urban unemployment rate has been steadily climbing in recent years.

6. Dense Corruption

Reforms turn out to make the problems even worse unless government is willing to move on to a full democratic system (with a multiplicity of competing parties). Implicit in all this is the most dramatic symptom of decay, the pervasive corruption, and the deep cynicism of the population about the integrity of its leaders. This is to leave aside spectacular scale of corruption—the giant quasi private Business Corporations of PLA, financing the largest part of the military budget outside the control of the Central Government. There has always been a surprising amount of corruption in China—it does with the discretionary powers allowed at the local level. Mao's Socialist Education Movement in the early 1960s revealed some of the spectacular abuses around then. But the market economy along with the close relationship between the party, local government and public or private business has opened up an immense area for new money making. A series recent cases have shown a level of gangster-party rule in major cities—Shenyang, Xiamen, Xingtai—which may extend much further than the cases already cited. Hundreds of officials have been arrested. And despite efforts to protect the party's top leadership, this cannot always be done—a politburo member has been sentenced to 16 years gaol, two executed for corruption; a Vice minister is awaiting trial for accepting bribes from smugglers. Reform, privatisation and strong protectionist local government are a recipe for unavoidable and dense corruption.[8]

7. Environment Degradation

China's air and water pollution, especially in the cities, is considered one of the worst in the world. Air pollution alone is estimated to cause around 3,00,000 deaths annually in China. The economic cost of Air and water pollution in China has been variously estimated to lie at 3-8 per cent of GDP.

8. China's Investment in India

Trade links are strengthening, investment links are non-existent. Chinese firms are still finding tough to do business in India, adding for good measure that the Chinese companies have not got a very good arrangement in India. The NIIT already runs 112 Computer Training Centres in China. Aurobindo Pharma, Ranbaxy, Dr. Reddy's and Orchid Chemicals, Sundaram Fasteners entered into China. Earlier India initiated the largest number of 153 anti-dumping cases against Chinese exports upto March 2003. Still India considers China as Non-Market Economies (NME). India will also need to modify its anti-dumping legislation in keeping with the global trends, international economic realities and need for intensifying the future potential of India-China Economic Cooperation.[9]

9. Single Party Rule

Chinese leadership, by maintaining the single party communist rule and reform from within, had no need to pay attention to this political argument for rapid privatisation. Rather political considerations in China dictated a slower approach. All these imply that the Chinese strategy of SOE reforms at a slower pace, without changing the political institutions, has turned out to be a better strategy. It is likely to go down as China's dependency ratio rises in future as children of the one child policy increasingly dominate the work force, the retirement population swells, and the one-child policy is relaxed under a more liberal political regime. The phase of shifting labour from low productivity agriculture to higher productivity manufacturing is nearly over in China.

10. Deng Xiaoping—A Visionary

Deng (Aug. 22, 1904—Feb. 19, 1997) introduced economic reforms in China much earlier in the late seventies. He is the first leader who visualised the impact of a stagnant economy. He argued vociferously that privatisation can be reconciled with socialism. Deng's popularity, power and prestige began to decline within the Communist Party of China (CPC) and Chinese Society after the Tiananmen episode (1989). He convinced that as long as the largest section of peasantry is well fed and well off, the CPC will remain in power. In India, all political parties were against this philosophy. Deng was convinced that the main conflict in Socialist China lay not between capital and labour but between backward productive forces and the advanced industrial system. He allowed economic liberalism but restricted political choice. The ultimate goal of Communism is to develop the productive forces for which economic development is essentially developed.

Inspite of the so-called revival of Maoist fever and the anti-corruption speeches made by Deng, China had "five million millionaires" by the end of May 1993. In 1993, there were two million stockholders in China and each week the number grows by 50,000.[10]

CONCLUSION

China introduced reforms first in agriculture, where much of population is associated, then market-based reforms. After the USA, next nation is China in inviting FDI flow in the world. China's low wage workforce has provided the basis for Chinese overseas firms. Entry into W.T.O. has been taken as a challenge and choice. By taking series of anti-poverty measures, it reduced poverty to 11.5 per cent level. Corruption is very dense. More millionaires have entered into the economy. Environmental degradation on Air and water are found deeper and wider. Unfortunately, India still observed China as a non-market economy.

Notes and References

1. P.S. Suryanarayana (2004), "Chinese Party to Promote Socialist Market Economy", *The Hindu*, Sept. 9.
2. Alok Roy (2002), "The Chinese Economic Miracle : Lessons to be Learnt", *Economic and Political Weekly*, Sept. 14th, p. 3839.
3. Gautam Sen (2000), "Post Reform China and the International Economy", *Economic and Political Weekly*, March 11, p. 932.
4. Arindam Banik, Pradip, Explaining FDI Inflows to India, China and K. Bhaumik, Sunday, the Caribbean: An Extended Neighbourhood O Iyare (2004), Approach, *Economic and Political Weekly*, July 24, p. 3400.
5. Eswar S. Prasad (2004), "Growth and Stability in China", *Economic and Political Weekly*, May 15, p. 2011).
6. Nigel Harris (2001), "China: The old Order Changes", *Economic and Political Weekly*, Oct. 13, p. 3897.
7. S.P. Gupta (1996), "Chinese Economic Reforms", Allied New Delhi, p. 11).
8. Nigel Harris (2001), "China: The Old Order Changes", *Economic and Political Weekly*, Oct. 13, p. 3900, Aug. 22, 1904-Feb. 19, 1997).
9. Ravinder Goel, (2004), MFN Status for China on Cards, *Sahara Time*, Oct. 2.
10. Ravindra Sharma (2004), Deng Xiaoping: Reformer, Innovator, Visionary, *Mainstream*, Oct. 2, p. 21.

Macro-economic Policy in China's Economic Growth

Jayati Ghosh

INTRODUCTION

China's truly remarkable pace of growth for a period of over two decades has been punctuated with concern about bouts of deflation or overheating. As a result, macro-economic management in China appears to have more to do with dealing with these cycles around a relatively high trend rate of growth, rather than with realising and/or sustaining that trend itself. Assessed in terms of growth performance as revealed by official Chinese statistics, the government of that country appears to have little to worry about. China has recorded an annual trend rate of growth of GDP of 9.8 per cent during the past quarter century. Within this, there has been some difference across sectors. There has been a persistent and significant deceleration in primary sector GDP growth from the first half of the Eighties.

There appears to be a similar deceleration in tertiary sector GDP growth as well, though growth rates appear to have stabilized at relatively high levels over the last decade. The growth of the secondary sector, within which industrial production has been the clear leader, has been the prime mover for the high aggregate economic growth.

Recurrence of "Overheating"

This structure of growth is of relevance because, despites the overall high trend rate of growth, discussions on the need to manage bouts of deflation or "over-heating" recur periodically in Chinese economic discussions. Thus, the Chinese economy is seen to have experienced a long period of deflation from 1997 to 2001, and recovered from that only in the second half of 2002. Yet, the annual rates of growth during 1998 and 2001 varied between 7.1 and 7.8 per cent in three of those years, and between 8 and 8.8 in the other two-rates which would be considered creditable in other contexts, Further, no sooner had growth recovered to touch 9.3 per cent in 2003 and 9.7 per cent in the first half of 2004, than economists and the media started speaking of the dangers of "overheating" and the need to ensure a "soft landing."

This is precisely what is happening at the moment, as Chinese policy makers attempt to impose a dose of what they call "deflation" on an economy which was seen as over-heating. To understand how this is done, it is first necessary to analyse the principal sources of growth in the Chinese economy. The proximate determinant of high average rates of growth has been the high investment rates. Available figures indicate that the ratio of fixed assets investment to GDP in China stood at 41.4 per cent in 2003 and 47.4 per cent in 2004. Since these are only figures of the ratio of investment in fixed assets to GDP, the rate of saving in China must be even higher than these extraordinary levels. And given the high levels of fixed assets formation, it is not surprising that growth rates tend to be high. Also, the figures suggest that fixed asset formation rates are extremely volatile, resulting in the fluctuations around the trend growth rates that are disconcerting to Chinese policy-makers.

Components of Capital Formation

This kind of volatility is partly facilitated by the manner in which capital formation is financed in China. Budgetary appropriations and foreign investment typically account for very small shares of less than 7 per cent of total fixed assets formation. The major finance comes from borrowing, in three ways. First, domestic loans, that is, loans of various forms borrowed by investing units from banks and non-bank financial institutions. Second, "raised" funds, that is extra-budgetary funds for investment in fixed assets received by investing units from central government ministries, local governments, enterprises and institutions. And third, "other funds", that is funds for investment in fixed assets received from other sources, including capital raised through issuing bonds by enterprises or financial institutions, funds raised from individuals, and funds transferred from other units.

The importance of such "off-budget" borrowing means that the purely fiscal stimulus for growth in China is limited. Fiscal revenues in 2000 stood at just 15 per cent of GDP, and it is the growing desire of the centre to control expenditures that is seeing an increase in that ratio to 20 per cent by 2004. But even of these expenditures a considerable share goes to current expenditures rather than capital formation. Clearly then it is the flexibility to acquire funds that enables different entities to undertake such investment expenditures that raises the investment income ratio and keeps growth going at high levels. Credit to finance such expenditures has indeed been easily available because the transition from a controlled to a more decentralized monetary system has implied a relatively lax monetary policy. This has resulted in a situation where local government functionaries, who influence appointment of banking and other functionaries at the local level are able to easily access funds for their projects.

Accumulation of Reserves

More recently, the decision to maintain a pegged exchange rate while liberalizing capital flows into and out of the country, has forced the central bank to buy dollars by selling yuan (RMB) so as to pre-empt any appreciation of the currency. This has resulted in the accumulation of reserves in excess of $ 500 billion. The increase in the foreign exchange assets of the central bank implies this is not easily sterilized, since the government has almost exhausted its holding of government securities because of past sales aimed at sterilising capital flows that lead to reserve accumulation. As a result, the high powered money base of the central bank has expanded and the Chinese economy has been characterized by an easy money situation that makes available the funds that finance capital construction projects.

This is not a problem inasmuch as it helps keep the Chinese economy growing at this rapid rate. The problem is that when growth is triggered with such expenditures, it propels further such expenditures and the resulting expansion soon runs into bottlenecks of various kinds, especially bottlenecks in the power, steel and other infrastructural areas. This can then cause inflation. The problem confronting the Chinese government is to deal with the inflation that results in such circumstances of "overheating." What the government can try and do is engineer an increase in (administered) interest rates. But, there is no evidence that the kind of investment expenditure being spoken of is interest rate sensitive. Further, increases in interest rates could create a host of problems. In the first instance they can, just as a possible revaluation of the yuan, result in a spurt in capital inflows into the economy, worsening the exchange rate management problem. Second, they would adversely affect the viability of the already weakened state-owned enterprises, default by whom would worsen the non-performing assets problem of the banks.

Derivatives

All this results in a situation where the Chinese government falls back on administrative measures, including the use of central "commands" and guidelines to hold back runaway rate of investment. So despite the overt emphasis on markets and capitalistic growth, Chinese macro policy remains still very reliant on the use of administrative measures which serve to dampen economic cycles.

13

In China : A Problem of Plenty

PALLAVI AIYAR

INTRODUCTION

Millions of bright-eyed college graduates in China are destined for disappointment this summer, their dreams of cashing in on the country's spectacular economic growth, shattered. According to a recent report by the National Reform and Development Commission, the country's central planning authority, there will be no jobs for 60 per cent of China's 4.13 million students who graduate this year. Only 1.6 million jobs will be on offer, according to the report, a decline of 22 per cent compared to the previous year—even as the number of graduates has risen by 22 per cent since 2005. The unemployment situation is expected to only worsen in the coming years with young Chinese going to university in record numbers.

Last year, colleges and universities enrolled 5.04 million students, 4.7 times the number of those admitted in 1998. The total number of students in various kinds of higher education in

2005 was 23 million—the highest in the world. Those among this thundering army of new graduates who do land jobs are increasingly finding themselves earning at a scale on a par with blue-collar migrant workers. In a recent column in the China Daily, columnist Liu Shinan recalled how only a few years ago college graduates in China were considered to be part of an elite and turned-up their noses at salaries of 3,000 Yuan ($ 375) a month.

However, a government survey in 2005 found that the average monthly salary of employed graduates was just 1,588 Yuan ($ 198). In Interviews with migrant workers in shoe factories in China's southern city of Wenzhou, this reporter found that wages for middle-school graduates at the larger factories were as high as 1,200 Yuan a month. Mr. Liu recounts a popular joke: When a company boss yells that he needs 10 workers, he is answered by five migrant workers, four college graduates and one M.A.

Way to Mobility

In China education has traditionally been seen as a way to upward mobility. Unlike India where caste and birth determined status, the Chinese imperial examination system remained theoretically open to all, so that through study even peasants could aspire to join the bureaucracy. As a result of this ingrained mindset parents are willing to invest their entire life savings in securing a university education for the one-child they are allowed by law to have. Rural families, whose annual income amounts to a few thousand Yuan, often borrow money to cobble together the 10,000 Yuan ($ 1,250) a year fees that many Chinese universities have begun to charge. But increasingly, as the disappointed faces and snaking queues at job fairs around Beijing indicate, this is an ill-afforded investment that provides low returns.

In an interview to China's official news agency Xinhua, Vice-Minister of the Ministry of Labour and Social Security Zhang Xiaojian blamed the lack of adequate jobs on "surplus production capacity, more trade frictions and the revaluation of the Yuan." The logical conclusion would appear to be that China is suffering from an oversupply of graduates. However, in his column Mr. Liu points out that China only has some 150 graduates for every 10,000 citizens, compared to 1,500 in the United States and 900 in Japan. According to Anna Westlake, a human resources consultant with over 10 years experience in the mainland, most companies are desperate to hire. Their problem lies not in the number of graduate applicants but the quality of those applicants. Few prove to be independent and creative thinkers and fewer still are equipped by their universities with the skills in demand in the job market.

Semi-Privatised Education

China's education system today is best described as semi-privatised. Formerly state-sponsored institutions increasingly must rely on raising funds themselves. However, the resulting high tuition fees are often not matched by improved teaching quality. This reporter was formerly a visiting lecuturer at the prestigious Communications University of China, the top journalism school in the country. Admission was competitive and only 50 students out of a total 10,000 applicants were accepted for a new major in "English Broadcasting." The students had to pay 10,000 Yuan a year in addition to another 1,200 Yuan for accommodation. The first batch from this new major graduated last year. Today only one out of the 50 graduates has been able to find a job in English-language broadcasting.

While others have found places with Chinese-language media companies, many work as secretaries or being unable to find a job at all have decided to study further in the hope that an additional degree might improve their employment prospects. "I ended up very disappointed with the degree," says Teresa Lee who was only able to find a job as a secretary at an investment bank, despite having done well in her exams. "We learnt almost nothing in the four years that was of actual use in the job market, as I was to discover," she adds bitterly. Ms. Teresa says that despite her disappointment she is aware that she is lucky to have a job at all and attributes it to the fact that the Communications University of China is well regarded. Graduates from the majority of non-elite universities have it much worse.

Social Time Bomb

Faced with a situation where millions of university-educated graduates are only able to land jobs that pay the equivalent of a factory worker's wage, China's authorities are scrambling to issue regulation they hope will alleviate the crisis. Thus, last month Beijing decided to restrict the number of future college enrolments. Local governments were also issued a notice asking them to "do a good job" in helping graduates find jobs and instructed to pay unemployment subsides to those who have been unable to gain employment. China's authorities are aware that they are sitting on a potential social time bomb. The last major challenge to the Government's authority came in 1989 from a student movement that spread into the wider community. Since then the Government has tried to "co-opt" the educated "elite" who have by and large benefited from the economic reform process. The majority of anti-government protests in recent times have come from the rural poor and laid-off workers, sections who have been left behind in China's economic boom. These disadvantaged groups, however, lack the clout and voice of college-educated graduates. With social inequality much worse today that in 1989, Beijing is well aware that dis-affection among the youth could conceivably once again fuse with wider discontentment. Improving the quality of university education and generating enough jobs to absorb the burgeoning number of graduates is thus a task of urgency.

II

REVAMPING UNIVERSITY EDUCATION

Having impressed the world with the creation of glittering, international quality infrastructure, the erstwhile Middle Kingdom has now turned its attention to transforming its universities into world-class institutions. "Our government realizes the connection between a nation's overall power and the quality of its higher education," says Weiying Zhang, Assistant President of Beijing University. In this latest bid to raise China's global prestige, its universities backed by massive injections of governmental funding are spending billions of dollars in wooing top foreign-educated and overseas-born

Chinese, building cutting-edge research centre, partnering with the world's best educational institutions, and developing new programmes taught in the international *lingua franca*—English.

Under a central government programme started in 1998, (called the 985 Project) started in 1998, 10 of China's leading universities were given special three-year grants in excess of RMB 1 billion, for quality improvements. Beijing and Tsinghua universities, the top two ranked institutions, each received RMB 1.8 billion ($ 225 million). These grants were awarded in addition to special financial support provided by the 211 Project, a separate programme aimed at developing 100 quality universities for the 21st century.

Second Phase of the 985 Project

In 2004, the second phase of the 985 Project was launched and the number of universities under its purview was enlarged to 30. Included in this second phase of special funding is Beijing Normal University (BNU), ranked 15th in the country. Its special "international department" alone receives some RMB 16 million ($ 2 million) annually from the centre. Han Bing, Deputy Director of the department, explains that the funds are used to hold international conferences, attract world-renowned academics as faculty, and support BNU scholars in attending conferences abroad. Dr. Han adds that BNU hosts 30-40 scholars from leading Western universities annually, Top professors are paid $ 40,000 a year.

Restructured Salary Scale

At Beijing University's Guanghua School of Management, of which Dr. Zhang is Executive Dean, full professors with Ph.Ds from prestigious universities abroad can expect $ 60,000 a year. The ability to offer internationally competitive salaries is key to attracting quality academics, says Dr. Zhang. The official national salary given to a full professor in China today as set out by the Ministry of Education (MoE) is a mere RMB 4,000 ($ 500) a month. But for the last few years the Government has permitted individual academic departments to supplement official salaries with private funds that the departments raise through fees, consultancies, and commercial spin offs. Thus the Guanghua School of Management makes-up the difference between official and actual salaries through the revenue it gains from its Executive MBA programme, for which it charges a hefty $ 35,000 a year. BNU in turn supplements salaries with the money it generates from the $ 2,700 a year foreign students learning Mandarin in its language programmes pay. The university has over 2000 foreign students enrolled in various courses and has academic agreements with 153 universities abroad including Princeton, which holds an annual summer school programme at the BNU campus.

As a result of its improved pay scales, the Guanghua school currently boasts some 50 "re-turned scholars" (Chinese nationals who return after studying abroad) and more than half of the faculty hold foreign Ph.Ds. "These are not Ph.Ds from any old university", adds Dr. Zhang, himself a D.Phil. from Oxford. "We only look at Ivy League or Ox-Bridge educated talent." In fact several of the research institutes at China's better universities have a minimum requirement of a foreign Ph.D. for faculty members. The first such centre, called the China Centre for Economic Research (CCER) was established in 1995 at Beijing University. One of CCER's earliest staff members, Professor Feng Lu, recalls the Herculean efforts required to persuade quality academics to return to China a decade ago. In contrast, he says, there are more than 50 application for every vacancy advertised today. Examples of world-renowned academic choosing China as their new homes abound. In 2004, Princeton Professor Andrew Chi-chih Yao one of America's leading computer scientists took up a place at Beijing's Tsinghua University to lead an advanced computer studies programme. Beijing University, in turn, successfully wooed Tian Gang, a leading mathematician from MIT, to set up an international research centre for mathematics.

Batch of the Best Students

"For a world class university it's necessary to attract the best students and faculty internationally. Eventually we don't just want the best Chinese students but the best from around the world," says Dr. Zhang. As a result Chinese universities are increasingly offering courses taught in English and in collaboration with internationally recognized partners. The

Guanghua School of Management offers a dual degree programme in English with the National University of Singapore. In addition, undergraduate courses and an MBA programme in English wholly administered by Guanghua are also on offer. In September 2004, the University of Nottingham, Ningbo, China (UNNC) began its first intake of students. The school is a branch of the U.K.'s Nottingham University and is China's first joint-venture university with an independent campus (there are, however, over 700 foreign affiliated colleges in China). At UNCC, all students are required to speak only English during study and even in social life.

The net result of all these joint venture projects is that it increasingly makes sense for Chinese students to stay at home rather than seek more expensive but largely similar degrees in the West. However, Dr. Zhang points out that collaboration with western partners and the promotion of English cannot in itself fundamentally transform the lacunae in China's current educational system. For him one of the most significant reforms pioneered at Beijing University has, in fact, been the end to lifetime tenure, for decades a defining characteristic of Chinese universities. Since 2003 professors at Beijing University are no longer promoted on the basis of seniority but with an eye to their research and publication records instead. If a new lecturer cannot make it to Associate Professor within six years, he or she is asked to leave. "This was the only way to change to orientation of our faculty towards academic research," explains Dr. Zhang.

India and China : A Study in Contrast

The combined results of these efforts are already paying off. Despite the common perception that Indian higher education with its IITs and IIMs is superior to the Chinese, China's universities in fact beat India's in almost every international ranking. According to the well-regarded Shanghai Jiaoton University (SJTU) Academic Ranking of World Universities, China has two universities in the top 300, while India has none. China features eight times in the top 500, India only thrice. The SJTU rankings are complied on the basis of university alumni and staff winning major academic prizes, the publication of highly cited research articles published in prestigious academic journals, and articles indexed in major citation indexes.

According to Subarno Chatterji, an English literature professor at Delhi University with a D.Phil. from Oxford, there are no special incentives in India to attract top quality academics from abroad. Salaries remain fixed at government-funded institutions by the University Grants Commission at Rs. 50,000 a month for full professors and there is "little concerted or organized interface between academia and the corporate world." Dr. Chatterji is currently contemplating leaving India to teach at Miyazaki University in Japan. "They pay their academics very well," he says. According to Calla Weimer, a Fellow at the Economic Department at the National University of Singapore, "The NUS Economics Department increasingly sees China as a competitor in attracting and retaining good faculty, but the same does not hold for India." She adds: "While Chinese economists are being lured back to universities in their home country, Indians see more content to remaining Singapore."

The long strides China has taken towards literacy and basic education have put India to shame for years. For example in 2000, only 47 per cent of all children in India had managed to complete grade 5 of primary schooling as opposed to 98 per cent of Chinese children. But China's remarkable recent renaissance in higher education means that even elite education in India is falling behind the standards being set to the north of the Himalayas. In 1978 only about 1.4 per cent of the Chinese population was enrolled in higher education. Today the figure is close to 20 per cent. Currently some 20 million students are studying in various kinds of higher educational institutions in China.

That China has a considerable distance to go before its aspirations to create truly world-class universities becomes a reality is evident. The absence of critical thinking hampers the development of academic debate. China is, in fact, still to produce a Nobel Prize winner. According to Michael Pettis, a professor at the Guanghua School of Management and former adjunct professor at Colombia University, "the fundamental problems with Chinese education, an intensive focus on rote learning and inability to develop arguments," remain despite the large inflows of university funding from the centre. Adds Dr. Zhang, "We still suffer from too much governmental control and have little lee-way to implement reforms without cumbersome permissions and procedures." Chinese universities are unable for example to develop new programmes or curricula without prior governmental approval. "We have been able to improve our hardware considerably," says BNU's Dr. Han. "But as is always the case in China, the software takes longer."

•

Rejuvenation of Asia

Chinese President Hu Jintao on Thursday (November 23, 2006) said "the 21st century would be a century of Asia" if India and China worked together in partnership and peaceful coexistence. Addressing the India-China economic, trade and investment cooperation summit, organized by the Federation of Indian Chamber of Commerce and Industries (FICCI), Mumbai. Hu, who is currently on a visit to the country, said he endorsed the views of Prime Minister Manmohan Singh that Asia was 'big enough' for the development of both India and China. It is my sincere hope that the business communities of the two countries will be future-oriented and will work together to boost the bilateral ties and contribute to the development of both the countries and the rejuvenation of Asia.

(Source: *The New Indian Express*, November 24, 2006)

14

Protecting Intellectual Property : The Guanxi Way

G. Narasimha Raghavan

"Is China a threat, challenge or a strategic partner?"[1]

INTRODUCTION

While the above quote refers to India's discretionary stance towards an equivalent cohort, such obligatory choice stares in the face of many nations, and they stand in awe and frightful wonder at the largesse of a nation like China. Likewise, it would not take long for a country to speculate whether India is a comrade or adversary. Nonetheless, there is one area that is of interest to many foreign investors, amongst the many differences that are noticed between China and India—the status of intellectual property. In this paper, the primary focus would be on the problem of intellectual property protection in China and how it is being resolved through the traditional relationship schema called *Guanxi*.

What is Intellectual Property?

Intellectual Property (IP) refers to property rights in creations of the mind, such as inventions, industrial designs, literary and artistic works, symbols, and names and images. World-over, IP is being touted as the next architect of corporate affluence. At any point, protecting IP is but a trade-off, taking cognizance of the need to strike an appropriate balance among the needs of creators, developers and users, in conjunction with various national and global legislations.

Status of Intellectual Property Protection in China

Despite China's accession to the World Trade Organisation (WTO), its legal regime is yet to be fully consistent with the WTO—mooted Agreement on Trade Related Intellectual Property Rights (TRIPs). Additionally, inadequate enforcement of IP rules[2] is the most observable reason for large scale blatant violation. In most cases, violation of IP in China takes on the garb of counterfeiting (selling bogus or fake merchandise)[3] and piracy (unauthorized production and sale of an IP protected good).[4] It must be realized that piracy and counterfeiting cause an enormous damage to the IP holders, who, out of the blue, identify that a cheaper version of the good is available in the market—a surefire signal that their investments in the production and marketing of the good has been hammered.

Some of the estimates of the losses from IP infringement are:

1. The losses suffered in China by foreign firms are at US $ 20 billion annually.
2. Two out of very five foreign manufacturers are losing more than 20 per cent of their revenue every year.[5]
3. Counterfeiting alone is estimated to be in the tune of US $ 16 billion, with counterfeits accounting for 15-20 per cent of all branded goods made in China.[6]

Modus Operandi and Reasons

In China, there are two methods used in producing goods (in the manufacturer's end) that are in the anti-IP dominion:

- *Overbuilding:* Legitimate factories producing additional products than what they are supposed to manufacture, with an aim to 'sell on the other side'.
- *Cloning:* Making exact replicas of products, along with packages.
- At the other end of the spectrum, we find three reasons for the widespread prevalence of down right disregard for IP in China.
- *Cultural ethos*: The Chinese are under the erroneously appreciated Confucius—influenced thought that 'ideas are not the property of any one.' Hence, there exists the tendency to categorize counterfeiting as a legitimate opportunity to make a living.
- *Geographical accessibility:* Being quite a big nation the enforcement mechanism is not all that effective, given the proviso of the existence of 'local protectionism'.
- *Economic case:* Agreed that China faces unemployment crisis, the authorities are not in a benign attitude to check the functioning of such small factories that provide the much needed employment to many nationals.

The Uniqueness of Guanxi

It is Confucius again, who comes to the rescue here. The Chinese society remains very a relationship oriented structure, undoubtedly a Confucian heritage that stresses the importance of human relationship in day-to-day transactions.

In the notorious haven of China, low-cost pirated versions of Western brand-name products are all too easy to find.[7] "Guanxi" plainly means "relationships", and stands for any type of relationship. In the Chinese business world, however, it is also understood as the network of relationships among various parties that cooperate together and support one another.[8]

In an unadorned way, Guanxi simply means building a rapport with a person, based on mutual trust and respect. This relationship could be with one's suppliers, buyers, and/or with the government officials. It is through these valued connections that the other parties sense the justification for not infringing the legal and agreed rights of the manufacturer.

The very need for an informal and effective system like Guanxi arises in China is fundamentally as a response to the highly unique enriching philosophy of doing business there. Besides, developing Guanxi helps business to obliterate the inherent lack of transparency in the business environment. All the more, it is only through Guanxi that the right kind of relationship with the government can be struck—a move that would in the long run articulate the importance of protecting IP for the nation as a whole.

Some examples are: building partnerships with the Chinese before doing business, collaborating with the Chinese government on issues of national importance, making donations to local government and institutions, educating employees about the illegality of engaging in anti-IP activities.

Establishing Guanxi and Protecting IP

There are four modes of cultivating Guanxi in China.[9]

(a) To start with, the relationship need not be based on money. Treating someone with decency while others treat him/her unfairly could result in a good relationship.

(b) Next, it starts with and builds on the trustworthiness of the individual or the company. If a company promised certain things and delivered as promised, the company is showing trustworthiness and the Chinese would be more inclined to deal with them again.

(c) Third, being dependable and reliable undeniably strengthens the affiliation. A good example is related to the 1989 political instability in China. Companies that stayed found their relationship with the Chinese strengthened as they were viewed by the Chinese as friends who did not abandon the Chinese when they needed friends.

(d) And lastly, frequent contacts with each other will promote understanding and emotional bonds and the Chinese often feel obliged to do business with their friends first.

As can be deciphered from the above explanation that Guanxi is not used solely for IP related quandaries alone; rather, it is a contrivance to comply with the Chinese commercial culture. In the case of IP, it is the high return, the case of copying and the low risk attached to the activity[10] that makes counterfeiting and piracy lucrative options. Guanxi situates these activities in a mutually revolting position, so that the associated parties do not engage in such IP defiant operations. Moreover, Guanxi is based on the twin principles of encouraging the moral uprightness of the individual and stimulating social order.

The most prominent counterfeited goods include medicines, soft drinks, processed foods, tobacco products, and clothing to sophisticated textile machinery and automobiles. Enterprises manufacturing and selling electronics products are particularly vulnerable. It is a truism to state that the preservation of IP provides one of the most difficult business concern and legal issue facing China.[11]

Derivative

India and China's impending power and muscle in the coming years, would give them a pan-Asian Character,[12] and they will hold sway over many international issues of importance, IP being one among the more prominent ones. It is here that India and China must take notice of the fact that a mere stronger IP regime would not suffice; a broader set of complementary initiatives has to be embedded into the system. Along with the development of human capital (through knowledge dissemination and awareness of IP), Guanxi is a typical complementary tool to maximize the potential of IP in the pro-competitive era in the long-run.

Notes and References

1. Title of an article, G. Parthasarathy, *The Hindu Business Line*, June 30, 2006.
2. Maskus, Keith E., "Intellectual Property Rights in the WTO Accession Package: Accessing China's Reforms," in Bhattasali, Deepak, Shantong Li and Will Martin, *China and the WTO*, World Bank, Washington, 2004, p. 60.
3. Here, the effort is taken to pass the fake as an original one. Eg. Imitation of a Parker Pen.

4. In this case, an unauthorized means is used for copying other's designs or technology, and sold without any compensation or permission. Eg. Copying Microsoft's Windows operating system software.
5. For more such estimates, see Chapter 5: The two-Dollar Rolex, in Shenkar, Oded, The Chinese Century, Wharton School Publishing and Pearson Educational Publishers, Singapore, 2005, pp. 81-99.
6. Besides counterfeiting, China also specializes in across-the-board trade mark infringement. Creation of fakes and shoddy goods is very good business, claim Beck, Daniel, Stephanie Feldman, Herman Grimoldi, and Susanna Ver Eecke, "Combating Piracy Through Guanxi", in Dayal-Gulati, Anuradha and Angela Y. Lee, Kellog on China, Northwestern University Press, Illinois, 2005, pp. 115-137.
7. Einhorn, Bruce, "Big Pharma Has a Friend in Guanxi", 7 December, 2004. Available at www.businessweek.com.
8. This boils down to exchanging favours, which are expected to be done regularly and voluntarily.
9. To understand the Chinese Business Culture and the predominance of Guanxi, visit http://chinese-school.netfirms.com
10. According to Jim T. Dwyer, Investigator, Regional Asia-Pacific Law and Corporate Affairs Digital Integrity, Microsoft, knowledge must be free, but its dissemination must involve costs. See report in *The Hindu Business Line,* "Call to protect intellectual", 7 May, 2006.
11. The limitations of China's current laws relating to IPR are given in Haley, George T., Usha C.V. Haley and Chin Tiong, *The Chinese Tao of Business,* John Wiley and Sons, Singapore, 2004 pp. 77-80.
12. Bhagat, Raheeda, "The China-India Matrix", *The Hindu Business Line,* 6 July, 2006.

15

Disinvestments : The Chinese Example

S. VENKITARAMANAN

INTRODUCTION

The latest news is that China initial public offerings (IPOs) of a number of its large State-owned Banks. The IPOs are being made on the Hong Kong Stock Exchange with a view to giving the shares to potential foreign as well as Chinese investors. Ahead of the IPOs, the Chinese Government has roped in strategic investors in the form of large multinational banks, Bank of America and HSBC to quote only two examples. Bank of America has put down $ 3 billion for a less than 10 per cent stake in China's fifth largest public sector Bank, China Bank of Construction. HSBC has put in $ 1.75 billion for a stake of less than 10 per cent in the Bank of Communications. (This IPO has just been successfully completed). The amounts proposed to be divested through the IPOs are mind-boggling. The list is still being extended.

Disinvestments : Initial Steps

Slated for further IPOs during the year are the Shanghai Investment and Trust Bank Investor (Temasek of Singapore likely investor), Bank of Beijing Investor (where ING Group of Netherlands is a likely investor) and a few others. The fact is that China has gone ahead with initiating divestment of its shares in public sector banks with a view to improving their management and performance, the FDI involved being an incidental benefit. China is aware that its financial system is in need of an overhaul. It is well-recognised that the banks have large non-performing loans on their books. Despite this, if Bank of America is willing to invest in a minority stake, it only means the acquirer has faith in the growth potential of the banking sector and continuing reforms of regulation and management.

The latest buzz is that the Government of China has also allowed Bank of America, to bring in 50 plus managers to strengthen the bank's lending management culture. China's zeal for catching up with the developed world has helped our own Leftists overcome their fear of foreigners gobbling-up shares even in a vital sector, like public sector banks. The transition from State control to commercial lending in the Chinese banking system has already started. The Chairman of one of the banks having an IPO is reported to have stated publicly that one of the first things he did on taking charge from his predecessor, was to put the Board of Directors in a position to take decisions. The local unit of the Communist Party, which was all long inspecting all lending decisions, was asked to step aside. This decision marks a sharp de-politicisation of banking. This is also a first step towards commercialisation.

Towards Commercialisation

Whether a new strategic partner, like Bank of America, with its minority stake and just one place on the Board will be able to effect a more complete transformation of the Bank, remains to be seen. One commentator in the international financial press has pointed out that it is Bank of America's tradition to take risk-oriented decisions. After all, it was Bank of America's legendary founder who had decided in the 1930s, purely on the basis of his gut-instincts, to finance an intinerant and insignificant film producers's proposal to convert cartoons into films. The film producer was Walt Disney and the film was *Snow White*. The founder of Bank of America, A.P. Gianinini, had to overrule his management-trained son and others who had advised him against taking such risks. It turned out to be a risk worth taking. So too did Bank of America take a risk when it financed *Gone with the Wind* a glowing success of the cinema industry in its time. May one hope that Bank of America's daring investment in Chinese banking follows-up this tradition of taking risks and succeeding in them.

Returning to China's divestment, its banking IPOs bring into focus the discordant line adopted by our Indian Leftist brigade against the divestment of a 10 per cent stake in BHEL and similar openings in the banking sector. This is contrary to what China's admittedly Leftist rulers are doing. Our Leftists' resistance is typical of a mindset, which "lacks" self-confidence in our being able to control the private investor, who is after all in a minority. Our banking regulator is ultimately Indian and competent. The Government of India sets the rules of the game. Why should one be afraid of the foreign or domestic minority private investor? Incidentally, the Chinese divestment story goes farther than banking. One of the major mining ventures in that country is also issuing an IPO simultaneously with the Banking IPOs, expecting to garner billions of dollars as a result.

Pragmatism

This shows the pragmatic way in which China has approached issues of State control and divestment. If there is a minority interest in State enterprises held by private shareholders, foreign or domestic, it cannot do harm to the efficiency of the enterprise. On the contrary, it may help increase the efficiency by setting benchmarks of market based return. This is not to say that all is well with China's banks. The Chinese banking reform is just beginning. A recent review of Chinese reforms in *Financial Times*, June 20, has pointed out that there are trifling problems faced by China's public sector banks. Among other things, Chinese banks share our problem of over-staffing and large number of branches, besides large non-performing loans.

To quote one instance of reform in Chinese banking, three years ago, one of the banks, ICBC, had a workforce of about

5,00,000. It has since closed down about half of its 40,000 odd branches and cut about 1,30,000 staff. The Bank Chairman said that he still has too many workers, but pleads "political sensitivities" when asked when he will reduce this further. He states, "We will gradually solve the problem through retrenchments." A familiar story, except that our Chairmen will scarcely give expression to such problems in public! And we claim that India has freedom of expression—but not for chief executives of public sector entities and banks in particular.

The example cited demonstrates the process of transformation, which China's banks have embarked on. Maybe, India's public sector banks are already cost-conscious, at least to a limited extent since some of their shares are listed on the stock markets and stock market prices are signals. But the Chinese experience shows that much can be achieved given the political will and executive grit to face political sensitivities. It is also important to note that the Chinese have scored successes in reducing non-performing loans from their earlier high levels.

Recapitalisation of Bad Debts

The Chinese Government has spent $ 30-50 billion of its own resources to recapitalise its bad debt liabilities. This must

TABLE

List of Banks in China Slated for Divestment

Date of Announcement	*Bank*	*Acquirers Name*	*Value of bid (in $)*
2005	China Construction Bank	Bank of America	3.0 bn
2004	Bank of Communications	HSBC	1.75 bn.
1997	Shanghai Investment and Trust	Tennessee Singapore	0.77 bn.
2005	Bank of Beijing	ING Baring (Dutch)	0.215 bn.
2003	Industrial Bank	Hang Shzhon Bank, Hong Kong	0.208 bn.
2005	Hang Shzhon City Commercial Bank	Commonwealth Bank of Australia	77 mn.

Source : *The Asian Wall Street Journal*, 20 June, 2005.

be one reason why international banks are willing to lend their hand to participate in China's banks' equity and to help reform Chinese banking. The progress of China's economic reform, especially in banking, has many lessons for us. In the context of the latest debate in India on BHEL, not the least important, is their courageous and pragmatic decision to invite private investors, both domestic and foreign, into our banks. As against this, we are still fighting shy of such an open invitation to multinational bankers.

Perhaps, the Prime Minister and the Finance Minister are quite frustrated already with the Left's "righteous" indignation about the limited divestment in BHEL. But is it too much to hope that given China's bold initiative on bank divestment, India's masters will moderate their stand at least in the near future?

Rising Inequality in China

C.P. CHANDRASEKHAR AND JAYATI GHOSH

INTRODUCTION

There is much international interest in China's economy, because of its remarkable growth over the past quarter century. Recently, attention has also focused on the fact that this growth has been associated with significant increases in inequality in both income and wealth distribution, which were relatively low during the central planning period. Two new reports also focus specifically on this issue of inequality in China, and provide important new information on recent patterns in this regard. The recently released China Human Development Report, 2005 of the UNDP in Beijing (which is prepared mostly by Chinese economists) has as its theme the issue of inequality in economic and human development indicators. And the OECD has just come out with a report on income disparities in China, as part of its series on China in the Global Economy.

Widening Inequality

Both of them reinforce the perceptions of observers and analysts that economic inequalities have increased sharply over the economic reform period since the early 1980s, and this has been especially marked since the substantial opening-up of the economy since the early 1990s. The Gini coefficient measure of inequality based on consumption data suggest some decrease from the mid-1970s to the mid-1980s, and increase thereafter. Intrarural and intra-urban inequalities also increased over the 1990s, despite an episode of declining inequality within urban and rural areas around the mid-1990s. Meanwhile, inequality between urban and rural areas rose steadily over the 1990s. The ratio of urban-rural per capita income (urban disposable income to rural net income) increased from 1.86 in 1985 to 3.11 in 1990. While there was a short period of declining differences between 1995 and 1997, the post-1997 period saw a dramatic and continuous increase in this ratio between 1997 and 2002, from 2.47 to 3.11. It is likely however that these are still underestimates of the actual rural-urban income gaps. As the China Human Development Report (CHDR) 2005 points out, "if public housing subsidies, private housing imputed rent, pension, free medical care, and educational subsidies were included, the actual per capita income of urban residents in 2002 would increase by 3,600 to 3,900 Yuan, bringing the urban-rural income ratio to about four-fold instead of the 3.2 fold acknowledged by official figures." (page 27). This would make rural-urban inequality in China among the highest in the world. The CHDR also points to widening inequality within rural and urban areas as well, based on data from a household survey conducted in 2002. These increases in inequality are ascribed to the economic growth process, which has meant that rural non-farm income opportunities are concentrated in a few areas, while some urban areas have grown more rapidly than others.

Regional Disparities

China's regional inequality had declined between 1979 and 1990, but reversed to a rising trend over the 1990s. In particular, the difference between inland and coastal China increased, especially in the late 1990s. According to the China HDR 2005, the ratio of per capita incomes of eastern to central regions increased from 1.42 in 1997 to 1.52 in 2003. Most of the regional inequality in China is to be found between three large regions and within provinces (that is, between districts within provinces). Coastal-inland inequality has been always much lower compared to rural-urban inequality, even though it has been rising more sharply in recent years. The three largest cities of Beijing, Tianjin and Shanghai account for a large part of the variation in regional incomes. These large metros, which enjoy a high level of industrialization and with over 71 per cent of their population living within 100 km off the coast or navigable waters, were able to reap the full benefits of public infrastructure expansion and export promotion, and therefore attracted substantial FDI inflows.

The central region, the agricultural heartland, reaped benefits from deregulation in the early phase of the reform period and had a growth rate of 7.7 per cent, higher than the national average, between 1979 and 1984. However, the subsequent period saw growth rates fall as agricultural expansion reached its limit. With the lack of access to the mainland, compounded by difficult terrain and lack of mineral resources, western China has lagged behind average growth rates in the post-planning period, especially in the 1990s. The movements in per capita income across regions indicate these trends.

Significant Trends in Employment

Employment in China has increased steadily over the last two decades, much of it fuelled by the industrial and services sectors, and has registered an average annual growth rate of 2.55 per cent between 1980 and 2002. However, growth has been much slower in the period after 1990 at 1.09 per cent per annum, compared to 4.33 per cent in the earlier decade. The share of agricultural employment in the aggregate has declined steadily from 68.7 per cent in 1980 to 50 percent in 2000-2002. However, rural employment is still dominated by agriculture, which accounts for two-thirds of rural workers, and therefore, slow rates of expansion of agricultural employment have reinforced the widening of rural-urban inequality. Total rural employment has been almost stagnant between 1995 and 2002. Employment has grown at a low 0.22 per cent per annum over 1990-2002, much lower than the 4.13 per cent of the previous decade of structural reform in agriculture.

Part of the stagnation in rural employment reflects an economy in the process of industrialization and development. The urban areas have absorbed part of the workforce from the rural areas reflected in large-scale migration, and this has compensated, at least partially, for stagnating rural employment. However, migration has also been partially the reason behind increasing urban unemployment post-1985. Unemployment (in terms of absolute numbers of people) has risen steadily since 1985, reaching a high of 7.7 million in 2002. This rise has been particularly sharp since 1990, recording an annual growth rate of 6 per cent, compared to –3.4 per cent between 1980 and 1990.

Influential Wage Structure

The disparity between rural and urban areas has been significantly accounted for by the growing gap between wages in agriculture which is dominant in rural areas and wages in industry and services which predominate in urban areas. The ratio of industrial wages to agricultural wages, which has always been high since 1980, has generally experienced a rising trend. This rising pattern is even sharper in the ratio between most of the service sector wages and agricultural wages, with declines only between 1993 and 1996. The remarkable rise in service sector wages and to a certain extent in industrial wages has, therefore, not benefited the rural population much.

Wage rates have also varied widely within the dominant sectors and between various sub-sectors within urban China, adding to urban inequality. Wages in new sectors such as telecommunications, banking and insurance, and real estate have increased significantly in recent years. Meanwhile, the government's recent attempts to stimulate domestic consumption have raised average wage levels in state-owned organizations dealing with healthcare, sports, education, culture, and scientific research and in government whereas wage levels in more traditional manufacturing industries with more older state-owned enterprises have stagnated throughout the decade because of the cut in government subsidies.

Resource Mobilisation

While external liberalization may have facilitated more rapid growth, it has also been a major factor behind increasing inequalities. Part of this is due to the basic nature of FDI flows, which choose safe destinations that are already somewhat developed. That is why foreign investment in the coastal regions exceeded that in the interior regions by far—in 2000, foreign investments in the eastern region were more than 85 per cent of total FDI. Public resource mobilization has shown an increasing inequalising tendency and a bias towards richer, coastal areas. Before economic reform, there was a centralized budget and an equitable distribution of resources, which were generated from the profits of and taxes on the state-owned enterprises (SOEs), since the rich provinces were required to turn over large surpluses to the government while the poorer provinces received large subsidies. However, as profitability of the SOEs declined in the reform era, the system was marked by chaos with local governments imposing other revenue raising measures. There was a proliferation of *ad hoc*, extra-budgetary projects monitored through the banking system, which continues even today. The share of central revenues and, consequently, the ability of the central government to spend on physical and social infrastructure, declined considerably.

Sectoral Dynamics

Industrial growth in the reform era has been very high, but even then, patterns of development have encouraged the forces of inequality. There has been acute capital-deepening in new enterprises, which have replaced traditional ones, so employment elasticity in manufacturing has been very low. Service sector employment growth has been inadequate to meet the needs of the labour force, and also typically service sector employment has required a higher level of skill which much of China's population, especially in rural interior areas, has not possessed. Further, reduced subsidies and greater external competition faced by SOEs have reduced their profitability and employment generation potential. Since 1984, when benefits of the agrarian reform was exhausted, agricultural growth has decelerated and lagged behind industrial and service sector growth rates. Unlike the industrial sector, this sector has not received much state patronage in terms of investment, nor has it seen proliferation of small enterprises on the scale of the industrial and service sectors. New agricultural policies that are now trying to regularize property rights in land in accordance with the structures of a market economy are likely to have a severe adverse impact on the rural population, since China's egalitarian distribution of land has had a strong equalizing effect on the distribution of farm income. Recently there have been sharp increases in wealth inequality, driven by land ownership in particular. (China, HDR, 2005)

Impact of Migration

Restrictions on labour movements have been one important factor behind rural-urban inequalities in China. The origin of this lies in the Hukou, or household registration system, which was started during the central planning era. Individuals were tied to their birthplace and given a household based residence status at birth. Only approved urban registered residents were allowed to live and work in urban areas, and in consequence rural residents were forced to stay and work within rural areas. More important, only the urban-Hukou holders were entitled to receive the guaranteed social service benefits such as education, housing and healthcare in the urban areas. From 1980s onwards, some rural migrants have been granted temporary residence permits that allow them to remain in cities and enable them to access some social services, though at excessively high fees especially when compared to urban residents. The larger part of the migrant population, however, did not qualify for temporary residence permits, and had to remain in the informal sector without access to the public utilities and other benefits available to urban residents.

It is estimated that about half of the total flow of migrants would have been denied any kind of legal status in the form of temporary permits or urban Kukous. In addition, rural migrant workers in cities often face discrimination as a result of local regulations, being charged various "administration fees",. (China, HDR, 2005) They also face harsher and more unhealthy and dangerous working conditions. All this has added to inequalities in access to income and public services among the migrant community and led to severe poverty among migrants.

Focus on Pro-poor Programmes

A case can be made that increasing inequality during this phase of economic transition in China is inevitable. Thus, recently a government official argued, "Looking at income inequality as a whole, it may be the case that rational, and thus inevitable, disparities are more significant than irrational disparities. The widening of income disparities occurred, on the one hand, during a process when overall incomes increased steadily and, on the other, where economic efficiency has also been continuously improved. In this regard, the process has helped overall economic growth and social development." (Han Wenxiu, 2005, page 11).

However, it is also accepted that widening income disparities can impose more and more negative effects in economic and social development. The government of China seems to have recognized the growing problems of inequality and poverty. Recent "White Papers" on employment, poverty and women acknowledge the need to correct regional imbalances as well as rural-urban and gender disparities. There has been a specific attempt to develop infrastructure and natural minerals of the interior regions to generate incomes. The recent strategies of developing the west and revitalizing the northeast have involved funding new infrastructure projects and increasing fiscal transfers to these areas. Other recent efforts include expanding the security net and providing pensions and unemployment insurance which was started in the 1980s, allowing some relaxation in migration norms, the launch of poverty relief programmes (including the aid-the—poor fund) on a much wider scale than before, extension and some decentralization of the banking sector to make credit accessible to interior and rural areas. Addressing the problems of poverty and inequality in China will require wide-ranging and multi-pronged policies. Fortunately, the Government still retains enough control over crucial economic levers to ensure a redirection of growth patterns in more progressive ways.

Winds of Change in China's Growth Strategy

S. Sethuraman

INTRODUCTION

China's 2.3 trillion dollar economy, the fourth largest, continues to power ahead but its leader have become more aware than ever before that more than half of its 1.3 billion people are getting caught in the ever widening rural-urban income disparities and regional imbalances which could potentially lead to a social explosion.

A New Socialist Countryside

The new strategy embodied in the Eleventh five-year plan (2006-2010) makes a major departure from the traditional focus on higher growth through its exceptionally high rates of savings and investment to achieving a more "balanced growth" for building a "prosperous, harmonious society" and with reduced dependence on energy, resource and capital-intensive modes of progress. Greater "self-innovation" in economic transformation is another thrust factor in the plan. Internally, Chinese leaders are beginning to view with greater concern the growing rural-urban income disparities and disturbing divide between thriving coastal zones on the east, the northern and western areas, the migration of surplus labour to cities aggravating the unemployment situation, and potential threats to social and political stability. They have, therefore, decided to lay greater emphasis, without giving up the centrality of relatively high and sustained growth, on bringing about a leap forward in modernization of agriculture, improving the welfare of farmers, building rural infrastructure to urban levels and laying the foundation for building "A New Socialist Countryside."

Redressing Imbalances

A UN report on China's development recently cited the wealth gap between urban and rural communities as one of the highest in the world and the "palpable" inter-regional inequalities. But it noted that the Government was coming to grips with the problem of redressing imbalances in economic and social development. The report called for spread of education, health care and social security protection as part of measures to bring down inequalities across regions. China's eleventh five year plan gives primacy to these factors and approved by China's supreme legislative body, the National People's Congress Session in March 2006. Beijing plans to spend more for agricultural development and infrastructure construction, which would help to boost grain production, ensure food security for the people and arrest the drift towards urban areas. Education and health care will get higher financing. Policies will be set in motion for protecting farmland, safeguarding rights of workers and providing employment and job training in the rural areas. The Government recently abolished the centuries—old agricultural tax as part of measures to improve the condition of farmers and increase transfer payments for the poorer segments. Other tax reforms have been under way. Including unification of corporate tax to do away with the wide difference between the rates of domestic companies at 33 per cent and of foreign-funded firms at 17 per cent, rise in personal tax exemption limit and incentives to encourage employment and re-employment which will also cover agriculture and rural development.

Growth Dynamics

The spectacular growth record of China over the last two decades, averaging more than 9 per cent, has not brought about any dramatic transformation in the countryside, and India would do well to learn from the Chinese experience that mere harping on 8-10 per cent growth will not take us far unless there is a more holistic approach to development. China's National Bureau of Statistics (NBS), has re-worked economic growth since 1993 after a census of productive sectors which revealed a much higher level of activity not so far captured in national accounts. Almost 90 per cent of the revision is accounted for by higher value-added in the services sector and faster price increases than assumed earlier. The revised data for 2004, the census year, showed a 16.8 per cent rise in the size of the economy with GDP growing by 10.1 per cent, a double digit for the third year in succession, to make China the sixth largest economy. With another 9.9 per cent rise in 2005, GDP exceeding 2.2 trillion dollars, China is now the fourth largest economy, having outpaced France and Britain, and behind only to the US, Japan and Germany.

China's per capita income is roughly $ 1,700 which, with its population, does not make it any the less a developing country. Apart from the significant rise by 9 percentage points in the share of tertiary sector (services) to GDP from 31.9 per cent (old) to 40.7 per cent (new) at the end of 2004, the census data does not alter the broad picture of the economy and its growth pattern, but it provides a more reliable base for the Eleventh plan formulations and its priorities in economic and social development. The revised composition of GDP shows, apart from the increase in share of services, a decline in that of industry (including construction) to 46.2 per cent from 52.9 per cent (old data) and that of primary sector (mainly agriculture) to 31.1 per cent. Although China's investment rate has been quite high, it was only 41 per cent in 2004 as against the earlier estimate of 48 per cent, but even this is relatively high in relation to most economies, including Asian countries.

No "Overheating"

NBS Director, Mr. Li Deshui, draws the inference that the economy at this level of investment is not overheating and is maintainable for "fairly fast and sustained growth" which the planners would want to stabilize at 8-9 per cent. He notes that in 2005 the share of consumer spending in GDP was 33.3 per cent—a sign of domestic demand taking over from exports as the driver of growth—while investment and exports contributed 48 per cent and 18 per cent respectively. There has been neither inflation nor deflation. China's long-term explosive growth and its emergence as the world's manufacturing hub and third largest trader and India's catching-up as a fast-growing economy with its abundance of skills are being increasingly seen as a transformation under way of the global economic landscape. While foreign investors may look at huge market opportunities, there are underlying concerns about their rising competitiveness. Developed nations, who have dominated the world, are weighing the impact that the two Asian giants can make on the global economy, earth's resources and environmental conservation. With a growing appetite for natural resources for the ongoing expansion, the two countries would account for a substantial increase in the world demand for energy.

11th Plan Perspectives

The Eleventh plan has indicated two targets for 2010: Doubling the per capita income of 2000 and reducing energy consumption by 20 per cent. The World Bank in an update on the Chinese economy considers per capita income doubling feasible with only 7 per cent average growth as against the trend rate of 9.5 per cent but is skeptical about the targeted reduction in energy use which shot up in recent years. The National Development and Reforms Commission, which is the planning body, has set up a task force to frame a new energy policy for security and is also working on a long-term plan to increase use of alternatives—nuclear, wind and solar energy. Increasing use of ethanol and coal liquefaction are also on the agenda. China's two-way trade last year totaled $ 1.4 trillion, exports growing by 28.6 per cent and imports by 17.6 per cent. Although in the second half of 2005, domestic demand overtook exports, the trade surplus tripled from the previous year level to $ 102 billion and reserves totaled $ 819 billion. With its decision to rely more on domestic consumption than exports, China expects diminishing surpluses. But the World Bank sees it as a gradual process and has projected the reserves to rise close to $ 1 trillion by the end of 2006.

Democratic India *versus* Authoritarian China is a theme that's been debated at world for a for very long now. But the curiosity has now given way to new economic and strategic concerns. With India's and China's share of the G-7 countries' dollar GDP set to move up from current levels of 2.6 per cent and 7.7 per cent respectively to 40 per cent and 79 per cent by 2050, the competition between the two is set to escalate. The world, and even India, has tried to play down the discord. They point to the supplementary roles being played by the two emerging powers. India's growing soft skills, mainly in the services sector, and China's hard skills in manufacturing were argued to be mutually compatible.

Source: Pyaralal Raghavan: "India-China growth race",

The New Indian Express, November 27, 2006.

Lessons from China

K. Subramaniam

INTRODUCTION

Currently, two economic forces are impacting global trade. One is Wal-Mart and the other is China. The former is the conduit through which massive retailing of goods worth billions of dollars takes place. The latter is the manufacturing hub churning out goods to feed those retail mills. A study of Wal-Mart's operations and China's manufacturing potential may have lessons for countries like India. Wal-Mart has been described as the Beast of Bentonville or an 800-pound gorilla. China is an authoritarian state run with an iron hand by a communist party. What do they have in common? For Wal-Mart to grow, it has to draw on the bottomless reserves of cheap or low-priced goods. For China to employ its millions, it has to exploit its capacity in manufacturing an infrastructure. If steady streams of goods do not feed Wal-Mart's super-centres, Wal-Mart cannot grow.

Wal-Mart Business Strategies

If steady exploitation of China's industrial and manufacturing capacities does not take place, the displaced labour from the hinterland cannot be absorbed and there will be social disruption. In the early years, the Chinese authorities looked at the Wal-Mart alliance with caution. Once they understood its potential, they latched onto it. Wal-Mart is unique as a business model. Sam Walton had a different vision of retailing. Instead of charging a little less than his competitors, he would slash prices as much as he could and yet make a profit. Rather than operating on price breaks from wholesalers to boost his margins, he would pay less at the wholesale end and pass on the savings to customers. He hoped to make up the difference in high volumes.

The company pursued cost reduction and efficiency so ruthlessly that it reversed the role of the retailer. Wal-Mart grew phenomenally and, by the mid-1980s, Sam Walton was on the top of the Forbes list of richest Americans. A 2002 McKinsey Global Institute report said: "Productivity growth accelerated after 1995 because Wal-Mart's success forced competitors to improve their operations." Wal-Mart's growth had social implications—it had grown too big and become self-destructive in its drive towards cost-reduction. It now has a work-force of around 1.6 million workers, including over a million in the US. It operates 3,200 stores in the US and around 1,100 outlets in nine other countries. Its dominance as a buyer is unparalleled.

As Prof. Edna Bonacich of UCLA put it, "They are the largest toy seller and grocer. There are large products they control. And then the manufacturers are basically stuck having to sell them. If they don't sell to (Wal-Mart), then they are in deep trouble. So there is big volume effect." With its dominance in the market, Wal-Mart could change the power relations between the manufacturer and the retailer. As Prof. Nelson Lichtenstein of the university of California, described, "The power of Wal-Mart is such, it reversed a hundred-year history in which the manufacturer was powerful and the retailer was sort of the vassal... Now the retailer, the mass global retailer, is the centre, the power, the vassal, who has to do the bidding of the retailer."

"Race to Use Bottom"

Several studies established that even as Wal-Mart contributed to higher poverty rate, it did not bear the full cost of its corporate practices and shifted them to the state. Employees were unable to cover the cost of medical insurance and their wages got reduced by as much as 40 per cent. Even as Wal-Mart opened super-stores in new towns, it displaced workers employed in regional chains. Not all the displaced labour could be absorbed by the employment created in Wal-Mart super-centres, as they adopted sophisticated technology requiring lesser manpower. This resulted in unemployment. Thus, Wal-Mart created islands of low wages even as the argument was advanced that it neutralized the impact of low wages by offering cheaper products to the poor. It had anti-union policies and discouraged the formation of unions to settle wage and related benefits. Many of these practices led to the perception that the operations of Wal-Mart were a 'race to the bottom' and the affluent blue-collar professionals who rose during the post-War years were being wiped out.

Soon this model created tension between the US manufacturers and the big box retailer. The manufacturers' profits were consistently reduced or eliminated by the fierce demands of Wal-Mart. This had implications on the US manufacturers and on Wal-Mart. More and more of Wal-Mart suppliers began to outsource and locate manufacturing units in Asia, especially China. Analysts have provided examples of companies driven abroad to maintain their supply contract with Wal-Mart and to say afloat. Levi Strauss is one such. After it commenced its dealings with Wal-Mart in 2003 it had to close down two of its last factories and lay off 2500 workers in the US.

As one report said, "A company that 22 years ago had 66 clothing plants in the US—and that was also one of the most socially responsible corporations on the planet—will, by 2004, not make any clothes at all. It will just import them." Even bigger companies like GE had to outsource their production in cheaper locations with lower wages resulting in job losses in the US. In its early years, Wal-Mart promoted US goods through it much publicized "Buy American" campaign and supported domestic companies. But, under growing economic pressure, it began to source imports as far back as the 1970s. Thus began its move towards the East and its alliance with China.

Wal-Mart buys so many Chinese products that if it were a country, it would be China's sixth largest export market and eighth largest trading partner. The company was said to have established a network of 10,000 suppliers for its China operation. Wal-Mart's eastward migration was signaled in 2002, when it decided to shift its procurement centre from Hong Kong to Shenzhen, the hub of South China's export industries. Shenzhen has the fifth largest port in the world and as reports go, the port was constructed to suit the interest of Wal-Mart. The preparatory steps taken years before, began to yield results only after China was admitted to the WTO. Under its WTO commitments, China agreed to permit foreign retailers to enter as fully-owned subsidiaries after 2002. Wal-Mart came to have the whole of China under its coverage. The relationship between Wal-Mart and its suppliers in China is more zamindari (akin to landlord and tenants) in nature. Some reports read, "In southern China, Wal-Mart has found all the ingredients it needs to keep its 'every day low prices' among the lowest in the world'."

Other reports suggest how meetings between suppliers and Wal-Mart China buyers would take place at "the negotiations centre." Suppliers make their offers to Wal-Mart China buyers. Those whose offers are not accepted are summarily sent out. For them to survive, they will have to cut down costs, which can only be through reduction in wages. Wal-mart gives suppliers specifications for its products. Suppliers have to meet the specifications as also the price, quality, delivery schedule and the whole lot. Thus develops a clear and continuing dependence between Chinese suppliers and Wal-Mart.

Lessons for India

Though Wal-Mart has reluctantly accepted the necessity to recognize labour unions in China, in the present conditions, wage levels take a down-ward spiral and working conditions deteriorate. Many observers feel that this phase of China's global integration is regressive and anti-poor. It is the fear of slowing down of the rate of growth that seems to have encouraged China to lean so heavily on Wal-Mart. The long-term prospects of China's relations with Wal-Mart are uncertain.

For any reason such as currency revaluation, US sanctions or embargoes, Wal-Mat will not hesitate to close down its China shop. In the wake of that event, China will be rudderless. Some of our economists in the Ministry of Finance and Planning Commission have strongly recommended FDI in retail trade in India and quote the Chinese experience. Are they fully aware of all the facts and the implications of their prescriptions for a country like India?

BHARTI PLUMPS FOR WAL-MART

Bharti Enterprises on Monday November 27, 2006 announced that it had signed an MoU with Wal-Mart Stores Inc, officially naming the world's largest retail chain its partner for the telecom major's foray into the retail segment, after months of speculation. "Ours will be a joint venture of equal partnership with Wal-Mart and we will function in the cash and carry format," said Mr. Sunil Bharti Mittal, Chairman and Group Managing Director, Bharti Enterprises. Wal-Mart will be an equal partner in the backed supply arena of the retail venture in terms of logistics and technological support, while Bharti will be Wal-Mart's franchisee and wholly own the front-end system.

Source: *The Hindu Business Line,* November 27, 2006.

Part III

India : The "Tiger's" Development Strides

India has Come of Age

Ashok Jacob

INTRODUCTION

Where does the rest of the world see India today? When I say 'India' I mean its progress, its future and perhaps the issues that stand in the way of its progress. As we stand today India is participating in a contagion that is sweeping the world and that is "the reshaping of the economies of the developing world." We in India are not insular or inward looking, but we tend to focus on what the developed world is doing rather than what is happening in the emerging markets around us. In some ways, therefore, we need to make sure that we are comparing apples to apples in terms of who India should compare itself with.

For example, the IMF expects developing countries to grow at 6.6 per cent next year the fastest pace in 30 years. Countries such as Brazil, Russia and South Africa are booming. The Middle East and even parts of Africa are enjoying high oil prices. Low global interest rates have reduced their service costs, and the fall of the US dollar had improved the competitiveness of those countries whose currencies follow the greenback as most of Asia does. Unlike previous booms, emerging economies have improved their fundamental financial health, introduced macro economic policy and structural reform to enjoy a sustained period of growth.

Collectively the developing world has run a current account surplus fox six consecutive years after being in deficit for the previous 20. Unlike previous debt financed booms which were invariably followed by some financial crisis, the current expansions are financed largely by domestic savings. Foreign debt is falling, Forex reserves are rising and many emerging economies use floating rates instead of fixed exchange rates which have often been a contributor to vast financial outflows.

EIGHT CATALYSTS OF ULTIMATE CONTAGION

So, to put things in perspective, India in some ways is only keeping pace with the progress of much of the developing world. It is not the star of the pack—China definitely is—but it isn't the laggard either. Although we in India see our progress and our country as something special, every other developing country sees itself in the same way. What does the future hold for this phenomenon of developing countries literally rising from the ashes? There are eight trends which are helping to create self-sustaining market dynamics across the developing world. I call them the Eight Catalysts of Ultimate Contagion and they are Technological Innovation, Expanded Credit Availability, Tax Reform, Improved Educational Opportunities, Institutionalized Property Rights, Deregulation and Foreign Direct Investment, Wider Distribution of Wealth, and Parents' Desire For Their Children's Success.

Technological Innovation

Firstly, Technological Innovation. Low-cost broadband access, wireless connectivity and things like that are the key to a regulatory framework that encourages competition. It has been demonstrated that advancing a country's telecom infrastructure directly correlates with GDP growth. Mike Best at MIT has shown that every 10% increase in teledensity results roughly in a 3% rise in GDP. South Korea is the star example of a telecom framework that promotes competition. To cut a long story short, 30% of South Korea's GDP stems now from e-commerce. The South Korean IT sector has grown at 16% per annum over the last five years and now accounts for 15% of GDP and 30% of total exports. The Government estimates that the country will generate US $ 100 billion in telecom equipment sales and US$ 50 billion in exports in two years time.

China now leads the world with the greatest number of both cell phones at 305 million and fixed lines at 295 million. These numbers are a year old so they are probably double that today! The number of telephone lines per 100 inhabitants in China rose from 6.96 in 1968 to 21 in 2003. The number of cell phones has risen from 23 million in 1998 to over 300 million today. Yet penetration is only 23%. In broadband, China has more DSL (digital subscriber line) connections than any other country in the world. The number of 15 million is double the level of last year.

When anyone talks about India, very often we hear someone moaning that India is different, there are too many people, our problems are unique. Well, our population is 300 million less than China's; but our teledensity is 4% versus China's 21%. We have 44 million fixed line phones and 45 million wireless subscribers, one-seventh of China's. But to look at this positively, the subscriber rate is growing at over 100% per annum, and this may well turn out to be one of the most important drivers of GDP growth. Remember China has five to seven times our teledensity and much, much higher GDP growth.

Expanded Credit Availability

Secondly, nowhere have we seen the change brought about by Expanded Credit Availability as in India. Simplistically, if a household can borrow against future income, it is better prepared to survive income shocks without sending its children to work. A move up in terms of access to credit is associated with the victories in child labour, one of the perpetual thorns in India's side. For example, HDFC and SBI launched the Credit Information Bureau prior to which banks in India had no way of checking on a borrower's creditworthiness—that was a major impediment to lending. Household credit in India today is only 5% of disposable income. This level will continue to grow and bring more prosperity to the country.

Educational Opportunities

Educational Opportunities obviously are nowhere as more pronounced as in India, which is probably the engineering capital of the world. Everybody hears about the IIT graduate. Tax Reform, deregulation and foreign direct investment, wider distribution of wealth, institutionalized property rights, and lastly—and perhaps most importantly—parents' Desire for their children's success are all factors playing a role in the most miraculous economic growth of the entire developing world today. Obviously some of these factors are more powerful driving forces in the rise of the Indian economy than others.

A Key Question for the World

Now this brings us to the key question which the whole world is asking. *Can India, like China, translate free market reform into economic prosperity?* India has come a long way in the past 15 years. Before 1990, the Indian Government modeled itself after the Soviet Union's Socialist Economic Model-although containing it within a democracy—only to realize later that this would be a recipe for disaster. In 1991, the country liberalized its economy, privatizing business and opening-up domestic markets to foreign investment. But the country still has not reached its full potential.

China with its authoritarian government but much freer economy has grown much faster than its neighbour to the west. Since 1980, China has grown at 12% annually versus India's 5% on a purchasing power parity basis. India still has some roadblocks to achieving this type of growth, most notably government deficit and an ever-present government bureaucracy. But the balance of risk and reward is now skewed to the positive. The stock market has doubled in the last two years and could well turn out to be the best performing emerging market for the remainder of this decade. There are numerous trends on the Indian landscape that could turn it into an economic colossus rivaling China some time during the next 10 to 15 years.

The work in progress that characterizes India has created more hope internationally than ever before. measured against more of the developed world, India's recent performance has been strong. The Indian economy is almost US $ 3 trillion on a purchasing power parity basis. Real GDP grew at about 4.5% last year, and India's National Council of Applied Economic Research projects a pick up to over 6% over the next few years. Furthermore, the Index of Industrial production has risen from 162 in 2001 to over 200 today. After a severe drought put a lid on growth in 2002, it appears that both the 2003 and 2004 monsoon seasons have supplied plenty of water to India's farms enabling the economy to reaccelerate. The IT services business has seen a rebound from the much over-hyped internet bubble years and has benefited from the trend towards outsourcing and offshore migration of hi-tech jobs to this country. But to put India's economy in perspective, last year's nominal output by industry sector was as follows: Agriculture, Forestry and Fishing: 23%; Mining and Quarrying: 2%; Manufacturing: 15%; Electricity, Water and Gas: 2.5%; Construction: 6%; Trade, Hotel, Transport and Communication: 22%; Financing, Insurance, Real Estate and Business Services: 13%; Community, Social and Personal Services: 15%

What does that Mean?

It means that India is still very much an agrarian society, although the growth of its services segment has made that an important contributor. But mining, manufacturing, utilities and construction are barely 25% of output. By contrast, China's industrial and construction sectors are over 55% of the economy and agriculture is less than 15%. If India succeeds it is very important in emulating China's performance, which is what the Government is trying to do, then the output from infrastructure related sectors will grow significantly in the years ahead. India's population is young with a segment that is very well educated and well suited for science and engineering. Citizens aged 14 and under comprise 32% of the population as opposed to 23% of China's. The median age of India's population is only 24 years, while it is 31in China. Now, while India's overall literacy rate of nearly 60% lags well behind China's 88%, it has a very well developed system of higher education that takes advantage of what the rest of the world sees as a genetic predisposition towards science and engineering. India has also made strong improvements in literacy in the last decade. For example, in the early 1990s, only half of the population was literate. It is India's youth and growing access to educational opportunities that will help spur the country to modernise its government and infrastructure further. India's Government is moving inexorable towards a free market economy. The Government has gone on a privatization spree in the past 10 years. Indian corporations are hungry for improved profitability and financial strength.

Commitment to a Pro-growth Culture

The establishment of Special Economic Zones demonstrates the Government's commitment to a pro-growth culture. India's relaxation of barriers to investment has enabled foreign exchange reserves to grow from US $ 59 million in September 2002 to well over US $ 120 billion today. That is, millions to billions! Even though the rupee is pegged within a range the dollar has declined 7%. Foreign Direct Investment has risen from under US $ 250 million in the early 1990s to over US $ 4 billion today. Total exports have risen from US $ 35 billion in 1998 to US $ 55 bullion plus this year. Sorely needed *infrastructure projects* are being undertaken. There is no ironclad test of a booming economy than jam-packed hotels, crowded airports, continuous traffic jams and cancelled and rescheduled meetings. We see all these in India today. The country has initiated a US $ 10 billion road construction programme. Road haulage and road construction require trucks and lorries. In turn commercial vehicle manufactures require more auto parts and more service outlets. Haulers require more financing and more maintenance work. Consumers receive goods faster and for less cost. Demand rises, more trucks are added to fleets, circulation of income begins again.

The deficiencies in the *electric power* grid have hampered growth. The gap between supply and demand for electricity has widened from 5.9% in 1999 to over 9% today. The peak power shortages have made it 12 to 15%. The root cause of the relative eve lack of power modernization is the antiquated system of State Electricity Boards, which are monoliths of socialist planning. These boards are highly inefficient and support themselves by charging minimum usage fees and other assorted tariffs that effectively prohibit private investments in and expansion of the power sector, GDP growth in India could be 2 or 3% higher if this infrastructure was not creaking as much as it is.

India's middle-class is benefiting from the *improved access to credit*. India has a booming middle-class estimated to be as large as 250 million or more. Like their counterparts in China, they are seeking a Western—style standard of living and consumption level. Historically, India's retail lending has lagged behind developed countries. But a new culture of credit has emerged, supporting growth in car loans and credit cards. Home-mortgage lending is growing over 30% annually, and further growth is heavily supported by the demographics as roughly one half of the population is under the age of 24, and the typical home-buyer tends to be in his mid-30s. Historically, Indians have been debt averse and savings oriented, but that is changing. From a lender's perspective, new foreclosure laws have made mortgage lending less risky from a credit standpoint, thus attracting more lenders to the market and furthering the progress of the economy. Additionally, car sales have been growing at 25 to 35% per year, a trend also fostered by loosening credit.

India's Government is displaying a *new pragmatism on the geopolitical front*. Talks with China and Pakistan are progressing, making foreign investors happier and more sanguine about the position here. But again, compared to China, India's most compelling growth remains unrealized. The differences in electricity and oil consumption, telephone use, GDP and poverty level all indicate considerably more upside for India. Consider that India's estimated population of 1.05 billion is only 19% below China's 1.29 billion. Yet its daily oil consumption is less than one half of China's. Its electricity consumption is less than 40% of China's. Its telephone penetration is less than 20% of China's. Its GDP on a Purchasing Power Parity basis is more than 40% below China's. An estimated 25% of the Indian population is still below the poverty line versus only 10% of the Chinese population.

India's Some Particular Advantages

Although India's Foreign Direct Investment of US $ 3.5 billion is less than 10% of China's and overall exports of US $ 50 billion are less than 20% of China's, India does have some particular advantages. For instance, it has carved out a stronger position in IT services and pharmaceutical industries, and that is really owing to the predominance of engineering and science graduates and widespread proficiency in the English language. India also has an established *system of property rights* that places it well ahead of China in this regard. It has a large pool of exceptionally well educated individuals and benefits from an increasingly open society. It is possible that India's focus on services has created an overall wealth disadvantage compared to the Chinese, where over 100 million people to the Chinese, where over 100 million people work in manufacturing industries, many times the number of Indians working in IT services. But India's growth in IT is likely to spread to manufacturing to promote a rising standard of living. Furthermore, it is likely that these two countries will be able to feed off each other's growth. Trade between India and China in the early 1990s was only US $ 100 million a year. It is now over US$ 9 billion. China has benefited from India's expertise on the IT side, while India has benefited from Chinese manufactured goods. As relations between the two countries improve, the potential for cross border investments likewise will improve.

Some Trouble Spots

Now, despite all these positive attributes, there still remain some trouble spots that must be addressed. These include India's need to improve its overall social system. India needs to bring its government spending down. Federal budget deficits are over 5% of GDP, 10% when state budget deficits are factored in. This might be an appropriate level for a recessionary period, but this is no recession. India is enjoying faster growth than most of the world. The problem would appear to be inefficient government spending. Inflation in India has been higher than in most places at 4 to 5%, which could be a result of this high deficit. And these deficits are only growing and forecast to grow. India must overcome the resistance to change in its bureaucracy. Commonsense dictates that the IT industry has only flourished because it has not been around long enough to be regulated to death. This idea needs to be recognized throughout the public sector.

INDIA HAS COME OF AGE FINALLY!

We equate India with an undermanaged company that has outstanding assets and the potential for much greater earning power, but in need of fewer layers and more efficient management. We think the positives outweigh the negatives, and the presence of China as a regional and increasingly global economic rival will ensure that the process of change accelerates rather than decelerates.

So to wrap up, India has come of age finally! This time it is different and permanent. The catalysts for India's coming prosperity are almost all in place. India will, like China, translate free market reform into economic prosperity. Capitalism is the juggernaut or the tsunami that is sweeping the world, especially the developing world that includes India. The thing about change, which many people do not realize, is that while this country will change less than what we expect in the next two years, it will be virtually unrecognizable ten years from today, particularly from an infrastructure view of roads, airports, telecoms, water, energy—just as China is not recognizable today from what it is was ten years ago. Nearly every other developing country in the world will also be unrecognizable in ten years time. And all India has to do is to stay on this global bandwagon and enjoy what I call the Ultimate Contagion.

20

India—The Land of People's Power

Ajai Chowdhry

INTRODUCTION

India is on the threshold of receiving rare global economic accolades, the kind it has only seen heaped on the much smaller Asian economies in the 1980s and the 1990s. But unlike the pride of Tigers, the Elephant is well and truly considered to be beginning to dance. From Wall Street to Oxford, toast is being raised to the success story that is India. The good thing is that this much vaunted success is owed much less to India turning a flat world's back-office or just its Information Technology prowess, but really to a number of factors that have combined to see the country rise phoenix-like from its many and myriad problems. Well, as they say big country, big problems, but none that its inherent strengths cannot overcome.

The recent stock market crash notwithstanding, Indian economy's excellent performance; the strong rupee (until recently); the growing exports; the improving communications and commuting infrastructure; the booming real-estate; the humming manufacturing; the soaring Information Technology sector; the revving automobiles; the soaring aviation, all suggest a confident stride into the 21st Century. It has also showcased its ability in design and research; outsourcing; medical and pharma research; tourism; retail; and petrochemicals. In music and arts, Bollywood and sport also it is making a mark.

Global Status

These are just some of the areas where India has either made rapid strides, or emerged a global leader. Was all this expected two decades ago? It is easy to lose one's bearing in the excitement; easy to get drunk on this new-found global status. But for anyone to honestly say that one knew so much was coming so soon is like being a pompous parakeet in the monsoon. Who had in the 1980s or the early 1990s thought of the Indian-techie wanting to leave the seemingly high life of the United States for a better piece of action back home? Those were the days when H_1B visas and the Green Card were as sought after expressions among migrating Indians as some of the very American euphemisms, or Brand America's corporate icons.

Perceptual Transformation

The alchemy of factors has turned that on its head in recent years. Today, the Indians working overseas and watching Indian television channels and their homeland being a toast of the Western media often feel restless, and it is not uncommon for them to enquire from friends and relatives about opportunities back home. Nothing else captures this better than the global perceptual transformation of India in the last few years. Today, the prevalent fear among many developed nations is about the loss of skilled immigrants—a vital resource—who today are increasingly moving back to India to explore the ample opportunities this land is throwing-up. Ditto for losing a number of other jobs that Indians can do better and at a fraction of price than their Western counterparts. Good morning America, the Sun is well and truly rising on a flat world and India could well emerge as the global capital. Tonnes of newsprint, covers of global business magazines and hundreds of international leaders are today hesitating to talk about India's greatness. Even as the West talks of all things India and not anymore about the land of great unfulfilled potential, there is a certain awe that Asian Tigers never evoked and which, in comparative terms, is only matched by the huge brand equity that China has built globally.

Technology Innovator

If manufacturing was China's apogee, services and IT prowess can definitely be said to have propelled India onto the West's horizons, Who would have imagined that a nation that had banned import of technology in the 1970s and the 1980s would become the hotbed for technological innovation by the turn of the century? This was made possible by Indians who had the faith and belief in what Indians can deliver anywhere in the world, if given the right milieu.

When some enterprising Indians took the courage to look within, rather than outside for opportunities, they established dream corporations, the stuff Harvard and Cornell case studies are made of. They took a pride in their country, and worked to make the world proud of it. A case in point is IT hardware development—India is the only country where Indian manufacturers still rule the market. The same market that few gave a chance until the 1990s, least of all for manufacturing!

The same market has metamorphosed today into what they now call 'a big pie', among the handful worldwide that are growing exponentially even as all other geographies slow each year, leading to closures and job cuts. Indian products, such as the rural PC platforms developed by HCL and Wipro, have led international majors like Intel to co-work with them and develop a specific range, which they would sell in the developing markets.

Mind India

HCL has created a forum called 'Mindia—celebrating the prowess of the Indian mind'. The platform, already 18 sessions old, has invited Indians from different walks of life, each deliberating on what he/she feels constitutes Indianness. This attempt has really been stimulating, exciting and needless to say, enriching. Though each individual brought his or her own unique interpretation of 'Mind India' at the forum, there was one thread of commonality and consistency that pervaded throughout—Clear sentiment of pride and esteem in being an Indian. And the continuing inspiration to contribute to this elevating image of India. I have no doubt that this century clearly belongs to India. Such is the power of Brand India that its billion plus people, who were tagged as its liability, are today being looked at as its biggest strength. The country's youth, which would constitute its active workforce for at least the next 25 years, is a lot more adventurous and enterprising. The pride and confidence of the youngsters will take the nation to great heights. That simply means that pride for India would only get stronger and inspire more technology innovations, more aggressively than ever.

21

Need for the Agriculture Renewal

M.S. SWAMINATHAN

INTRODUCTION

In an article published in the December 31, 2005, issue of *The Hindu,* I had summarized the main features of the Year of Agricultural Renewal programme recommended by the National Commission on Farmers (NCF) in its 3rd Report presented to Sharad Pawar, Union Minister for Agriculture and Food. The 4th Report of NCF submitted in April 2006 contains the draft of a National Policy for Farmers, titled "Jai Kisan," for widespread discussion.

Farmer

For the purpose of this policy, the term "farmer" includes landless agricultural labourers, sharecroppers, tenants, small, marginal and sub marginal cultivators, farmers with larger holdings, fisher men and women, dairy, sheep, poultry and other farmers involved in animal husbandry, pastoralists, as well as those rural and tribal families engaged in a wide variety of farming related occupations such as sericulture, vermiculture, production of biofertilizers and biopesticides, and agro-processing. The term also includes tribal families sometimes engaged in shifting cultivation, and in the collection and use of non-timber forest products. In all cases, both men and women will receive equal attention.

Year of the Farmer

The Year of Agricultural Renewal, better referred to as the Year of the Farmer, is due to begin on June, 1, 2006, with the onset of the South West Monsoon. Soon after Independence in 1947, Jawaharlal Nehru remarked: "everything else can wait, but not agriculture." He said this in the context of the Bengal Famine of 1942-43 and the acute food scarcity prevailing in the country in 1947. In fact, I recall that at the wedding of my elder brother in September 1947, there was a strict rule that not more than 30 guests could be provided with food. Our population was then 350 million. Today, our population is over 1.1 billion and thousands of persons are fed in the weddings of the rich, since where there is money, there is food. However, a recent report by UNICEF says India has the largest number of malnourished children in the world, nearly 57 million out of a total world figure of 146 million, an index of widespread poverty and deprivation. Farmer's indebtedness is rising and farmland even in Punjab, the heartland of the green revolution, is being referred to by the electronic media as "killing fields." Yet, the economy is estimated to have grown at 8.1 per cent during 2005-06, on top of the 7.5 per cent growth recorded in the previous year. The services sector continued to be the major driver of economic activity, accounting for almost three-fourths of overall GDP growth. Indian companies raised an unprecedented $ 40 billion in equity and debt. Merchandise exports rose by 25 per cent crossing the $ 100 billion level. Unfortunately, more than 50 per cent of our population living in rural areas have no option except to remain silent onlookers of this new-found urban prosperity, conveyed night and day on television channels. This is the Indian enigma.

Agriculture cannot Wait

Having declared failure in achieving most of the Tenth Plan goals in agriculture, the Union Planning Commission is now busy preparing the Eleventh Plan. The NCF in its 4th report has pointed out that a business as usual approach in agriculture, ignoring Jawaharlal Nehru's "agriculture cannot Wait" exhortation, would have at least the following three major consequences:

- Spread of agrarian distress and rural discontent, and spread of the Naxalite movement;
- Returning to a "ship to mouth" era, and the consequent erosion of national sovereignty in foreign policy;
- Jobless or even job-loss growth resulting in the expansion of urban slums.

What then should we do to end this sad chapter in our agricultural history and fulfil the "Jai Kisan" commitment made by Lal Bahadur Sastri? The steps to be taken are simple, doable, and affordable. They, however, need a change in mindset from regarding farmers as "beneficiaries" of small government programmes to treating them as partners in development and custodians of food security. Integrated action on the following five points will help to get our agriculture back on the rails.

Five-point Plan

First, undertake soil health enhancement through integrated measures in improving organic matter and macro- and micro-nutrient content, as well as the physics and the microbiology of the soil. Gujarat has already issued soil health cards to farm families and other States can do like-wise. Secondly, promote water harvesting, conservation, and efficient and equitable use by empowering gram sabhas to function as "pani panchayats." Such "pani panchayats" should foster the establishment of community managed water banks and the recharge of the aquifer. A sustainable water security system should be put in place, particularly in rainfed areas lacking assured irrigation facility. This will be facilitated by mandatory water harvesting and greater attention to dryland farming.

Thirdly, initiate immediately credit reforms coupled with credit and insurance literacy. The Finance Minister has announced a reduction in this should be regarded as the first step in a series of measures including the revitalization of the cooperative credit system. The farm families' agriculture, health, and domestic credit needs should be attended to in a holistic manner. Also in chronically drought-prone areas, the repayment cycle should be extended to four to five years. Credit delivery systems should be made gender sensitive—only a small proportion of women cultivators have been issued kisan credit cards. Adequacy and timelines of credit availability are vital for institutional credit to be meaningful to small farmers.

Fourthly, bridge the growing gap between scientific know-how and field level do-how both in production and post-harvest phases of farming. This could be done through a slew of measures including the training of one woman and one man of every panchayat as farm science managers, establishing farm schools in the fields of outstanding growers, adding a post-harvest technology and agro-processing wing in every Krishi Vigyan Kendra, and organizing nation-wide lab-to-land demonstrations in the areas of agricultural diversification, food processing, and value addition.

Village Knowledge Centres

Also knowledge connectivity as proposed under Bharat Nirman should be accomplished by establishing village knowledge centers or "gyanchaupals" throughout the country. Small farmers should not be subjected to administrative and academic experiments in the area of crop diversification without first linking the farmers with the market for the new commodities. Crop-livestock-fish integrated production systems are ideal for small farmers since this can also facilitate organic farming. Success in agricultural progress should be measured by the growth rate in farmers' income and not just by production figures. Low economic risk, high factor productivity, avoidance of ecological harm, and assured income must be the bottom line of all agricultural research and development strategies. Had we adopted a pro-small farmer biotechnology strategy, we would by now have had Bt-cotton varieties whose seeds farmers could keep and replant, unlike in the case of the hybrids marketed by private companies.

Focus an on-farm and Non-farm Livelihoods

Scientific strategies should include attention to both on-farm and non-farm livelihoods. We should confer the power and economy of scale on families operating one hectare or less though management structures such as cooperatives or group farming as well as contract cultivation based on a win-win model of partnership situational structures such as small holders' cotton, horticulture, poultry, and aquaculture estates can be promoted by stimulating the formation of self-help groups at the farm level. Concurrently, we should launch an integrated rural non-farm livelihood initiative by revamping and integrating numerous isolated non-farm employment and income generation agencies such as the Khadi and Village Industries Commission, Small Farmers' Agri-business Consortium (SFAC), textile, leather and food parks, agri-clinics, and agri-business centers. Unless market-driven multiple, livelihood opportunities are created, the pressure of population on land will grow, the indebtedness of small farmers will increase, and the agrarian distress will spread. Poverty will persist so long as asset-less rural families remain illiterate and unskilled. The National Rural Employment Guarantee Programme provides a unique opportunity for imparting functional literacy using computer-aided joyful learning techniques. We should use new technologies to leapfrog in the area of human development in villages. At the same time, knowledge without access to the inputs to apply that knowledge will have no meaning. Input supply systems need review and reform.

Finally, the gap between what the rural producer gets and the urban consumer pays must be made as narrow as possible, as has been done in the case of milk under Dr. V. Kurien's leadership. The National Horticulture Board was created for this purpose over 23 years ago, but like the SFAC, it also lost its way. It can only be hoped other expensive new programmes such as the Fisheries Development Board, the National Rainfed Area Authority, and the National Horticultural Mission will learn from the success achieved by agencies such as the National Dairy Development Board, the Indian Space Research Organisation, and the Atomic Energy Commission in achieving specific goals in a time-bound manner, and benefit from strong professional leadership.

There is an urgent need for a National Land Use Advisory Service, structured as a virtual organisation on a hub and spokes would cover the major agro-climatic zones and farming systems, for providing proactive advice to farmers on land and water use through an integrated analysis of meteorological, agronomic, and marketing data. There is also need for an Indian Trade Organisation mandated to protect the livelihood and income security of farm and fisher families. At the same time, farmer-centric Minimum Support Price (MSP) and Market Intervention Scheme (MIS).

End Message

Agriculture in our country is based on the technology of production by the masses. As a consequence, it is the backbone of the national of extensive poverty and deprivation persisting under conditions of impressive progress in the industrial and services sectors will continue so long as we refuse to place faces before figures. The NCF has suggested the mainstreaming of the human dimension in all agricultural programmes and policies, the adoption by the National Development Council of a National Policy for Farmers, and the establishment of a State Farmers' Commission by every State Government. This is to give voice to the voiceless in the formulation of farm policies including the preparation of the 11th Five Year Plan. Let the year of the Farmer help to shape our agricultural destiny in a manner that farming once again becomes the pride of the nation on the occasion of the 60th anniversary of our Independence on August 15, 2007.

22

On Growth, Poverty and Opportunity

G. SRINIVASAN

INTRODUCTION

The euphoria generated by the country's average Gross Domestic Product growth rate of 8 per cent during the last three years beginning 2003-04 apart, the United Progressive Alliance Government's economic policy lays much emphasis on conferring benefits to the Eleventh Five Year Plan, commencing from fiscal 2007, also underscores the importance of adopting an inclusive growth strategy that considers the aspirations of the rural and urban poor for a decent standard of living. A recent development policy review by the World Bank titled *Inclusive Growth and Service Delivery: Building on India's Success* rightly draws attention to the disconcerting reality of the growing gap in economic progress and service delivery for the best and worst segments. "India is an emerging global super-power, joining the elite club of acknowledged nuclear powers; and India has child malnutrition rates among the highest in the world", it rues.

The Contrasts

"The headcount poverty rate in rural Orissa (43 per cent) and rural Bihar (41 per cent) is higher than similarly measured poverty rates of African countries such as Malawi or Ghana. While parts of the country are competing successfully not just in low-skill services such as call centers but in high-skill areas of consulting, soft-ware engineering and biomedical research, over half the labour force works in agriculture, often in appalling conditions...," goes the review. In a recent independent evaluation of learning achievement in Rural India, the World Bank found that in the bottom five States half the Standard V students surveyed could not read at Standard II level while more than two-thirds could not do simple division.

All these issues were raised by the Planning Commission Deputy Chairman Mr. Montek Singh Ahluwalia, in the Dashrathmal Singhvi Memorial Lecture on "Growth and Poverty Reduction: Is the Glass Half-full of Half-Empty?", in New Delhi on August 18, 2006

Ambitious Proposition

"Historically the approach to reducing poverty relied heavily on achieving rapid growth. Pandit Jawaharlal Nehru, who was Chairman of the National Planning Committee set-up by the Indian National Congress, recalled the aim of the Committee as getting rid of the appalling poverty of the people for which it thought a five or six times increase in wealth was necessary. Deeming this as too ambitious, it concluded that doubling or trebling of national income in 10 years was a more practical proposition. This involved a growth rate of 7-11 per cent per year. In 1944, there was the Bombay Plan, which was more modest and spoke of trebling national income in 15 years, which involved a growth rate of 7 per cent.

"In the early 1960s Ram Manohar Lohia questioned whether the poor were benefiting and compared India with China. The Perspective Planning Division of the Plan panel came out with a paper, "Perspective of Development, 1960-61 to 1975-76", with the aim of achieving minimum standard for all in 15 years. It concluded that this required 6.5 per cent growth with special programmes for marginal groups. The actual trend in the 1960s and the 1970s showed that we did not achieve our growth targets. GDP growth was 3.5 per cent, instead of the target of 5 per cent. So, unsurprisingly, not much happened to poverty in the 1960s and the 1970s.

"These led critics to contend that we should not focus only on the elusive growth front but on programmes that would really help the poor. The 1970s therefore saw a raft of targeted anti-poverty programmes, while the Green Revolution raised farm production. The 1980s saw the beginning of policy change aimed at accelerating growth and the growth rate did improve to 5.4 per cent in the 1980s which got further accelerated to 6.3 per cent in 1992-2005. The last three years have seen 8 per cent GDP growth while the Eleventh Plan growth target could be even higher and close to 9 per cent.

No Uniform Growth

"While our growth performance has improved there are concerns about whether this is doing enough for the poor and excluded groups. There are several reasons for this. First, growth acceleration is not uniform across all States. Gujarat, Uttranchal, Tamil Nadu, West Bengal, Karnataka and Andhra Pradesh are doing well, while Uttar Pradesh, Madhya Pradesh and Orissa have done poorly in the past ten years or so. Even in States that are doing well, some of the regions within them may be worse off than others as in the case of Maharashtra, Andhra Pradesh and Karnataka. Hence, the challenge to ensure that the growth in all parts of the country is as close as possible to the average."

"A basic and long-standing concern pertains to whether the growth strategy has bypassed the poor, excluding them from the benefits of growth. There is no doubt that the proportion of people below the poverty line has declined over time but not fast enough. The official figures for poverty in 1999-2000 showed that the percentage of the population below the poverty line had declined from 36 per cent in 1993-94 to 26 per cent in 1999-2000. The comparability of the two figures was questioned and concern was voiced that the pace of reduction in poverty is over stated."

Poverty on a Decline

"Preliminary estimates from the latest NSS thick sample

conducted in 2004-05 now provide data that are fully comparable to 1993-94. This comparison shows that the percentage of population below the poverty line in 2004-05, which is comparable to the 1993-94 figure of 36 per cent, was about 28 per cent. This is higher than the official figure of 26 per cent for 1999-2000, but if the 2004-05 data comparable to 1999-2000 are used then the poverty estimate is 22 per cent. In short, adjusting for comparability there is a continuous decline in poverty of around 0.8 percentage points per year.

"It must be recognized however that this is at best a modest rate of decline. One reason for this is that agricultural growth has only just kept pace with population growth during the last decade. There is a need to accelerate farm sector growth and also shift from agriculture to non-farm operations. But labour-absorbing manufacturing growth at the levels contemplated requires labour reform not a hire-and-fire policy but flexibility in employing labour through skill-building and vocational education. Organised sector employment is low, causing real concern, and low quality employment does not get the country out of poverty.

"Poverty measured in terms of consumption is only one of its dimensions, It is necessary to focus on the broader issue of lack of access to basic public services such as health and education, which should be provided to all. Viewed from this point the extent of deprivation is much larger. Half the children drop out before completing primary school. Malnutrition of children in 1998 was an high as 47 per cent.

Issue of Opportunity

"There is also the issue of equality of opportunity. There is no doubt that in the post-reform era the population in the middle segments is moving upwards. What is not clear is if people who are traditionally poor and from the weaker sections are getting equal opportunity? I give you an instance. In most rural schools, they don't teach mathematics. If the name of the game in the knowledge economy is science and technology and if the rural child is not getting an opportunity to enter these areas, we are not creating equality of opportunity. Non-equality of opportunity and concept of fairness must be addressed squarely."

23

FDI : Will India Edge Out China?

S. MAJUMDER

INTRODUCTION

In Asia, foreign investors are in a quandary about where to go. By the barometer of Foreign Direct Investment, China seems to be the place to be in, but if it is economic competitiveness, India appears more attractive. Paradoxically, though China ranks lower than India in terms of global competitiveness, its FDI was ten times more than India's. As per the Global Competitiveness Index, 2006 of the World Economic Forum, China was ranked 54 and India 43 in the ascending order. This apart, between 2005 and 2006, China's ranking slipped from 48 to 54, whereas India's moved up from 45 to 43.

There has been much debate about the measures used to assess the FDI potential of the two countries. While China's attractiveness is viewed mainly in terms of cheap labour and better infrastructure, India's potential is leveraged by the Global Competitiveness Index, which includes nine parameters–infrastructure, institutions, macro-economy, health and primary education, higher education and training, market efficiency, technological readiness, business sophistication, and innovation.

Contrasting Models

China and India follow diametrically opposite growth strategies. China wants to cool its overheated economy. At the recent annual meeting of the Central Committee, the Communist Party of China endorsed a new doctrine, that is, to build "a harmonious socialistic society," which goes against Deng Xiaoping's vision of a growth-oriented society. India, in contrast, is pursuing faster economic growth, with the manufacturing sector as the base. It has set a GDP growth target of over 9 per cent in the Eleventh Plan (2007-2012). China, on the other hand, is looking to contain its 10 per cent growth.

India's rise in the competitiveness index ranking can be attributed to innovation, a well-developed corporate sector, qualitative use of technology and accelerated transfer of technology. In contrast, China, despite soaking up GDI, trails in ushering in innovative technology, even in industries where it dominates. Dr. Yasheng Huang, noted economist and Professor at the MIT Sloan School of Management, cautions India against blindly following the Chinese model. He makes a distinction between the two economies, and states that the Chinese model is not a strong platform for sustainable development.

He commends India for improved corporate governance and fostering private sector development. For instance, India has adopted Public-Private partnership in infrastructure development programmes. In China, however, more than 90 per cent of the infrastructure development has been through government funding, leaving little for harmonious socialistic growth. In terms of fund flows, more than 60 per cent of the FDI China receives is from its Diaspora. These investments are capital-intensive with hardly any technology component. In contrast, more than 70 per cent of the FDI in India is from the West and other developed countries and includes technology transfers. The capacity of Indian industry to innovate and adapt quickly has helped to improve it technology standards. And this has also been made possible by the timely opening-up of the economy.

In China, the slow privatization of national enterprises, even after reforms, prevented them from adopting modern technology. This has resulted in a big gulf between home-grown and FDI-based industries. In contrast, India's home-grown units have tasted greater success following the reforms-Bajaj Auto's is a case in point. The company regained its position through investment and research. So, too, Tatas, Ranbaxy, Reliance and Videocon have established their brand image globally since the reforms. China and India have followed entirely different growth models—China's growth being led by FDI and exports, and India's by domestic demand and investment. The Indian Diaspora contributes a mere 9 per cent of the FDI, but it is helping bridge the technology divide.

Infrastructure Trends

According to Prof. Yasheng Huang, China has scored in terms of providing better infrastructure—between power, roads, port facilities and industrial sites. But in terms of 'soft infrastructure', such as corporate governance, and legal, financial and political systems, India has the edge. China's weak legal structure, inadequate Intellectual Property Rights system and the not-so-transparent banking organisation are areas of concern for foreign investors.

China draws much praise for overtaking India in macro-economic parameters. But in terms of micro-economic indicators, such as return on capital, development of domestic enterprises and corporate governance, India is ahead. With an FDI deluge into industry, China has emerged as the world's manufacturing hub, making products ranging from toys to electronic gadgets. India, on the other hand, has become a major source of skilled manpower. Though China is catching up, it still has a long way to go, especially in R&D outsourcing. According to a survey by the Boston Consulting Group, R&D investments by foreign companies in India will surpass those in China. Of the seven areas of R&D investment, in four—automobile, IT, telecommunication and financial services—India has attracted more funds.

Red Signal!

Economists fear that if China pursues only investment—led growth, it will run up huge bad loans. Total Factor Productivity (TFP) is the key to sustainable economic growth. TFP is backed by technology and efficiency growth. In China, FDI enterprises contribute most to TFP; local businesses are lagging. Unless national enterprises are privatized further and institutional funds used more efficiently, TFP-led growth will slacken in China.

> Investment flows from China have also been haphazard. Chinese investments into India in the last one and a half decades (until end—2005) was just $ 2.91 million—lower than Sri Lanka's—and constitutes just 0.01 per cent of total FDI flows. Yet India has emerged as the single largest destination for Chinese FDI, ahead of both Russia and the US. But India's security concerns and regulatory norms have thrown a spanner in the works. The Chinese don't want a replay of the experience in the OECD countries where cross-border buy-outs by Chinese companies have been largely unsuccessful primarily on account of the lack of transparency and security concerns. This leaves China even more keen to tap Indian markets. But economic and strategic concerns come in the way of greater cooperation. Only a visionary Chinese leadership that substantially addresses these concerns will be able to break through the current stalemate.
>
> *Source*: Pyaralal Raghavan: "India-China Growth Race", *The New Indian Express,* November 27, 2006.

24

China's Lessons for India

DAN STEINBOCK

INTRODUCTION

In January 1975, Deng Xiaoping and Zhou Enlai drafted China's modernization initiatives in agriculture, industry, science and technology, and national defence. The transition from import substitution to export orientation led to China's 'reform and opening'. China is no longer just a destination for foreign direct investment (FDI)—it is the home for Asia's new multinationals. The Chinese experiences offer pertinent lessons to another emerging great power India.

1980s: From Low-tech to Natural Resource Development

As foreign corporates entered China around 1979, a few state-owned trading companies and technology firms began to invest overseas, typically on the basis of existing overseas trade linkages in South east Asia. By 1985, only 143 Chinese enterprises had established and invested $ 170 million in some 45 countries that is, less than 3 per cent of China's total inflow of FDI. These businesses were mostly in low-tech services, as exemplified by Chinese restaurants, which were located in the major cities of Chinatowns of host countries, including the US, Japan and Thailand. In the latter half of the 1980s, some 620 new Chinese businesses invested over $ 860 million in over 90 countries. Now natural resource development projects, along with assembly and transport, dominated Chinese overseas investments. The growth rate of Chinese FDI was almost 50 per cent faster than the growth rate of multinationals worldwide. However, China accounted for only 0.1 per cent of total outward FDI world-wide.

1990s: From Manufacturing to Electronics

After the Tiananmen Square events, the Chinese Government introduced market-oriented reforms to re-attract American and other investors. Now, China also showed-up on the radar screens of US corporations. Over the latter half of the 1990s, US capital flows to China averaged $ 1.1 billion annually. Through foreign multinationals the so-called foreign-invested enterprises (FIEs)—FDI has played a critical role not just in China's economic reforms and opening, but in the rise of Chinese multinationals. After the mid-1990s, the FIEs replaced the small-and medium—size enterprises of the overseas Chinese as major investors. Capital inflows soared from $ 11 billion in 1992 to $ 50 billion in 1999.

After the mid-1990s, two-thirds of the US investment in China was directed at the manufacturing sector, especially industrial machinery and electronic equipment—the very same sector and segments the Chinese government was now promoting in overseas investment.

Rise of Chinese Challengers

During the past decade or so, China, along with the US, has been one of the most attractive country market for inward FDI world-wide. Meanwhile, Chinese challengers have emerged in industries as different as mobile communications, car manufacturing, detergents, oil, petroleum and petrochemicals. In 2004, *Business Week's* Global 1000 List featured 423 US companies with a combined market capitalization of $ 10.8 trillion. Japan had 137 companies with a market cap of $ 2 trillion. Hong Kong's 15 and China's six companies. meanwhile, had a market cap of $ 190 billion and $ 104 billion, respectively. China was just behind Russia's nine companies with $ 196 billion, but it did better than, say, Mexico's six companies with $ 75 billion, or Brazil's five companies with $ 71.2 billion.

Global competitiveness indicators tell the same story. In business competitiveness, the US leads world-wide. During the past few years, Japan (8th) has steadily improved its position, but China (45th) remains behind. FDI of Chinese multinationals is barely 6 per cent of the foreign capital inflow.

Lessons

The Chinese experience may offer important lessons to Indian reformers.

(1) First, the Special Economic Zones were set-up close to Hong Kong and the bamboo network of the overseas Chinese. In the same fashion, Indian reformers can take advantage of the expatriates, particularly Americans of Indian descent who have played a substantial role in the US technology revolution.

(2) The second lesson underscores the dual nature of China's economic liberalization. In China and India, reforms arrived only after the failure of decades of socialist experimentation. In India, however, the winds of change have focused on internal economic reforms, which is necessary but not sufficient for full transformation. As China's experience demonstrates, it is the external reforms—opening of the economy—that is truly critical. Unlike Japan and East Asia's Tiger economies, China has opened its domestic market and is not building an export power house behind a wall of protective tariffs, but growing a massive marketplace that promises extraordinary opportunities world-wide. With the right mindset, comparable accomplishments are now within India's reach, as well.

(3) The third lesson involves the twofold nature of foreign direct investment. During the past quarter of a century, the goal of China's reformers has been to attract FDI into China, while stimulating the emergence of Chinese

FDI abroad. Still, it was the arrival of world-class multinationals that stimulated the rise of Chinese challengers.

India has already given rise to several world-class multinationals, particularly in ICT software and services. From the standpoint of the national economy, however, these companies form a thin layer. It is only when sheltered industries are opened to international competition that Indian challengers can emerge across industries.

Key lessons for India

- Take advantage of the expertise and enterprise of Indian expatriates world-wide, particularly in the US.
- Internal economic reforms are necessary, but not sufficient. To capitalize on globalisation, the economy must be opened to foreign investment capital. In the long-term, inward FDI is an opportunity, not a threat. Through transfer of technology and expertise, it can rapidly stimulate the rise of indigenous producers.

Part IV

"The Asian Giants" : Global Economic Power Dynamics

India and China through Fresh Eyes
Part IV

Qiu Yonghui

"The Asian Giants" Global Economic Power Dynamics

INTRODUCTION

"The journalists in both China and India have been a very long time." This is one of the several opinions during the annual conference of the Chinese A South Asian Studies, which was held in Shanghai A participant, a journalist by profession, reacted arguing her claims on being healthy and balanced news reports concerning India. I myself, as a reader of Indian newspapers for a long time, about various news reports on China published media. My working days always began by clicking samachar.com and grasping the news stories interested in. I can therefore easily and more balanced reports concerning China from the Indian

India and China through Fresh Eyes

QIU YONHUI

INTRODUCTION

"The Journalists in both China and India have been sick for a very long time." This is one of the several opinions I heard during the annual conference of the Chinese Association of South Asian Studies, which was held in Shanghai in May 2006. A participant, a journalist by profession, reacted immediately by arguing her claims on being healthy and balanced in her own news reports concerning India. I myself, as a regular Chinese reader of Indian newspapers for a long time, started thinking about various news reports on China published in the Indian media. My working days always begin by clicking the website samachar.com and grasping the new stories as much as I am interested in. I can therefore easily add more examples of balanced reports concerning China from the Indian side.

In *The Hindu* alone, only recently in May 2006, in their reports both Pallavi Aiyar and Harish Khare have commented on almost all aspects of the leading developing country in the world. Their stories covered different places in China: the sandstorm-suffering capital; the shops on Huai Hai road in the commercial city of Shanghai: a huge market in a small town called Yiwu in Zhejiang; a Buddhist Temple called Shaolin in Henan. They even commented on the Indians working or studying in China ("The Return of the Hong Tou A—San"—the Sikhs with their red turbans—and "Made in China—Indian Doctors"). It is really a wonderful experience having seen these two Indian journalists covering lots of interesting topics. As far as I am concerned, such Indian newspaper reports have undoubtedly enriched my discovery of India.

Compared with these extraordinary reports, we, both Indians and Chinese, can't deny the fact that preciously we used to read all the boring reports, most of them covering catastrophes, road accidents, conflicts and so on for whatever reasons they might have been. Later on, we could only read the arguments and talks concerning the Sino-Indian border conflict of 1962, which were later followed by news stories perhaps on the doubts about the reforms and opening-up in both countries. In one word, we really did not know what was happening in our neighbourhood.

Great Surprises

And of course, we paid heavy prices for this. As one of the outcomes of reading those deadly stories in newspapers, both Indians who visited China and Chinese who came to India after 1990 were taken aback by what they saw with their own eyes. For Indians, it's a great surprise that the infrastructure in China, particularly in the big cities, has been developed well. For Chinese, "I wonder if all people in India are Buddhists," for instance. Even this year, an Indian visiting scholar in Beijing University complained: "Since I am here, I have seem a completely different picture of China. They made us fools for long. Now I know even the Chinese food I take in India is not really Chinese."

In this condition, we fail to understand why the representatives from India and China shared the same or similar views on numerous issues on the international stage without consulting each other in advance, even during the most difficult period in their bilateral relations. Maybe it is due to the fact that journalists in both China and India had been sick in the past. Let's hope they do not remain the same any more, not any longer. In fact, it's not difficult to understand some very complex, and yet simple, familiar words like socialism or communism. Harish Khare has made a good attempt by wandering along the streets in Shanghai ("Broad-mindedness on Huai Hai Road," *The Hindu,* May 27, 2006).

And for the Chinese, as the gap between the rich and the poor is getting wider, they may come to understand that something much better has happened in India to narrow the gap between the two segments of the society, something like the reservation policy being implemented and debated now-a-days.

A Comparative Study of Growth Pattern in India and China : A Review

Md. Abdus Salam

INTRODUCTION

The attainment of sustained high economic growth is a necessary condition for improving the quality of life of the people throughout the country. Both China and India have been undergoing a period of economic transitions during the last many years. The central objective of transition through economic liberalization is to improve the competitive efficiency of the economy in the global market to sustain accelerated rates of economic growth and thereby continuously improve welfare of the people. India launched its market-oriented economic reforms in 1991. China launched similar reforms from 1978 and is now well ahead of India in integrating its national economy with the global economy. The contrast in the experiences of these two countries with economic reforms under different political systems with sharp inter-party differences on many issues is remarkable. This paper tries to make a comparative study of growth pattern in India and China during post reforms periods of both the countries. For this, some important Indicators of economic and social development like GDP, life expectancy, literacy rates, the proportion of population employed in agriculture, etc. are being used to characterize the difference between the two countries.

The Performance of the Indian Economy

India in its more than fifty-seven years of independence has waged a long battle against hunger and poverty. To remedy this situation, India's economy went through several episodes of economic liberalization in the 1970s and the 1980s under Prime Ministers Indira Gandhi and, later, Rajiv Gandhi. However, these attempts at economic liberalization were half-hearted, self-contradictory, and often self-reversing in parts. India suffered a major economic crisis in 1991, due largely to the effects of oil price shocks (resulting from the 1990 Gulf War), the collapse of the Soviet Union (a major trading partner and source of foreign aid), and sharp depletion of its foreign exchange reserves. The economic crisis led India to implement a number of economic reforms, including cut in the budget deficit, sharp cuts in tariff barriers, liberalization of FDI rules, exchange rate and banking reforms, and dismantling of the industrial licensing system. The major structural economic reforms carried out since 1991 have been primarily in the areas of Trade, Industry, Infrastructure, Finance, and Foreign Direct Investment. The thrust of the reforms in all areas has been to open India's markets to international competition, remove exchange rate controls, and encourage private investment and participation in industry and the finance markets. According to C.P. Chandrasekhar and Jayati Ghosh (downloaded from the website http://www.ilo.org/public/english/employment/strat/publ/etp55.htm) the principal aims of the structural adjustment policies adopted as a part of the reform process were: (i) to do away with or substantially reduce controls on capacity creation, production and prices, and let market forces influence the investment and operational decisions of domestic and foreign economic agents within the domestic tariff area; (ii) to allow international competition and therefore international relative prices to influence the decisions of these agents; (iii) to reduce the presence of state agencies in production and trade, except in areas where market failure necessitates state entry; and (iv) to liberalize the financial sector by reducing controls on the banking system, allowing for the proliferation of financial institutions and instruments and permitting foreign entry into the financial sector.

Post-reform industrial policy has moved in three principal directions. The first was the removal of capacity controls by "dereserving" and "delicencing" industries, or abolishing the requirement to obtain a license to create new capacity or substantially expand existing capacity. The second area of industrial reform related to the dilution of provisions of the MRTP Act, so as to facilitate the expansion and diversification of large firms or firms belonging to the big business groups. The third type of liberalisation in industry involved foreign investment regulation. The proponents of policies such as trade liberalisation, agricultural export promotion and the reduction of per capita food subsidies, have argued that they would necessarily lead to an acceleration of output growth in agriculture by increasing market-based incentives for agricultural investment and output. But such acceleration has not occurred, and indeed agricultural growth has decelerated in the 1990s compared to the earlier decade.

Structural Reforms

The major structural reforms carried out by several state governments include:

(i) Measures to improve quality of life through improvements in basic public services such as primary health, primary education, and rural infrastructure services such as electricity, water, and roads.

(ii) Clustering high-tech industries and services (for example, in software parks).

(iii) Setting up Special Economic Zones and Agric-Economic Zones to promote exports.

(iv) Formulating state-level industrial policies to attract investments.

(v) Power-sector reforms that restructure state Electricity Boards by separating generation, transmission and distribution activities, encouraging independent power producers in the private sector to invest in the power sector, and setting up independent state Electricity Regulatory Authorities.

Agricultural production in India is an important determinant of overall economic growth. Total foodgrain production in 2001-02 (April-March) amounted to a record 209.2 m tonnes, including 89.5 m tonnes of rice and 75.6 m tonnes of wheat. However, yields per acre remain low by international standards. Other major crops grown include oilseeds, cotton, pulses, sugar, tea, coffee, rubber, jute and potatoes. Two-thirds of India's populations work in agriculture and agriculture, forestry and fishing account for around 25% of GDP. However, the majority of farming families live below the poverty line. Without a rapid and sustained increase in overall rates of economic growth, reducing poverty will remain a considerable challenge. A policy of import substitution in the decades after independence encouraged the development of a broad industrial base. However, a lack of competition contributed to poor product quality and inefficiencies in production. Several sectors have now been opened up to foreign participation under India's liberalizing reform programme, contributing to a significant expansion in the production of durable consumer goods, including cars, scooters, consumer electronics and computer systems. Services have proved India's most dynamic sector in last few years, registering rapid growth in telecom and information technology (IT). Services like airlines, banks and construction etc. accounted for over 48% of GDP in 2000. The most notable weakness of the reform process has been in fiscal Consolidation. Indian governments at both the central and state levels have failed miserably to reign in growing revenue deficits and reduce the overall fiscal deficit. The foundations for a sustainable high growth rate in any economy lie in maintaining fiscal discipline. Indian policy-makers have not adequately achieved this. The structure of revenue expenditure and political obstacles to any reduction of subsidies and downsizing the government at all levels has been primarily responsible for the lack of progress on fiscal reforms. India's record on social development expenditure has been poor considering Indian requirements and poor also in relation to many developing countries. India has some of the lowest human development indicators in the world, particularly in rural areas. At the other end of the scale, India also has a large number of highly qualified professionals, as well as several internationally established industrial groups. Studies revealed that larger investment in the social sectors is 'necessary not only because social development is an end in itself, but also as a precondition of accelerating growth'. The massive shift required in the pattern of government expenditure in India in favor of social sectors and infrastructure can only be carried out through structural fiscal reforms.

The Performance of the Chinese Economy

China had introduced market-oriented reforms in 1980, that is, a decade earlier than India. As a consequence during the 1980s, industrial and agricultural output in China grew by an average 10 percent per year. Between 1982 and 1990, per capita income tripled; by 2002, it had grown by about 40 percent. China now accounts for about 4 percent of the world's economic output. Exports of China rose by about 35 percent in 2003, Imports were up by 40 percent in the same period. In 2003, the Chinese economy was the sixth largest in the world, at $ 5.989 trillion. The power behind the growth of Chinese economy is manufacturing, which provides more than half of China's GDP and is expanding by more than 12 percent per year, on average; in 2003, industrial production rose by 16 percent. Wages that average only $ 0.60 per hour have made China the low-cost producer in fields from textiles to telecommunications auto parts. Heavy industries such as steel and chemicals are a mainstay of the Chinese economy. This has also attracted large-scale investment from foreign companies eager to cash in on cheap labour. In 2002, foreign direct investment in China reached an estimated $ 52.7 billion. Trade contributes an estimated 40 percent to China's GDP. Economic growth has allowed China to overcome some of its social problems in last few years.

India and China : A Comparison

China and India both are going through economic transitions.

Fundamental concerns in India include the massive overpopulation, poverty, unemployment and environmental degradation. India's economy has shown relatively healthy growth since 1991 when an economic crisis caused the government to implement various economic reforms. Yet, many analysts view India's economy as falling below its potential, especially when compared to a country such as China, which has achieved far greater economic success over the past decade. The central objective of transition through economic liberalization is to improve the competitive efficiency of the economy in the global marketplace to sustain accelerated rates of economic growth and thereby continuously improve the security and well-being of the people. India launched its market-oriented economic reforms in 1991. China launched similar reforms from 1978 and is now well ahead of India in integrating its national economy with the global economy. However, India is slowly but steadily catching up in this race. The contrast in the experiences of these two countries with economic reforms under different political systems is noticeable. China and India are similar in relative population size and affluence. In 2001 China had a population of 1.276 billion and a GDP per capita of US $ 909, while India's population was 1.029 Billion and GDP per capita US $ 496.There is also similarity in terms of the proportion of the population that is urban. China's was estimated at 37% in 2001, compared with 33% for India. In China average urban household income in 2001 is estimated at US $ 2,657, whereas for India it is estimated at US $ 2,847. According to H.E. Mr. Robert D. Blackwill (2002), the two countries China and India launched their economic reform programmes from different historical experiences. Nonetheless, the fact remains that in the last 10 years, China has forged ahead on most economic measures. He has examined the economies of India and China respectively with the following statistics:

(1) Over the last 20 years, China's GDP has grown at about 10% a year, compared with India's 6% growth rate.

(2) A decade ago, India and China had close to the same per-capita income. Today China's per-capita income is about $ 900, roughly twice that of India.
(3) In 1991, China produced 670 billion kilowatt hours of electricity, India 290 billion. In 2001, China's production was 1.14 trillion kilowatt hours while India's was about 450 billion.
(4) In 1991, China's receipts from tourism were $ 2.8 billion. This had grown to $ 14.10 billion by 2001. The comparative figures for India were $ 1.4 billion in 1991, and $ 3.04 billion ten years later.
(5) In 1991, India and China started off from about the same base, with less than one computer for every thousand individuals. By 2000 China's rate is three times India's, with more than 15 computers for every thousand persons, compared to 4.5 in India.
(6) In 1990, manufacturing in China was about 37% of the economy; today that relative weight has increased to about 45%. China now produces 50% of the world's cameras, 30% of the air conditions and televisions, 25% of the washing machines and 20% of the refrigerators. In the last 12 years, manufacturing as a percentage of the Indian economy has decreased, falling to about 24% of the economy from 30%.
(7) China's trade in goods and services as a percentage of GDP grew for 35% in 1991 to 49% in 2000. During the same period, India's percentage rose from 18% to 30%.
(8) Since 1980, China has welcomed over $ 336 billion in foreign investment; India has received only $ 18 billion.
(9) In 1990, China's exports were $ 62 billion, which were three-and-a-half times greater than India's. Today China's annual exports are over $ 266 billion, and the comparative gap has widened to over five-and-a-half times India's current exports.
(10) And we all know what an enormous investment China is putting into its domestic infrastructure—airports, roads, port facilities, telecommunications, and so forth.

India : To tap more Potential

Many studies reveal that India's economy has failed to live

up to its potential, especially relative to other developing countries like China, which has a comparable population size, but has enjoyed far greater economic development. The relative position of China and India in different fields can also be observed from graphs 1, 2 and 3. In a nutshell, it can be observed that China is relatively in a much better position than India. As Table 1 indicates both India and China experienced significant growth in population, GDP and per capita GDP (both measured on a PPP basis), trade, and FDI during post reform periods. However, on several economic fronts, India lost significant ground to China. In 1990, India's economy (GDP, PPP basis) was about three-quarters the size of China's, but by 2002 it was less than half. India's living standards (per capita GDP, PPP basis) was slightly greater than China's in 1990, but by 2002 it had fallen to 55.5% of China's. India's exports relative to Chinese exports fell from 28.9% in 1990 to 15.7% in 2002, while imports dropped from 55.3% to 19.8%. India made small gains in FDI flows relative to China over this period (rising from 2.3% to 5.9%). However, the total level of FDI stock in China was substantially higher than that going to India in both periods. In fact, FDI flows to China in 2002 alone (nearly $ 53 billion) were more than double the cumulative stocks of FDI in India through 2002 ($ 26 billion). Many economists attribute the sharp widening economic gaps between India and China to differences in the pace and scope of economic and trade reforms undertaken by each country, where China has substantially reformed its trade and investment regimes (which has contributed to sharp rises in GDP growth, trade, and FDI flows), India's economic reforms have been far less comprehensive and effective. Between 1986 and 1999 the GDP growth rate of China was maintained at a pace that made for a wide gap with India's. During 1996-98 China's average growth rate was 74 per cent higher than India's rate. (But in 1996-99, this gap narrowed considerably to just 8 per cent higher than India's). The per capita income, which was about the same in 1980 for both countries, had diverged in the two decades that followed. Evaluated in PPP terms, the gap was 86 per cent in favour of China, not only because of a higher growth rate of GDP but also because of a lower growth rate of population. In 1952, China's population was 57 per cent higher than India's. In the 1990s it was just 28 per cent higher. At present, China's population is growing at 1.0 per cent a year (target for 2000-2001: 0.92 per cent) while India's population is expanding at 1.9 percent a year. At this rate, India's population will overtake China's by 2025. China has an ambitious plan to reach zero population growth by 2020 to level at 1.5 billion people. If so, then India will overtake China by 2016, unless it implements some drastic plan to curb population growth.

An editorial of *The Hindu* (December 8, 2004) highlighted that "despite the fairly high Gross Domestic Product growth over the past decade, India has not been able to mobilize anything like the kind of FDI or domestic investment needed to build world-class infrastructure. FDI annual inflow into India has touched $ 4.7 billion. For an economy of India's size, given the huge investment requirements in core areas such as telecommunications, highways, power, mining, airports and seaports, this is still minor league. Despite India's political diversity and sharp inter-party differences on certain issues, the Centre and the States need to work in tandem to create attractive investment destinations. With private investment, domestic or foreign, tolls will become the order of the day. Some States, notably in the west and south of the country, have done very well in developing infrastructure and attracting FDI. But all this is only a fraction of what is needed to achieve Chinese-type rapid industrial expansion, world-class infrastructure development, increased trade, and higher levels of growth. Prime Minister Manmohan Singh's target of securing $ 150 billion FDI in 10 years is not beyond reach but it asks for tremendous work from the system."

The Global Competitiveness Report, 2003-04 of the *World Economic Forum* has ranked India several notches above China. In the Business Competitiveness Index (BCI), India's rank is 37 out of 102 countries as against China's 46. The BCI is an index of a country's micro-fundamentals and focuses on the quality of the business environment as well as the sophistication of companies in the country. India is the world's top-ranked country when it comes to the presence of a large number of competitive firms. On the availability of engineers and scientists, it is third in the rankings and No. 6 in terms of its policy on allowing foreign technology. As far as the quality of management schools is concerned, it is No. 8. Both India and China, however, have slipped on the Growth Competitiveness Index—which measures the long-term sustainability of growth. China's fall, though, has been sharper than India's. The reason for the fall in India's case is a very sharp deterioration in the Macroeconomic Environment Index—India's ranking fell from 18 in 2002 to 52 in 2003. Within the constraints of democratic politics and the relatively 'soft' nature of the economic reforms implemented since 1991, the Indian economy has reaped several welcome rewards from its reforms. These have strengthened the conviction that the broad direction of the reforms is right and, in that sense, made the reform process irreversible. India's economy has also successfully moved into a higher trajectory of growth and displayed strong dynamism in selected sectors. This encouraging performance brightens the prospects for stepping up India's growth rate and improving the competitive edge in the years to come through further appropriate economic reforms. Local manufacturers are learning to innovate and compete globally, and the middle class is expanding. India's foreign-exchange reserves have reached about $ 130 billion. That is not a lot compared with China's $ 403 billion. However, given the comparative advantage of a skilled workforce available at low costs, backed by huge foreign exchange reserves India has a potential to compete in the world economy.

CONCLUSIONS

Through reform, India overcame its worst economic crisis. In post economic reforms, the Gross Domestic Product (GDP) improved from an average of about 5.7 per cent in the 1980s to an average of about 6.5 per cent in the Eighth and Ninth Plan periods, making India one of the ten fastest growing developing countries, where the dismantling of the industrial licensing system, free investments by foreign companies, lowering of import tariffs on capital goods all contributed. Encouraging progress was also made in other sectors. The percentage of the population in poverty continued to decline, even if not as much as was targeted. Population growth decelerated below 2 per cent for the first time in four decades. Literacy increased from 52 percent in 1991 to 65 per cent in 2001. Software services, entertainment and information technology-enabled services emerged as new sources of strength, creating confidence about India's potential to be competitive in the world economy. The share of India's trade as proportion of GDP rose from 13.1 per cent in 1990 to 20.3 percent in 2000. India's growing middle class of more than 350 million people, with a reasonably affluent standard of living, provides a huge market for foreign corporations, especially since April 2003, when all quantitative restrictions on imports were lifted. Along with its fairly good growth rate (which is far below the potential growth rate of eight percent targeted by India's Tenth Five-Year Plan), India has been successful in reducing poverty. The poverty ratio that is people below the poverty line, as a percentage of the population as estimated by the Planning Commission at the national level came down from 36 percent in 1993-94 to 26.1 percent in 1999-2000. The poverty ratio during this period declined both in rural areas and in urban areas. There is little doubt that poverty in India has been reduced during the last decade. The Planning Commission has set a poverty ratio target of 19.3 percent by the end of the Tenth Plan period (upto March 2007).

An important indicator of gains from economic reforms, reflecting the attractiveness of India as an investment destination, is shown by the increasing inflows of both FDI and Foreign Institutional Investment (FII) into India. Several measures to boost FDI have been taken. Projects for electricity generation, transmission and distribution as also roads and highways, ports and harbors, and vehicular tunnels and bridges have been permitted along with foreign equity participation up to 100 per cent. Inflows of both FDI and FII into India have increased during last few years. India's economy clearly is on the move and most certainly has the potential to emerge as a global economic power within next twenty to twenty-five years. Commenting on mid-year economic review of Government of India an editorial of The Hindu (December 17, 2004) highlighted that "Investment as a proportion of GDP is low in India compared with what it is in China even though the requirement is higher, particularly for infrastructure. The bottleneck to infrastructure investments is not a shortage of funds but a lack of clarity on regulatory issues. Unless this is sorted out investments will remain choked. The Golden Quadrilateral highway project, which ought to have been completed, is just half done. Ports are struggling to cope with increased trade volumes, as slow policy making crimps new investments. Air passenger traffic has risen 22 per cent, leaving airports inadequate; yet procedural hitches have meant that neither the expansion of existing airports at Mumbai and New Delhi nor the green-field projects at Bangalore and Hyderabad have got off the ground. Months after the Electricity Act, 2003 was passed in Parliament, the Government has not been able to put together the National Electricity Policy that promises to infuse competition and efficiency into a sector that has under-performed for many decades." Economic reforms in the future must be more people-friendly. They must be given a human face so as to continuously enhance the social empowerments of the poorer and most vulnerable sections of the society. The burden of adjustment to structural reforms must be more heavily borne by the richer sections of the society. While some agricultural reforms have already been carried out, these are highly inadequate. Priority must be given to the agriculture sector in all future reforms since many more jobs can be created in the agricultural sector. There is an urgent need to raise investment in agriculture in the areas like irrigation; watershed development; rural infrastructure; drinking water; housing and sanitation etc. That will raise incomes of farmers and rural labour on a sustainable basis and also help in raising the productivity of Indian agriculture to all-around economic growth. Future economic reforms in India must be based on the long-term vision of transforming India into global economic power in the next twenty to twenty-five years. These reforms must aim to raise the productivity of Indian labour and improve the work culture. Growth With Employment is the most effective strategy for eliminating poverty and proving the quality of life of the people. India must concentrate on accelerated growth in agriculture, IT, services and exports during the next two decades, and make efforts fiscally to raise the rate of investment to start closing the gap with China.

TABLE 1

(*Units*)

Area	*China*	*India*
Total	9,596,960	3,287,590
Land	9,326,410	2,973,190
Water	270,550	314,400

GRAPH 1(a)

Comparison of Area

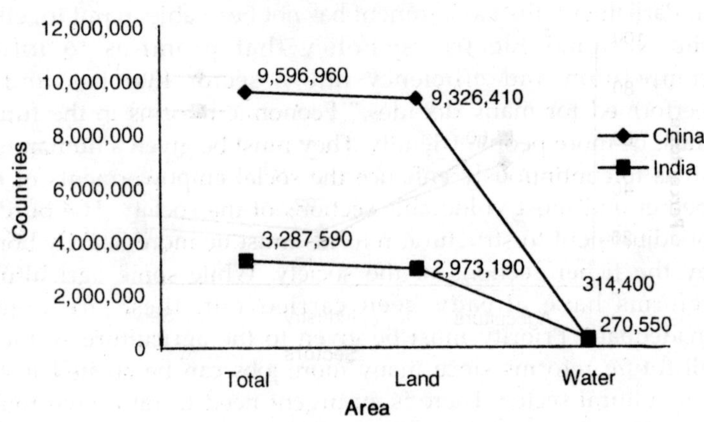

GRAPH 1(b)

Comparison of Area

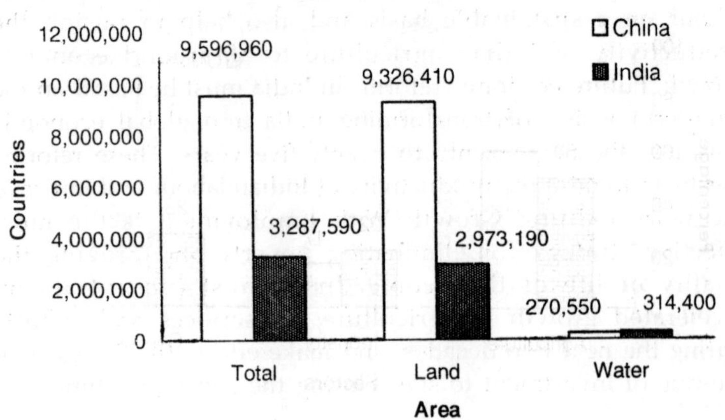

TABLE 2

(in 2000)

Labor force—by occupation (in %)	China	India
Agriculture	50	60
Industry	22	17
Service	28	23

GRAPH 2(a)

Comparison of Labour Force Engaged

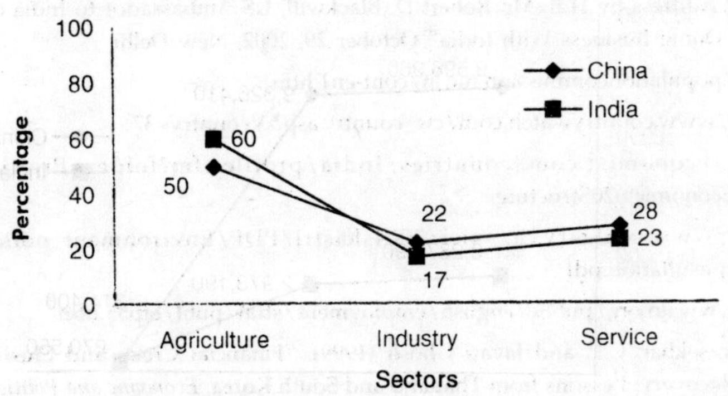

GRAPH 2(b)

Comparison of Labour Force Engaged (in 2000)

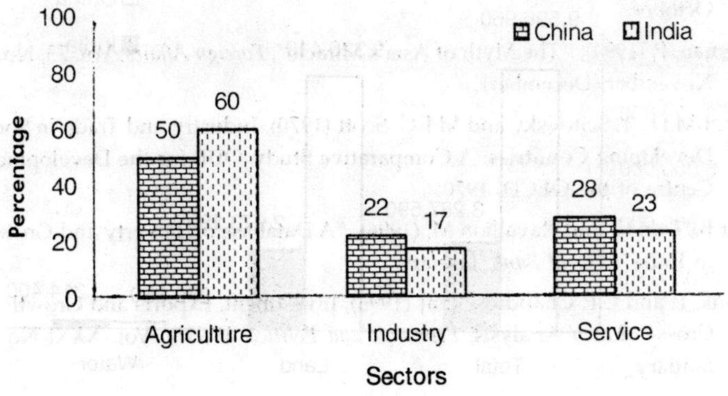

References

http://hdr.undp.org.

Jean Dreze and Amartya Sen, India: Economic Development and Social Opportunities, (New Delhi: Oxford University Press, 1995).

Government of India, Export Import Policy, 2002-07, New Delhi: Ministry of Commerce, 2002.

Government of India, Tenth Five Year Plan 2002-07 (in three volumes) (New Delhi: Planning Commission, 2002).

Abhijit Roy (2003), India set to rank third by 2040, The Hindu, Dec. 29, 2003.

http://www.bisnetworld.net/bisnet/index.htm

Special Address by H.E. Mr. Robert D. Blackwill, US Ambassador to India on "Doing Business With India" October 29, 2002, New Delhi.

http://populationcommission.nic.in/cont-en1.htm

http://www.countrywatch.com/cw_country.asp? Vcountry=37

http://economist.com/countries/India/profile.cfm?folder=Profile-Economic%20Structure.

http://www.ucalgary.ca/~sici/2004shastri/PDF/Environment_policy consultation.pdf

ttp://www.ilo.org/public/english/employment/strat/publ/etp55.htm

Chandrasekhar, C.P. and Jayati Ghosh (1999), "Financial Crises and Elusive Recovery: Lessons from Thailand and South Korea, *Economic and Political Weekly*, February.

Ghosh, Jayati (1997), "India's Structural Adjustment: An Assessment in Comparative Asian Context", *Economic and Political Weekly*, May.

Ghosh, Jayati, Abhijit Sen and C.P. Chandrasekhar (1996) "Southeast Asian Economies: Miracle or Meltdown?" *Economic and Political Weekly*, October.

Krugman, P. (1994), "The Myth of Asia's Miracle", *Foreign Affairs*, Vol. 73, No. 6 November/December).

Little, I.M.D., T. Scitovsky and M.F.G. Scott (1970), Industry and Trade in Some Developing Countries: A Comparative Study, OUP for the Development Centre of the OECD, 1970.

Ozler B., Datt G. and Ravallion M. (1996), "A Database on Poverty and Growth in India", *World Bank*, January.

Patnaik, P. and C.P. Chandrasekhar (1996), Investment, Exports and Growth: A Cross-country Analysis, *Economic and Political Weekly*, Vol. XXXI No. 1, January.

Sen, A. and Patnaik, U. (1997), "Poverty in India", *CESP Working Paper*, JNU, Delhi.

Singh, Ajit (1995), How Did East Asia Grow So Fast? Slow Progress Towards an Analytical Consensus, UNCTAD Discussion Paper, No. 97, February.

Young, A. (1994), Lessons from the East Asian NICs: A Contrarian View, *European Economic Review*, Vo. 38, No. 3/4 (April).

World Trade Organisation (1997), Annual Report, Volumes 1 & 2, Geneva: WTO.

http://www.adb.org/Documents/Books/Key_Indicators/2004/default.asp

http://www.adb.org/Documents/Books/Key_Indicators/2004/pdf/IND.pdf

The China-India Matrix

RASHEEDA BHAGAT

INTRODUCTION

At a recent conference of Economic editors in Singapore to discuss the findings of the latest survey sponsored by Master Card International as part of its ongoing research and analysis on business dynamics, financial policies and related activities in the Asia-Pacific region, it was a little disappointing to note that journalists from Thailand, Malaysia, the Philippines and Singapore showed very little interest in seeking information on the India economy. They were very keen to get the latest on China, though. Granted the title of the survey report was 'China and the New Global Economy,' but it did contain a lot of information on how India had come on the global stage with its strategic contribution to the services sector. Also, the crux of he report was that by 2020, China and India would have a middle-class consumer base of one billion people, a number that should have any manufacturer of consumer goods drooling.

Middle-Class Defined

Of course the definition of a "middle-class" person given by Dr. Yuwa Hedrik-Wong, who led the economists' panel that conducted the survey, was one with an annual income of or above $ 5,000. His survey estimates that with a "conservative" projected growth of the economies, by 2020, China would have 650 million "middle class" people and India 350 million. In 2004, this number was 79 million and 12 million respectively. But the most fascinating aspect of the report, which also explained to a certain extent the South-East Asian journalists' interest in China, was how that surging economy has changed the economic equations in the entire region, drawing the major produce from these countries, including India, to emerge an exporter to the Western world.

Might of Middle Kingdom

Dr. Yuwa used World Bank data to illustrate China's growing importance on the world stage and drive home why it can no longer be ignored by global businesses. In 1990, China's share of global GDP growth, on a purchasing power parity basis, was only 10 per cent. But by 1995 it had increased to 23 per cent, by 2004 it was 33 per cent or one third of the global economic growth rate "and I guess the figure for 2005 would be even higher." Coming to China's mighty labour force on the manufacturing side, Dr. Yuwa said that "between 2000 and 2005 about 30 million Chinese workers could be construed to be producing directly for the global market, by 2005-2010 this workforce is estimated to double to 60 million, an increase by 30 million people, which is the entire population of Canada!." This, he added, would have far-reaching implications for the rest of the world. An increase in the global supply of labour would mean that in the next few years wages could be suppressed, unless a country had a highly specialized labour force.

The India Story

It is in this context that the importance of India, "which is yet to make inroads into the manufacturing sector," is emerging, Dr. Yuwa said. "At the moment India's impact in the global arena is one of service exports and it is going from very, very basic to increasingly complex and sophisticated areas—from mere call centers, to low value add and then increasingly to R&D activities, what people now call business process outsourcing." While this was bound to continue, the only constraint for its future growth is "India's supply of skilled labour force. We're talking about 200,000 Indian graduates passing out every year, but according to a McKinsey report, only 20-25 per cent of these graduates are good. Thanks to the shortfall in quality we're already seeking a huge amount of job-hopping in the services sector in India; with a marginal increase in pay people switch jobs because the competition is keen," he said.

Leveraging China's Growth

While this had the potential of "slowing down India's growth in the services sector, at the moment what we're seeing is that on the manufacturing side China is providing huge supply in terms of both labour and capacity." The trick, therefore, lay in corporates in the region leveraging China's growth, its huge domestic market and its lower manufacturing costs, to drive economic growth in their individual countries by building-up a partnership with China. Japan had been an early bird in doing exactly this; many Japanese corporates had shifted their manufacturing base to China, and gained the advantage of cheaper labour and cheaper logistics, while maintaining the quality of Brand Japan, said the report.

Explaining how China's impact on Japan was dramatic, Dr. Yuwa said: "Today Japan's recovery is not only sustainable, but it is also putting the country on a completely high growth trajectory because of what Japan has managed to do with the China market. The profit of Japanese corporates is at an all time high." In 2003-04, the sales of 30 Japanese corporates grew by only 1.5 per cent, but their profit grew by 15 per cent and this was thanks to their leveraging China. "The equation is very simple; it was the same brand and the same global market, except the product was made in China, allowing the project margins to boom. Increasingly in Japan they no longer talk about 'Made in Japan', but 'Made by Japan in China", Dr. Yuwa, said, giving the example of how Toshiba today no longer makes a single colour TV in Japan, having shifted its entire manufacturing base to China.

Key Service Supplier

Terming the phenomenon of China emerging as a pan-Asia supply chain and India's foray into the services sector as a "positive supply shock", and underlining the importance of synergies among various players. Dr. Yuwa said: "India's $ 40 billion dollar per year service exports are reducing by 2 to 3 times the business operating costs of its outsourcing clients. Manufacturing is becoming increasingly service intensive and India now is actually becoming a key supplier in the service dimension of manufacturing. My message is that globally there is no escape from leveraging from countries which have different advantages. Manufacturing for China, and services for India."

He added that sometimes at business conferences people came up to him and said "Oh, but that is happening in China or India. How will it affect the rest of the world?" To which his reply has been that today you can't be a company in the US Midwest and say you never export to global markets and it doesn't matter to you what's happening in China or India. "My argument is that you still cannot escape the impact. If your competitor can tap into India for a bit of what they do in terms of service outsourcing or buy from China because it is cheaper there, then you competitor will beat you in the domestic market. So even if you have nothing to do with the global market, you cannot escape the impact of this positive supply shock coming out of Asia."

Pointing out how growth of China had positively impacted growth in the region—in the last 10 years India's annual export growth rate to US was only 12.5 per cent, but its annual export annual export growth rate to China was 50.21 per cent—he said, "That gives an idea of how growth in the region has changed. Taiwan was discussing whether they could impeach their President or not; its domestic economy is in deep depression, in fact it does not have an independent economy on its own, for all practical purposes its economy is integrated with that of China. This explains why in the 10-year period from 1994-04, while its export to its traditional market-the US—grew at an annual rate of 1.26 per cent, its exports to China grew by a huge 75.86 per cent. Today Taiwan is completely dependent on the China market."

Asian Integration

Dr. Yuwa said that, ultimately, there was no getting away from regional integration in Asia for the benefit of each participant. He was optimistic that this would happen, and was already happening in many areas, because "fortunately, economic integration in Asia is not driven by governments but businesses. In terms of government policies, it's a mess. Some people are pessimistic and ask: Gee, when are we going to see an Asia Free Trade policy, and my answer to them is: 'Probably never'. But that's not the point; the point is that economic integration is driven by business, the way they position their productions centers, maintain their supply chain, etc." A win-win situation for all would be when there is extreme integration "without government policy intervention, or despite that lack of government policy initiatives!" And one hopes that very soon a time will come when the South-East Asian media will be as interested, if not more, in India as in China!

28

Growth Sustainability of China and India

ANDY XIE

INTRODUCTION

At the recent 2006 International Monetary Fund/World Bank Annual Meeting in Singapore, I participated in a panel entitled "The Nature of Growth in China and India: Challenges Ahead and Implications for the Rest of the World." While acknowledging cyclical risks, I believe that the two economies can sustain high growth rates with substantial structural adjustments. China needs to shift wealth from the government to the household sector to engineer a decade of consumption-led growth. India must invest in infrastructure to support manufacturing-led growth. The cyclical risk for both is their dependence on global liquidity, which fuels China's exports and India's stock and property markets. The ultimate source of liquidity has been US consumers spending above their income, which pumps dollar liquidity into emerging economies through the vast US current-account deficit. The downturn in the US housing market is a big threat to the liquidity boom, as the US consumer may cease to borrow to spend.

In the longer term, both countries must overcome difficulties in sustaining pro-growth policies. Wealth concentration may lead to a popular backlash against growth for its own sake. In both countries, the political leaders may have to focus on income distribution rather than growth. Indeed, the trend may have already begun, with the global liquidity boom covering the growth implications for now. The biggest external risk is protectionism in the West. Globalisation has led to marked income concentration everywhere. The worry is that the middle-class in the West may vote against globalisation due to stagnation of their income levels.

The Crowd Came

Martin Wolf of the *Financial Times* was the moderator for the panel at the Singapore meeting. The other panelists were India's Deputy Chairman of the Planning Commission, Montek Singh Ahluwalia; a political scientist at the Carnegie Endowment, Minxin Pei; and an economist at the Center for Global Development and the Institute of International Economics, William Kline.

I was worried that no one would come. The facilities were guarded like Fort Knox, and negotiating security was a challenge in itself. People did show up, though. In fact, the crowd was so big that initially the doors couldn't be closed, although this was eventually achieved at Wolf's insistence. The level of interest was due probably to the title of the panel. If one puts China and India together in a title now-a-days, it tends to draw a lot of attention. While China and India have great future prospects, levels of enthusiasm have now reached bubble proportions, in my view. After the tech bubble burst in 2001, the global media and the financial community started looking for another hot topic. Along came the growth boom in China and India. This sentiment bubble will likely burst along with the end of the growth cycle. The current global cycle is all about liquidity and risk appetite. I believe it will come down either with an inflation problem that forces central banks to withdraw liquidity or with a collapse of risk appetite due to an accident.

Judging from the crowd size in our session, the bubble is quite alive.

Different Perspectives

Montek made the case for an increase in India's sustainable growth rate to 9% from 8%. He pointed out the importance of building-up the manufacturing sector to sustain India's growth rate. Key to this argument is that only manufacturing can create enough jobs for India's large population. Montek emphasized the importance of building-up infrastructure for manufacturing development. I quite agree with his messages. India's current growth is too dependent on the global liquidity boom. Strong stock and property markets are powering its consumption-led growth. It needs to build-up its manufacturing sector quickly to sustain growth beyond the liquidity boom.

As regards China, I argued that it falls within the East Asian model of investment—and export-led growth. The difference is the overwhelming power of China's bureaucracy, which is extraordinarily effective in mobilizing resources for capital formation. The system has a big advantage in terms of building capital-intensive infrastructure. At an early stage of development, the efficiency gains from capital accumulation far exceed the costs from inefficient methods of resource mobilisatgion. In particular, strong exports have overcome the tendency towards overcapacity in this growth model.

Pei argued that China has accumulated enormous social costs in pursuing rapid growth. As the tension over income inequality rises, the country may have to increase expenditure on social issues to maintain stability, which would slow down the economy. He noted that China's system is not supportive of high growth at first glance, and suggested that bureaucratic competition may have created the inefficiency in China's government-led development.

I agree with the view that China has not paid fully for high growth. A pliant population has allowed the government to side-step many social costs. What gives the government so much power is the availability of food at affordable prices and with variety. This is probably the first time that the Chinese population as a whole has been well-fed. This has come about due to the introduction of technologies in food production. The "full stomach" effect will likely wear off as new generations grow-up without fear of hunger. This could limit the government's power, with the result that development costs may well have to rise.

Kline spoke about the need for China to appreciate its currency, largely attributing the US' worsening trade balance to China's exchange rate regime. He argued that everything else has moved except China's currency, and that this is where the problem lies. Frustration over China's currency regime is widespread in the government and academia, particularly in the US. After years of pressure on China, the renminbi has moved by 4%. Many in the US were expecting China's currency to follow a path similar to that of the yen after the Plaza Accord in 1985. As I see it, the problem is that the US cannot make a case that a substantial renminbi move would be good for China, and it cannot force China to act against its will.

Short-term Issues

The Question and Answer session focused mostly on short-term issues. China's exchange rate system was at the centre of the discussion. There seemed to me to be much ado about very little. China is not going to make a decision that may undermine its stability. The Chinese government seems to accept that some appreciation is necessary, but is unsure how much is appropriate. Hence, it is appreciating its currency slowly to inch towards an equilibrium point. The main criticism of this approach is that global imbalances are likely to worsen during the slow process of adjustment.

One complication in the renminbi story is that a significant portion of the economy now depends on expectations of appreciation, especially in the property sector. If the currency appreciates quickly, these expectations might reverse, such that the economy could suffer a hard landing. This effectively rules out the possibility of a maxi-revaluation.

Another complication relates to the sustainability of US debt-led consumption. If US consumers break their habit of "borrow and spend", China's trade surplus could vanish. Hence, China should be cautious about making a currency adjustment on the premise of its large but unsustainable trade surplus.

Asian Renaissance Still to come

Despite the considerable enthusiasm towards Asia in general and China and India in particular, the current boom in Asia is part of a global cycle. Asia has passively supported this cycle, principally through China's role in suppressing global inflation during the liquidity boom. Ultimately, the liquidity comes from the US trade deficit, which depends on US consumers borrowing and spending.

Montek made it clear that India will have to repeat China's manufacturing success to sustain its growth rate in the long run. China's exports were 7.5 times India's in 2005, while its GDP was 2.8 times. China's exports look set to increase 1.6 times as fast as India's total exports in 2006. Without building-up its infrastructure, India's manufacturing sector cannot be successful. India is increasing expenditure on infrastructure, but the amount is still small. China's infrastructure growth per annum in many areas is equal to India's existing stock. It will take time for India to switch from liquidity-led to manufacturing-led growth. Strong asset markets on foreign liquidity are driving India's consumption boom, which is leading its economy. This is why India's trade deficit rose to 5.5% of GDP in fiscal 2005-06 from 1.7% in 2001-02. Hence, capital inflow is vital for keeping interest rates low and asset markets buoyant. If the global liquidity boom dissipates, India could suffer a period of low growth.

While China is successful on the supply side, it is dependent on exports on the demand side. Its GDP appears on course to double to an estimated 21 trillion renminbi ($ 1 approx. five renminbi) in 2006 from 10 trillion renminbi in 2001. Its exports look set to rise to an estimated US $ 950 billion ($ 1 approx. US $ 0.63) in 2006 from US $ 266 billion in 2001. Its incremental export/GDP ration is 53%, more than twice as high as the same ratio in 2001. This shows the extent of China's economic dependence on exports.

US-dependent

Apart from China's rising competitiveness, the US debt-led consumption boom is a major driver of China's export success. If the "borrow and spend" habit of the US consumer comes to an end, China's exports may languish. Its export-led growth model would become less effective. However, if it so chose, China could switch to consumption-led growth by redistributing government-owned wealth to the household sector. The government owns land, natural resources and major enterprises. Most of the country's wealth does not support consumption. This is the most important reason that China's household consumption is so low.

I estimate that China's government-owned wealth may exceed 100% of GDP. These assets could, for example, be packaged into traded funds, with shares in these funds distributed among the population. Such a step would double household wealth overnight. It would, for example, give Chinese farmers some capital, affording them the opportunity to purchase properties in cities and become urban residents. This would be a huge boost for urbanization, which would boost domestic demand. I believe that the resulting consumption boom could support high growth for another decade.

In short, if the US economy collapses, I would expect both China and India to suffer a period of slow growth—but to come back with reforms. China needs to shift its government-owned wealth to the households, while India requires a massive infrastructure build-up to support the development of its manufacturing sector. Once these steps have been taken, a real Asian renaissance should follow.

29

Agricultural Development and Poverty Alleviation in China and India : A Comparative Analysis

M.S. KALLUR

INTRODUCTION

Following factors make it imperative to have the comparative analysis of growth experience of China and India. Firstly, China and—more recently—India are striking economic success stories. A few decades ago, both countries were clearly among the world's poorest countries; now they are among the world's fastest-growing economies and are responsible for nearly all the recent global progress in poverty reduction. China and India are the world's two most populous countries of the world accounting for nearly 2.5 billion or 40 per cent of the total population of the globe. Secondly, these two economies are predominantly agricultural, in nature, notwithstanding the fact that both of them have, in recent years industrialized and their service sector is also growing fast. Thirdly, despite different political systems China and India are aggressively pursuing economic liberalization for growth. Lastly, both of them have broken from ideologically stultified external policies, which marked their existence for previous decades.

Objectives

It is a difficult task to analyze all the developmental policies pertaining to the three sectors of the economies of these two giants; therefore, an attempt is made to give an exhaustive comparative analysis of policies of them pertaining to agricultural development and poverty alleviation in both pre-and-post globalization periods. This becomes the first objective of this paper. Secondly, relative merits or otherwise of policies oriented to agricultural development and poverty reduction are looked into. Lastly, it also suggests the possible future actions to not only strengthen but also to remove imbalances in the primary sector of China and India.

The analysis is mainly based on secondary data. The structure of the paper is as follows. Section I deals with the primacy of agriculture as an introduction. Section II discusses the development pattern of the agriculture and its allied sectors of China and India, in both pre-and-post reform periods. Section III presents the relative merits and defects of the development policies pertaining to agriculture and poverty alleviation in both countries. In this section, there is also a mention about WTO. Section IV contains the conclusions and the future course of the developmental policy pertaining to agriculture and poverty alleviation in both countries.

The Place of Agriculture in the Indian and Chinese Economy

The story of the development of agricultural sector of both of China and India is having both similarities and differences. In a representative developing economy such as India, the importance of agriculture to the national economy is both crucial and pervasive. In some cases, this has not been fully appreciated, and endeavors to quickly transform the economy from basically agrarian to industrial have not led to any cascading growth. However, India is, even today, a predominantly agricultural economy. Agriculture has been the backbone of the Indian economy and despite concerted efforts towards industrialization in the last five decades it occupies a place of pride.

Like that of India, in China also the primary sector is all important. In fact, with the advent of the Communist Party into power in 1949, leaders emphasized agricultural development and implemented land reforms. Achieving self-sufficiency in food-grains production for supplying basic raw materials to the industry and sufficient food grains to industrial workers was considered as a basic policy for many decades.

II

AGRICULTURAL DEVELOPMENT IN THE PRE-AND POST-REFORM ERA

Recognizing the primacy of agriculture, both countries wisely started emphasizing and developing agriculture, from the beginning. For instance, India's First Five Year Plan was an agricultural Plan. In fact, with the advent of the Communist Party into power in 1949, leaders in China emphasized agricultural development and brought out land reforms. Achieving self sufficiency in the food-grains production for supplying basic raw materials to the industry and sufficient food-grains to industrial workers was considered as a basic policy for many decades. In China the egalitarian access to land ensured by the land distribution and tenure system performed a crucial welfare function, providing the bulk of the rural population with access to a basic means of subsistence and limiting the number of landless. New Agricultural Strategy which ultimately resulted in Green Revolution in India refers to the principle of concentration of efforts in selected areas and adoption of package of practices. Although first tried under the Intensive Agricultural District Programme [IADP] along with Intensive Agricultural Area Programme [IAAP] and High Yielding Variety Programme [HYVP] which were initiated in the year 1960-61, the year, i.e. 1967-68, in which entire package of these programmes bore fruits in it, is called the partial Green Revolution year. In 1970s it spread to Southern states. Production gains from Green Revolution technologies continued through the mid-1980s and we achieved not only self-sufficiency but also achieved 'surpluses in wheat and rice. However, in 1990's the sector lost it growth momentum. In India, on the other hand, even though overall economic growth was high, it is clear that slower growth in agriculture was the major reason behind the slower poverty reduction. Prompted by macro-economic imbalances, India's reforms began with macro-economic and non-agricultural policy changes. The reforms led to impressive rates of economic growth in the 1990s, but since reforms were largely focused on the non-agricultural sectors, they had limited impact on poverty reduction. Agricultural policy changes occurred only at later stages, and even then were only partial. Therefore, the evidence suggests that successful agriculture-led reforms reduce poverty faster. Right now, government is seriously trying to improve this sector and it has the target of 4 per cent growth per annum for agriculture which is essential to maintain 8 per cent growth rate of the entire economy. China also achieved food self-sufficiency and, further, witness extraordinary growth in basic grain production in late 1970s and her basic grain production is now much higher than that of India.

China was first to introduce reforms in 1978 and then India in 1991. Further, sequencing of reforms is also somewhat different in the two countries. China reformed its agriculture first by abolishing collectives, introducing the household responsibility system, and reducing mandatory deliveries of output to the state by farmers and thereby enabling farmers to produce for the market. The experience of China shows that the achievement of food self-sufficiency and the extraordinary growth in basic grain production experienced by the late 1970s was a necessary precondition for diversification of her economy. The availability of food surpluses provided the government with enough leeway to feed the increasing population and relax controls over the food-grains sector. Once food self-sufficiency was achieved, China gradually abandoned the policies biased in favour of rice and wheat, encouraging farmers to diversify production. In India, on the other hand rising minimum support prices artificially boosted production of major cereals, discouraging diversification of production towards non-grain commodities. Although India initiated reforms in 1991, reforms have been rigorously implemented in secondary and tertiary sectors but not in the primary sector. In other words, our agriculture in particular and rural economy in general, has not been reformed systematically at all even now and until it happens not much acceleration in the rate of reduction of rural poverty can be expected. India's agriculture, while always in the private sector, was insulated from world markets, riddled with government interventions the domestic market for agricultural inputs and outputs, whose net effect was to disprotect agriculture. On the other hand, China wisely reformed agriculture first and achieved spectacular results for several years, not only provided credibility of its reform process but also increased incomes of the poorer segments of the Chinese economy.

III

Perhaps one of the most striking results of China's agricultural reforms was that it led to the creation of a whole new economic sector that became the most dynamic in China's economy—the rural non-farm sector—the small-scale food-processing plants, machinery repair shops, and increasingly more modern and technology intensive industries that cropped up to meet growing demand among increasingly well-off farmers and to employ the millions of people whose labor was no longer needed on farms. Indeed, the whole structure of China's economy shifted. Agriculture provided more than half of the country's GDP in 1952, and it fell to 14 per cent in 2004. Over the same period, the rural nonfarm sector went from providing almost none of GDP to more than one-third. The growth of this sector not only played a large role in reducing rural poverty in China, but also put pressure to reform on the urban sector, which has been the main engine of growth since the 1990s. In contrast, India is attempting to leapfrog from a predominantly agricultural economy that to without reforming it to a knowledge-based service economy. Neither reforms increased the growth rate of the agriculture nor did it reduce the poverty in an impressive manner. This has caused urban-rural economic divide more in India.

In India, past government spending on irrigation, dominated by creation of large surface irrigation schemes, played an important role in promoting agricultural growth and poverty reduction, but today similar spending has smaller marginal returns, in terms of both growth and poverty reduction. It might be the case that investment in rain fed areas or traditionally lower-potential areas have higher returns today. Indeed, studies have shown that investments in rain fed areas of both countries have had high marginal returns for agricultural growth and poverty reduction. So major investments in harvesting rainwater through watersheds, through public-private partnerships, may help usher in a "multicolored revolution" (not just a "green" one) in agriculture. In both countries there is also vast scope for improving water use efficiency through institutional and management reforms of the existing water systems. India has had useful experiences with water user associations in some selected states, participatory watershed schemes, and community-based rain harvesting. But these successful experiments need to be scaled up to make a significant difference for agriculture growth and poverty reduction. In China providing irrigation system managers with incentives to improve user efficiency had a positive effect on crop yields, the groundwater table, and cereal production.

China has made more progress on rural infrastructure than India. Chinese government investment in power grew at 27 per cent a year from 1953 to 1978 and rural electricity consumption grew at a rate of 27 per cent a year from 1953 to1980, then slowed to 10 per cent a year from 1980 to 1990. In India rural infrastructure did not receive as much attention, particularly in the rural power sector, and thus rural electrification and the establishment of telecommunications connections proceeded more slowly in Indian villages. This slow pace severely affected the growth of agro-processing and cold storage in the rural nonfarm sector. Therefore, it is natural that the levels of processing in Indian agriculture are abysmally low.

In China agro-processing activities are of advanced nature and she has achieved much progress in retail food chains and supermarkets. In other words, there has been some kind of vertical coordination of production, processing, and marketing in China. She has been successful in attracting Foreign Direct

Investment [FDI] in the agro-processing, which India has not done. India can learn so many things from China in this regard. China has been successful in implementing fully land reforms and providing the egalitarian access to land to all. Thus it has succeeded in providing the bulk of rural population with access to a basic means of subsistence and limiting the number of landless. In India, on the other hand, land reforms to make the agrarian structure more equitable after independence were not as successful and left a relatively large number of landless agricultural laborers exposed to the negative consequences of unemployment and underemployment.

It is not true if we say that China is ahead in all respects in developing agriculture. India seems to be better off than China in areas particularly with regard to the institutional infrastructure of rural credit and marketing, although the reach of its services may not be perfect. China has to foster institutions providing timely credit and marketing facilities to marginal and small farmers.

WTO China and India

The inevitable restructuring and adjustments involved in opening-up agricultural trade flows on account of the fact that both countries have become members of the WTO will produce both winners and losers. India has been benefited partially from WTO in more than one way. Of late, exports of fresh fruits and vegetables, mango, grapes flowers etc. have been possible in a substantial quantity. For instance, exports of mango have increased from Rs. 30 crores in 1999-2000 to Rs. 70 crores in 2001-02. So is the case of grapes, pineapples and apples where India has the comparative advantage. In the field of vegetables also India enjoys one of the greatest competitive advantages despite a substantial transport cost; she exports fresh vegetables to number of countries in EU and with ever growing interest in India's cusine, the demand for her vegetables will increase, in future. Another area, which is allied to agriculture and where in we have achieved impressive growth in recent years, is 'Aquaculture'. It has emerged as a big industry in India, employing 1.2 million people in places like Cochin, a trading and fishing port ruled over the centuries by the Portuguese, Dutch and British that call itself the Queen of the Arabian Sea.

India exported shrimp and other marine produce worth $ 1.42 billion in the year (March) 2003, with the United States accounting for nearly 30 per cent of the revenues. Shrimp Farming and its growth owes a lot to the liberalization, as in 1991 it was wrapped in gold and full of dollars and it continued to be so for over a decade. Now, U.S. is levying anti-dumping duties on our shrimp exports and the business has slumped a lot. However, things can be sorted out with the US government, in the near future. Exports of organic products are another promising area. The U.S.A. has been the biggest market for India's organic produce exports, followed by European countries. To be specific, India exported about 6,412 metric tonnes of organic farm products in 2004 including spices, rice and fruits. Further, exports of them to European countries is set to shoot-up with the country expected to get the much-awaited status of "equivalence with European Union", regarding certification of organic produce by January 2006. Besides this, Karnataka would stand to gain from the equivalence status with the European Union as that would provide wider scope for exports of state's organic horticulture produce and fruits to European countries. A major shift in farm production toward non-food grains such as livestock, fish, and horticulture has been well under way in India and China since the 1990s. As European Union (EU) countries switch more to organic foods for value addition the two big developing countries, and also others in Latin America are beginning to catch up Now, China and India are emerging as new giants in production of organic food. Organic farming could also create new jobs in rural areas and help reduce urban migration. Such farming is now becoming more organised in India and China, "which together host more than half the world's farming households in India, there has also been remarkable growth, but primarily in the domestic markets, with about 2.5 million hectares now under organic certification and 332 new certifications issued during 2004. Currently more than 26 million hectares of farmland are under organic management world-wide, but that is believed to be just one to two percent of all agricultural production. Further, in China, organic farming offers the potential for sustainable poverty reduction.

However, domestic producers of crops for which the country lacks a comparative advantage (such as edible oils in India and wheat and maize in China) have suffered increasingly from falling prices induced by an increase in imports. It has already happened in India. However, membership in the WTO can provide useful external pressure to improve efficiency and implement reforms, particularly for tradable inputs such as seeds, fertilizers, farm machinery, and pesticides, where markets are regarded as inefficient because of either government intervention or lack of infrastructure. The implementation of the various agreements under the WTO can facilitate the role of the government in providing services related to information, marketing facilities, technical assistance, and laws and regulations related to standards and quality control. In addition, broad-based structural adjustments in the economy may depress rural incomes and increase opportunities in the manufacturing and service sectors, located primarily in urban areas. These inter-sectoral adjustments are likely to result in a reduction in the size of the primary sector, which will release additional unskilled labor into the labour markets. The rural population will gain if it is able to shift to more profitable off-farm occupations. Investment in rural education will be crucial in increasing farmers' ability to move out of farming. It will also be important to increase investments in rural R&D and infrastructure in order to enhance productivity.

Further, both China and India can gain tremendously by learning from each other, as WTO policies are dictated by the present three economic power houses, i.e. USA European Union [EU] and Japan. China has already attained economic height and India is started to gather momentum in this regard, and they can play an active role in uniting other developing nations when it comes to protect the interests of them. At the same time, both need to address their weaknesses and build on their strengths in order to achieve their national goals and fulfill the aspirations of their people. If both of them fail in ending the exploitation of strong member countries of WTO [what is nick-named Whose Trade Organization] then the same organization provides an opportunity to them to join hands and create a third bloc of countries besides the EU and US in trade negotiations. However, from now onwards, both the countries have to promote rural diversification and vertical coordination in a speedier way.

Poverty Alleviation Programmes and their Implementation

To begin with, both India and China were very poor. Historical analysis suggests that China and India had the same real per capita income in 1870. However by 1950, when the Communist regime took over, China's per capita income had declined by 17% while India's had increased by 16%. It took nearly two and half decades, for China to recover the lost ground with double India's rate of growth of per capita income. However, although both countries experienced acceleration in growth during 1980-2000 compared to the previous three decades, China's average growth rate of per capita income, at nearly 9% per year, far exceeded India's 4% per year, so that China's per capita income was nearly 70% higher than that of India in 2000. Official data for China suggest that rural poverty declined by 85% between 1978 and 1998, while in India it declined by 50% during more or less the same period. Perhaps, two reasons may be given for India's lackluster performance. Firstly, money spent on poor is not reaching them. Former Prime Minister late Mr. Rajeev Gandhi rightly remarked in a meeting that only 15 paisa out of one rupee is reaching the really needy persons. Notwithstanding the fact that there have always been and still are an enormous number of schemes aimed at poverty alleviation, but their aggregate effect in reducing poverty was negligible until late 1980s when things started improving. Secondly, we have not yet implemented 'reforms' in the agricultural sector. Until it happens not much of acceleration in the rate of reduction of rural poverty can be expected. Ours is a 'debating society' in which political differences are expressed freely, policy-making is exposed to pressure by various interest groups, and thus there will be long debates before decisions are made. As a result, implementation is slowed by the lengthy bureaucratic procedures, set-up to ensure checks and balances. China under communist regime in the past and a strong and dictatorial government has been able to take decisions faster and, that is why, the implementation is faster and effective. Democracy is both a plus and minus point as it can avoid disastrous courses of action such as the 'Great Leap Forward' in 1958, which resulted in massive famine and the Cultural Revolution from 1966 and 1976 which resulted in killing of 20 million people who were against the communist policies. At the same time, it will also dilute the seriousness of reforms like 'land reforms'.

Of late, reforms have also been slowed down at the implementation level by the regulatory environment and enforcement bureaucracy. In particular, as 'agriculture' is the state subject in India and regional parties rule the States, the agricultural reforms pronounced by the Centre are not taken seriously at all. Other things being equal, this makes India to lag behind in implementing agricultural reforms than in China. China has gone ahead of India and during the reform years she relaxed regulations on mobility between rural and urban areas, which gave impetus to the development of the non-farm sector and increased migration for purposes. In addition, the rapid growth of rural non-farm sector in China has been a critical factor in the success of its reforms, in relation to poverty reduction also. China's Township and Village Enterprises [TVEs] provided increasing job opportunities outside agriculture, thereby diversifying and expanding the sources of household income.

Notwithstanding the achievements in the field of poverty reduction which are mentioned above, even now there are some serious regional imbalances in China's development, and 60 per cent of the population still lives in poverty-stricken Western China. However, China has a planned approach to develop interior areas by building large industrial parks and the required infrastructure for the movement of physical goods. Despite disparities in development across the regions, there is little doubt that the living standards for a large fraction of Chinese have improved dramatically over the last decade and this is not the case in India.

IV

Both countries now face tremendous challenges on the path to further prosperity. The task of developing agriculture and poverty reduction is only half completed. Continued growth is a must, owing to pressure from population growth and- the need for employment. It is also a condition for a more stable society. Given the high expectations of their citizens, the lack of growth or even slower growth could lead to unrest in both countries. The limited natural resource base can be a critical constraint to growth. The future economic growth of both countries increasingly depends on imports of energy, for which future prospects are uncertain. Both countries are also among those most severely affected by water shortages. Consequently, future growth must be based on higher efficiency and will require China and India to invest in science and new technologies to harness energy and water, optimize their economic structures for allocative efficiency, and reform their fiscal, financial, banking, and insurance systems. Both countries must also pursue more pro-poor growth, which is not only a development objective in itself, but also a precondition for future growth in the long-term. The Indian experience shows that small-holder agriculture needs strong institutional support in these areas to grow and prosper. Given the key role of agriculture in poverty reduction and growth in China, public investments that boost agricultural productivity appear warranted. Significant increases in public investments seem unlikely because of budget pressures, so China and India will need to invest existing resources more efficiently. Studies have found that investments in agricultural research, education, and rural roads hold the greatest potential to promote agricultural growth and poverty reduction in both countries for allocative efficiency, and reform their fiscal, financial, banking, and insurance systems. Both countries must also pursue more pro-poor growth, which is not only a development objective in itself, but also a precondition for future growth in the long-term.

China and India can both gain tremendously by learning from each other, as both nations still face a long road ahead. The dragon, i.e., China, has attained height and the elephant, i.e. India, is starting to gather momentum, but both need to address their weaknesses and build on their strengths in order to achieve their national goals and fulfill the aspirations of their people. The lessons learned from the experiences of China and India is also of relevance to other developing countries and the fight against global hunger and poverty. Further, reforms are needed in both countries.

In all, a number of factors help to explain the difference in growth during the pre-reform era: initial conditions, the sequencing and pace of reforms, and the political system, institutions, and regulatory environment. Yet special mention must be made of the fact that China and India achieved remarkable development and growth even as aid as a percentage of GDP in the two countries remained low. This is in direct contrast to most other developing countries and regions, where aid is much higher but commensurate development and poverty reduction outcomes have not been realized. This fact bears an important lesson for developing and developed countries, multilateral agencies, and local NGOs and groups. It questions the very basis of current policy prescriptions that accompany aid packages, not only raising issues related to the efficiency and effectiveness of external aid but also, conversely, revealing the extraordinary and often underestimated capacity of national initiatives and policy actions to halt—and in fact turn—the tide of poverty. In sum, what can we learn from the process of economic reform in these two countries? To reduce poverty faster, one has to begin with Agricultural Reforms.

References

Ahluwalia, M.S. (1978), "Rural Poverty and Agricultural Performance in India", *Journal of Development Studies*, Vol. 14 No. 3 (April).

Ahluwalia, M.S. (1986), Rural Poverty, Agricultural Production and Prices: A Re-examination, in Agricultural Change and Rural Poverty, (Eds.) John W. Mellor and Gunvant M. Desai, Oxford University Press, New Delhi.

Ahluwalia, M.S. (1996), New Economic Policy and Agriculture: Some Reflections, *Indian Journal of Agricultural Economics*, 51:3, July-September.

Datt, G. (1997), "Poverty in India: An Update", International Food Policy, Research Institute (Processed).

Datt, G. (1999), "Has Poverty in India Declined Since the Economic Reforms", World Bank (Processed).

Kallur M.S. (1995), 'Liberalization of Indian Economy with Particular Reference to the New Industrial Policy of 1991", in Liberalization and Globalization of Indian Economy, K.R. Gupta (Ed.) Atlantic Publishers, New Delhi, 1995, pp. 175-169.

———, 'Agreement on Agriculture of WTO Indian Agriculture: Issues and Concerns", in Gopal Reddy (Ed.) Institutional Policy Options for Sustainable Agricultural Development, Dept. of Economics, Osmania University, Hyderabad, March 2004, pp. 96-102.

Maddison, A. (2002), Growth and Interaction in the World Economy: The West and the Rest over the Past Millennium.

Ministry of Finance (2002), Economic Survey 2001-2002, New Delhi, Government of India Press.

Park, A and S. Wang (2001), "China's Poverty Statistics" *China Economic Review*, 12, pp. 384-395.

Prabhakaran Nair, P.K. (2001), "Farm Sector from Green to Gray", *Business Line*, Vol. 8, No. 81, March 23, p. 4.

Ramesh Chand (2001), "Trade Liberalization, Grain Trade Pattern and Food Security Issues in Asia and the Pacific", Working Paper of National Centre for Agriculture Economics and Policy Research, New Delhi, pp. 1-41.

Saha (1996), "Internal Migration, Centre-State Grants and Economic Growth in States of India" IMF Staff Paper, 43, pp. 123-71.

T.N. Srinivasan (1980-2000), China and India: Growth and Poverty.

Srinivasan, T.N. (1989), "Growth and Poverty Alleviation: Lessons from Development Experience," published in French with the title "Croissance et allégement de la pauvreté: les leçons tirées de l'expérience du Développement" in Revue d'économic du développement, 1-2/2001, pp. 115-168.

World Bank (2000), India-Policies to Reduce Poverty and Accelerate Sustainable Development, Report 1971,Washington D.C.

World Bank (2002), World Development Indicators, Washington D.C.

Mobile Industry in India and China : A 'Must-Win' Market

DAN STEINBOCK

INTRODUCTION

In the mobile industry, the road to three billion subscribers in 2010 is paved with a global strategy that must capitalize on seemingly contradictory objectives—winning in the most lucrative markets, where growth is declining, and in the poor but emerging markets, where growth is exploding. In this global strategy, India and China will play a critical role.

'Must—Win' Markets

In 2003, the 10 most populous mobile markets had 846 million subscribers. A great untapped and underserved subscriber population existed world-wide. Only 1.2 billion people lived in developed nations, with about 5.1 billion in the less developed nations, some half of them in India and China.

In the mobile business, the world's most populous country markets in key regions included the following:

- North America: The United States and Canada;
- Western Europe: Germany, Italy, the UK, France and Spain;
- Asia-Pacific: India, China, Japan, Korea and Taiwan
- Eastern Europe: Russia and Poland;
- Latin America: Brazil, Mexico;
- Middle East : Saudi Arabia, Israel and Iran; and
- Africa: South Africa, Morocca and Egypt.

In each case, two to four most populous nations accounted for the majority of subscribers in the region. In the mobile business (as in many other technology-intensive sectors), global industry leadership does not mean leading in all markets. Rather, it means dominating about a dozen strategic 'must-win' markets. In the 1980s, the Asian market was Japan. Like Nordic leadership in western Europe in the 1990s, this superiority was not sustainable. At the end of 2000, China had overtaken Japan as the leading country market in the Asia-Pacific. It had one-third of the regional market share, against Japan, Korea and Thailand. These four market leaders accounted for 80 per cent of the total market and were the lead markets of the region. India held significant potential, but the country's wireless penetration was very low until the late 1990s.

The Next 'Next Big Markets' : Penetration Level

Ideally, the next 'next big markets' should have a large population, rising per capita income and relatively low penetration. In 2003, China led the World Bank's rankings of the most populous nations with 1.3 billion inhabitants. India was second, with 1.1 billion people. And the two were followed by Indonesia (215 million, 4th), and the Philippines (82 million, 13th). Average income per capita should be measured with purchasing power parity (GNI per capita 2003). In the world-wide rankings, China was 119th, followed by the Philippines (128th), Indonesia (142nd), and India (146th). What about penetration? Between 1998 and 2003, India's mobile population grew from 1.2 million to 26.2 million, which translates to 85 per cent in annual growth. That was well ahead the explosive growth in China (62 per cent), Bangladesh (79 per cent), Indonesia (78 per cent), Pakistan and the Philippines (66 per cent). Furthermore, mobile penetration was already 27 per cent in the Philippines, 21 per cent in China, and close to 9 per cent even in Indonesia. In India, it was still just 2.5 per cent. After China, India was the next 'next big market'. Indeed, compared to the massive hyper growth markets of China and India, none of the potential 'next big markets' are quite as impressive.

Drivers in the Emerging Markets

Success in the emerging markets has often resulted from the interplay of three drivers-consolidation among mobile operators, CPP (calling party pays), and, particularly, prepaid services. Initially an instrument to raise revenues among low-income users in Europe, once excluded by monthly payments and credit cheques, prepaid services drive the mobile boom in many emerging markets. In 1995 fewer than 2 per cent of people in most Latin American countries had cell-phones. The introduction of prepaid service sent use skyrocketing. Mobile subscribers jumped from 21 million in 1998 to 176 million in 2004, turning one in three Latin Americans into a cell-phone user. Today, three multinational operators (America Movil, Telefonica and Telecom Italia) serve about 76 per cent of the Latin American market.

The 'calling –party pays' model was widely adopted in the late 1990s. Some 90 per cent of net additions in Latin America are prepaid subscribers. Many of the advanced data services are available for prepaid users. The darker side of the story is that, by end-2008, average revenue per user (ARPU) in Latin America is expected to be less than $ 13, posing a profitability challenge to operators. In both maturing and emerging markets, effective acquisition and retention strategies are becoming critical to survival. Keeping current subscribers is a lot cheaper than attracting new ones.

Dynamics of Maturing/Emerging Markets

The mobile industry is not only innovating in the world's most developed economies. It is also globalising. This evolution has two faces. On the one hand, the most novel technologies and advanced systems are giving rise to sophisticated new services, which are first pioneered, marketed and sold in the mobile lead markets. Most subscribers, however, are outside these OECD markets. In addition to disruptive innovation, the mobile industry is driven by double-digit growth markets. These are no longer in the US, which enjoyed superiority in the mobile business from the 1910s to the mid-1990s. Nor are they in Western Europe, which captured innovation leadership amidst the digital transition, or in Japan, which has dominated service innovation since the end of the 1990s.

In 1998, there were some 200 million mobile customers world-wide. At the end of 2004, the figure had climbed to some 1.6 billion. By 2006, it is expected to be close to 2.6 billion. Rapid growth markets are no longer in the OECD economies, but in emerging markets—particularly in China and India. By the year-end, the number of subscribers in China is expected to exceed 400 million. In India, the growth in mobiles reached 55 million in early 2005. Mobile industry has been globalising for years, but now this process has proceeded to a qualitatively new stage. Maturing markets remain necessary to industry growth, but are no longer sufficient for industry leadership. Emerging markets have become critical to industry leadership. Because of scale economies, size matters. Big is beautiful, but scale does not make emerging markets attractive. Rapid economic growth does—as evidenced by India and China.

It Takes Two

In the maturing markets, high-growth years are behind, penetration is saturating, rivals are consolidating, and competition is about replacement demand and value. In the emerging markets, high-growth years have only begun, penetration is low, rivals are often fragmented, and competition is about original demand and volume. In the maturing economies, the handset market is evolving into a mature consumer electronics segment, with a huge user population that periodically upgrades devices to take advantage of new offerings. In the emerging economies, digital cellular and prepaid markets are still growing rapidly and gaining new, first-time users. Smart industry competitors do not attempt to fight the change; they embrace it. Nokia outlined its strategy to bring

The Next "Next Big Markets"

Economy	*Population 2003*	*GNI/Capita 2003*	*Cellular Mobile Subscribers Per 100 (2003)*
1. China	1,288.40	4,990	21.4
2. India	1,064.40	2,880	2.5
3. United States	291	37,500	54.3
4. Indonesia	214.5	3,210	5.5
5. Brazil	176.6	7,480	26.4
6. Pakistan	148.4	2,060	1.8
7. Russia	143.4	8,950	12
8. Bangladesh	138.1	1,870	1
9. Nigeria	135.6	900	2.6
10. Japan	127.2	28,620	68
11. Mexico	102.3	8,950	25.5
12. Germany	82.6	27,400	78.5
13. Philippines	81.5	4,640	19.1
14. Vietnam	81.3	2,490	3.4
15. Turkey	70.7	6,690	40.8
16. Ethiopia	68.6	710	0.1
17. Egypt	67.6	3,940	8.5
18. Iran	66.4	7,190	5.1
19. Thailand	62	7,450	26
20. France	59.7	27,460	69.6

the benefits of mobility to new growth markets, while introducing two new mobile phones-Nokia 1110 and 1600—for first–time users and consumers in growth markets like Africa.

By the end of this year, Nokia anticipates Africa will be home to 100 million subscribers and expects the African subscriber base to double to 200 million by 2009. With mobile voice and data, the mobile leaders seek to accelerate the adoption of mobile multimedia services in maturing markets—while enabling emerging markets to leapfrog dated technology solutions.

The interplay of innovation and diffusion is under transformation. Think of the car industry in the early post-War era. The most innovative and desirable models were designed, produced and marketed in the US; first for the wealthy but, over time, for the not-so-wealthy too. Today, this interplay occurs on a worldwide basis.

The Future

The faster the growth of the mobile in China and India, the better will be the chances of profitability for the mobile giants in Europe and the US—as the world's industry giants begin to look more like the customers they are supposed to serve.

In the 1980s, world-wide fashions still originated from California. Today, new fads and influences can pop up in many corners of the world, from Silicon Valley to Helsinki and London, from Seoul to Tokyo. Tomorrow, these feedback effects will escalate, from Hong Kong to Shanghai, from Bangalore to Mumbai.

31

India-China Trade : A Long Road Ahead

PALLAVI AIYAR

INTRODUCTION

Indian Industry is gearing up to flex its muscles in the heart of China, with the fourth Made in India show was held in Beijing from September 8 to 11, 2006. Organised by the Confederation of Indian Industry (CII) in partnership with the Indian Embassy in Beijing, the multi-sectoral exhibition will open amidst a backdrop of booming bilateral trade. Recently released statistics from China's customs authorities reveal that Sino-Indian trade in the first seven months of 2006 has reached $ 13.6 billion, up 27 per cent from the same period the previous year. It is thus widely expected that the trade target set during Chinese Premier Wen Jiabao's visit to India in April 2005, of $ 20 billion by 2008, will be met by the end of this year itself. Indeed, since the start of the new century, every ambitious target set for bilateral trade has proved not to be ambitious enough, the statistics zooming ever upwards with a momentum seemingly of their own.

"Chindia"

In 2005, India-China trade increased by 37 per cent over 2004 to touch $ 18.7 billion. Just three years earlier in 2002 the total volume of bilateral trade was a paltry $ 5 billion. China replaced Japan as India's top trade partner in North East Asia a few years ago and is now on track to overtake the United States to become India's number one trading partner within the next few years. Indo-U.S. trade stands at about $ 30 billion. Last year, more than 100 bilateral trade delegations crossed the Himalayas to seek out opportunities for trade and investment. Over 80 Indian companies have opened shop in China and some 45 Chinese firms now have operations in India. On the surface, this is a veritable economic renaissance providing evidence for the emergence of an economic colossus, 'Chindia,' that bring together the might of two of the world's fastest growing economies. But scratching the surface reveals any celebration of 'Chindia' to be chimerical. Serious, continuing flaws in the structural composition of trade and a disappointingly low investment engagement mean that there are many miles to go before the Sino-Indian economic relationship can have the kind of significance that exists in China's relations with its truly weighty trading partners.

Burgeoning Trade

Moreover, despite considerable improvement in political ties the lack of a final settlement on the boundary dispute between the two neighbours makes it difficult to totally dispel the mutual suspicion that has characterized bilateral ties for long. While burgeoning trade has helped provide momentum to the sweetening of previously sour relations on the political front, economic engagement can never be truly unfettered until full normalization of political ties is complete. In 2005, China's total trade volume was worth $ 1.4 trillion. Sino-U.S. bilateral trade reached $ 204.7 billion and Sino-Japanese trade $ 189.4 billion. India was merely the 16th largest exporting nation to China in 2005, a drop of one place compared to 2004 and the 13th biggest importer of Chinese products. In the first seven months of this year, India accounted for only 1.47 per cant of China's total imports and 1.46 percent of China's aggregate exports.

Composition of Trade Basket

Longer-term commitments are even less impressive. Indian investment in China currently stands at $ 130 million. By contrast, by the end of 2005, U.S. businesses had actually invested $ 51.1 billion in China and set up 49,000 enterprises in the country. Last year alone, China's total RDI inflows were worth $ 72 billion. Chinese investments in India are not much cause for celebration either. According to the Indian Government, FDI inflows to India from China between August 1991 and October 2005 worked out to a grand total of $ 2.03 million. Chinese statistics put the figure considerably higher at about $ 47.35 million but given that India's total inward FDI for the same period stood at $ 36.2 billion, even this number is distinctly unimposing.

On the trade front, the major continuing worry is the composition of the trade basket. India's exports to China are overwhelmingly dominated by low-value, primary products with a huge reliance on iron ore. In 2005, ores, slag, and ash comprised 56 per cent of India's exports to China with a year-on-year growth rate of 28 per cent. Despite Indian trade officials having repeatedly expressed concern over the lopsided nature of this export composition, in the first seven months of this year iron ore continued to dominate exports to China and comprised some 50 percent of total exports. Undue reliance on a single commodity is far from ideal. If the iron and steel industry in China were to experience a new direction it would dramatically impact on Indian exports. China's ongoing construction boom cannot be expected to last forever. Driven by fears of overheating, the authorities in Beijing have in fact been trying to tighten growth at the macro-level for then last several months. The impact of these measures on Indian exports is already being felt. In the first six months of 2006 Indian exports of iron ore thus decreased for the first time in years, by almost 16 per cent (in contrast iron ore exports had exploded by almost 23.3 per cent in 2004). As a result, despite a sharp increase in exports of some commodities like raw cotton, overall Indian exports to

China declined by 1.16 per cent in the first half of this year compared to the same period during 2005.

Bucking the trend of the last few years, India has thus developed a trade deficit with China of $ 858.5 million. Last year India's trade surplus with China stood at $ 843.2 million, itself a decline from the $ 1.74 billion surplus in 2004. The fact that primary products such as iron ore and raw cotton dominate India's exports also means that the benefits of value addition including increased employment, higher profitability, technological upgradation, and so on are lost. By contrast China's top exports to India include electrical machinery and machinery. These together accounted for 43.9 per cent of total Indian imports from China in 2005. Trade associations such as CII and the Indian Embassy in Beijing have identified certain sectors they believe have strong potential for growth in trade including dairy products, machine tools, power and energy sector ancillaries, and certain segments of apparel. The upcoming Made in India Show will feature products from some of these sectors.

However, trade alone cannot provide long term stability to a bilateral economic relationship, given that it is affected by a gamut of short-term circumstances and can as a result prove fickle. The example of iron ore is a case in point. Mutual investments are thus crucial to a truly sustainable economic engagement. Indian companies have begun to be attracted by the opportunities China offer in recent years. Its high volume, low-cost investment environment, connectivity to global markets, productive labour force, and the presence on Chinese shores of large numbers of multinational clients have lured a small but steady stream of Indian investors in diverse sectors including IT, pharmaceuticals, banking, wind farm equipment, auto components, and tire manufacturing.

Yet the majority of these investors in both the manufacturing and services sectors either sell to MNCs in China or export their products out of China to their traditional buyers. The meaty Chinese domestic market remains an imposing Great Wall that few Indian firms have been able to scale so far. Even the much-hyped synergies between India's software prowess and China's hardware might have failed to materialize. All the big Indian IT companies such as TCS, Wipro, Infosys, and

Satyam have invested in China. However, despite predictions that Indian companies could come to account fro up to 40 per cent of the $ 30 billion domestic Chinese market for software, so far none of India's IT heavyweights has been able to make a dent in this market.

Foreign-owned companies continue to be kept out of the really Large, multimillion dollar IT deals at the state-owned enterprises and Indian companies have found barriers like language and culture more challenging to overcome that expected. Conversely, low levels of Chinese investments in India are explained by Sujan Chinoy, former Indian Consul General in Shanghai, as there simple "being very few commercial reasons for them (the Chinese) to invest until such time as India acquires the importance of a high-value market to them with the attendant weightage that a large bilateral economic engagement brings."

In addition, Chinese investments in Indian infrastructure projects continue to repeatedly be blocked due to "security" concerns. For example, New Delhi has reportedly decided that it does not want any Chinese companies investing in or managing any Indian ports. Chinese telecom companies such as Huawei have also been refused permission for investments in India in the recent past, out of fears of Chinese espionage. Such fears underline the continuing vein of mistrust that lies deep in Sino-Indian ties even as Beijing and New Delhi attempt to forgo a new "strategic partnership."

From running scared of China, there does seem to be an increasing willingness to engage with it on the part of India Inc. The fact that he upcoming Made in India Show is taking place in China for the fourth year running is evidence. But both industry and policy-makers need to go beyond cheering the numbers for bilateral trade and look to address the underlying fundamentals that are in need of transformation if India and China are to develop the kind of economic linkages that would give real depth to their bilateral ties and forge the type of formidable partnership that advocates of 'Chindia' hope for.

32

Can India and China Emerge as Superpowers?

S. IYYAMPILLAI AND P. BALAMURUGAN

INTRODUCTION

After the Independence, India adopted a mixed economic policy to achieve socialistic pattern of economic development. However, since 1991, after the introduction of New Economic Policy in 1991, the severe liberalization process has been unleashed. In parallel, structural reforms were also introduced in a strict socialistic country, namely China, in the last two decades mainly in the form of market reforms. With the introduction of structural reforms, these two countries are expected to emerge as economic superpowers within the 21st century. The story of rise and fall of many superpowers in the past tells us the fact that no country in the world could sustain the eternal superpower. In the 1900s, the United Kingdom was also one of the superpowers in the world, which lost its superpower status after the Second World War. The former

USSR due to policy changes there, lost its superpower status and thus USA became the only world superpower. In future, the USA may be replaced by some other country. Thus, the privilege of superpower status is not a permanent phenomenon of a country. Now, India and China have entered into a new phase of economic development. In this context, the present paper attempts to understand the real meaning of the slogan of "India and China—The Emerging Superpowers in the 21st Century."

Meaning of Superpower

A superpower is a state with the first rank in the international system and the ability to influence events and project power on a world wide scale. Naturally, the superpower comes when a country is having sound economic and military background. The word superpower was popularized at the international level during the Cold War period between the USA and the USSR.

Criteria for Superpower

The criteria for superpower are not clearly defined. However, the following factors are all generally associated with the superpower status of a country.

1. State of the Economy

A world superpower should have a sound economy characterized by good access to raw materials, large volume of production of goods and services with high productivity, a leading position in international trade as well as global financial markets, innovation, and the ability to accumulate capital.

2. Military Status

A superpower should have a strong military characterized by relative invulnerability and ability to deter or cause great damage to its opponent country and should have the capacity to effectively project unified military power globally, including nuclear weapons. However, nuclear weapons alone do not necessarily make a nation superpower.

3. Geographical and Demographic Status

In general, a superpower should have a wide land under

its control. Territory allows a country to mine minerals and grow food, assuring its self–sufficiency. It is an important factor in warfare time. Even a richer country with smaller territory is more vulnerable in military sense. A superpower should have healthy and well educated citizens accompanied with strong cultural background. The gender equality should be maintained and the women participation in the workforce should be appreciated. During the Second World War the women participation in the American workforce increased to a remarkable extent. This was very helpful to tempo the economic development of America at the global level.

THE HISTORY OF ECONOMIC DEVELOPMENT IN USA AS A SUPERPOWER

At present, USA is the only existing superpower in the world. It is a federal republic in North America, founded in 1776. The USA originated from thirteen colonies in British North America that declared their independence in 1776. After winning the American Revolutionary War, it was recognized as an independent nation by the British following the Treaty of Paris in 1783. Since then, the nation has expanded across the North American Continent and also has acquired a number of overseas territories, adding 37 more states in the process. By the 1830's, the nation was in a compulsion to address the problem of states right, the role of federal government and the expansion of slavery. The nation's failure to resolve these problems led to American Civil War. During the Civil War time there were lots of technological advancements made in the country. After the Civil War, a large number of unprecedented immigrants were settled in the country. They provided labour to the American industry together with national infrastructure building. They were responsible for the country's rise to international power.

During the 1920s, USA enjoyed an unbalanced prosperity as farm prices fell and industrial profits grew. A rise in debt and an inflated stock market culminated in a crash in 1929, triggering the Great Depression. The nation did not fully recover until 1941. The USA did not directly involve in the Second World War until the attack on Pearl Harbor by the Japanese. The World War II was the costliest war in American history, but helped the nation to pull the economy out of depression as the required production of military material provided much–needed jobs. After the World War II, the United States and the Soviet Union became rival superpowers in the world. This led to series of proxy wars between these two countries. During the Cold War period, the American society experienced a period of sustained economic expansion. In 1991, the Soviet Union was disintegrated owing to various socio and political reasons. Since then, the United States continues to be the only superpower in the world.

India in Brief

India is the largest democratic and secular country in the world with the seventh rank in geographical area in the international order; and stays as a second most populated country in the world. At the time of Independence, India was an agricultural country with a higher contribution by agriculture in the country's GDP. However, now it is developing towards an industrialized country with a comparatively lower concentration of agriculture in the country's GDP. The textiles, chemicals, food-processing, steel, transportation equipment, cement, mining, petroleum and machinery are the major industries in India. Still, agriculture plays its rightful role in the country's economy with the huge volume of production of rice, wheat, oilseed, cotton, jute, tea, sugarcane, potatoes, and cattle like buffalo, sheep, goats, poultry and fish. With its rich natural resources, huge level of man power and its planned development, now India becomes the fastest growing major economy in the world, with a GDP growth rate of 8.4 per cent at the end of the first quarter of 2006.

China in Brief

The People's Republic of China is a country in East Asia with a population of over 1.3 billion people. With its fast growing population, China has been the most populated country in the world for a long time. The Communist Party of China has led the country under a one-party system since the country's establishment in 1949. In China, greater attention is paid to develop both agriculture and industrial sector simultaneously. China ranks first in the world in farm output;

around half of China's labour force is engaged in agriculture. It produces rice, wheat, potatoes, sorghum, peanuts, tea, millet, barley, cotton, oilseeds and livestock and fish on a larger scale. In industrial output, China ranks third in the world. In China, the main industries are iron and steel, coal, machine building, armaments, textiles and apparel, petroleum, cement, chemical fertilizers, footwear, toys, food processing, automobiles, consumer electronic, telecommunications and electronic information. Machinery and electronic products have become China's main exports. With its huge volume of production of agriculture and industrial products along with its market reforms now China has entered into a new phase of economic development and thus it becomes the fastest growing economy in the world.

Barriers Broken

Before the 1950, China and India had no much political or economic ties. In 1962, these countries had a war on border disputes. In continuation of the war, these countries had worsened relations during the rest of 1960s and early 1970s. During the 1980s, China and India renewed efforts to improve their relations. In 1981, Chinese Minister of Foreign Affairs was invited to India. After the Chinese Minister's visit to India, they held eight rounds of border negotiations between December 1981 and November 1987. These talks raised hopes that progress could be made on the border issue. Since the 1990s, there has been a gradual improvement in these countries' trade and diplomatic relations.

COMPARISON OF MAJOR SOCIO-ECONOMIC INDICATORS OF INDIA AND CHINA WITH THE UNITED STATES OF AMERICA

Social Indicators

China ranks first in world population followed by India. USA ranks fifth in world population. India is having highest population growth rate of 1.38 per cent when compared with the growth rate of 0.91 per cent and 0.59 per cent of USA and China respectively. The literacy rate is 99 per cent in USA. China is having the satisfactory literacy rate of 91 per cent. Whereas, in

India, almost half of the population is illiterate. The life expectancy is very high in USA when compared with China and India. Though China is the highly populated country in the world, it has a very low unemployment rate of 4.2 per cent when compared with 5.1 per cent and 9.9 per cent in USA and India respectively. Even after the 50 years of Independence, 25 per cent of India's population lives below the poverty line. Though USA is the richest country in the world with superpower status, 12 per cent of its population lives below the poverty line, which is higher when compared with China. In China, only 10 per cent of population lives below the poverty line. China follows USA in many social indicators and even performs better than USA in certain social indicators like unemployment rate, population below the poverty line and the population growth rate. Whereas in India, many social indicators have to be improved to a remarkable extent (Table 32.1).

TABLE 32.1

Social Indicators in USA, China and India in 2005

S. No	*Particulars*	*USA*	*China*	*India*
1.	Population (In Crores)	29.84	131.39	109.54
2.	International Rank in Population	5	1	2
3.	Population Growth Rate (In Percentage)	0.91	0.59	1.38
4.	Literacy Rate (In Percentage)	99	91	59.5
5.	Life Expectancy (In Years)	78	73	64
6.	Unemployment Rate (In Percentage)	5.1	4.2	9.9
7.	Population Below Poverty Line (In Percentage)	12	10	25

Source : Compiled from The World Fact Book—2006, USA.

Recorded Crime Rate

The major crimes like homicide, rapes, robberies, thefts, burglaries and drug offenses are very high in America when compared with China and India. The crime rate is almost same in China and India. In the year 1999, the crime rate was recorded at 8517.19 in USA, which was higher when compared to 179.95 and 176.82 recorded in China and India respectively. In the same year the rape was recorded at 32.05 in USA and it was recorded at 3.15 and 1.55 in China and India respectively. Thefts were recorded at 2502.66 in USA and it was recorded a very low rate of 115.79 and 27.25 in China and India respectively. It can be strongly concluded that USA ranks top in all the reported crime incidence when compared to China and India (Table 32.2). Underreporting may also be a reason for lower crime incidence in India.

TABLE 32.2
Crime Rate in USA, China and India in 1999
(Rate per 1,00,000 inhabitants)

Recorded Crime	*Country*		
	USA	*China*	*India*
Homicide	4.55	NA	3.72
Assaults	805.21	7.42	23.68
Rapes	32.05	3.15	1.55
Robberies	147.36	15.89	2.85
Thefts	2502.66	115.79	27.25
Burglaries	755.29	NA	11.15
Drug Offenses	560.11	NA	2.02
Bribery	NA	NA	0.36
Grand Total	8517.19	179.95	176.82

Source : Compiled from the Seventh United Nations Survey of Crime Trends and Operations of Criminal Justice Systems, covering the period 1998-2000.

Economic Indicators

In the Gross Domestic Product (GDP), USA ranks first in the world with a GDP of $ 13.36 trillion followed by European Union and China. In its GDP, the service sector contributes more than 78 per cent. India ranks fifth with a GDP of $ 3.61 trillion. In its GDP, the agriculture contributes 20.6 per cent which is higher when compared with 1.0 per cent and 14.4 per cent in USA and China respectively. In USA, agriculture plays only a minor role. China and India have favourable growth rates of

GDP with 9.9 per cent and 7.6 per cent respectively. However, China and India recorded a low level of per capita income when compared with USA. The per capita income in USA is more than 12 times larger than that in India and more than 6 times larger than that in China. China has the highest industrial production growth rate of 27.7 per cent when compared with 3.2 and 8.2 per cent of USA and India respectively. The USA and China have favourable balance of payment, while India has deficit balance of payment. When compared with the US and China, the external debt management in India is relatively better (Table 32.3).

TABLE 32.3

Economic Indicators in USA, China and India in 2005

Sl. No.	Particulars	USA	China	India
1.	GDP (In Trillion Dollar)	12.36	8.86	3.61
	Components of GDP (In Percentage)			
	Agriculture	1.0	14.4	20.6
	Industry	20.7	53.1	28.1
	Services	78.3	32.5	51.4
2.	Growth Rate in GDP (In Percentage)	3.5	9.9	7.6
3.	Per Capita Income (In Dollar)	41800	6800	3300
4.	Industrial Production Growth Rate (In Percentage)	3.2	27.7	8.2
5.	Export (In Trillion Dollar)	9.28	7.52	0.76
6.	Import (In Trillion Dollar)	1.73	6.32	1.13
7.	External Debt (In Trillion Dollar)	8.84	2.42	1.19

Source : Compiled from The World Fact Book—2006, USA.

Military Status and Other Indicators

The USA ranks first in the world in military expenses followed by China. USA spends more than 6 times larger than what China spends and more than 27 times larger than what India spends. With larger military expenses, USA has got the strongest and the most powerful military in the world. India ranks ninth in its military expenses. The percentage of military expenses in GDP is relatively higher in China when compared with USA and India. Chinese army is the largest one in the world with a manpower of more than 2.5 crores. The US ranks third in its geographical area after Russia and Canada. China follows USA. India gets 7th rank in its geographical area (Table 32.4).

TABLE 32.4
Military Status and Other Indicators in USA, China and India in 2005

Sl. No.	*Particulars*	*USA*	*China*	*India*
1.	Military Expenditure (In Billion Dollar)	518.1	81.48	19.04
2.	Military Expenditure in GDP (In Percentage)	4.06	4.3	2.5
3.	Manpower Engaged in Military (In Crores)	0.42	2.55	2.21
4.	Geographical Area (In International Rank)	3rd	4th	7th

Source : Compiled from The World Fact Book—2006, USA.

Can China and India Attain the Superpower Status?

In the 21st century, it is widely talked that China and India have the potential to become world superpowers. In the first decade of the 21 century, China and India are receiving the global attention to a remarkable extent. With increased participation in the global trade, they play an important role in the global economy. When compared with India, the China's impact on the global economy has been more visible. Comparing India, China records a better performance in terms of many of its socio and economic indicators like the volume of GDP, growth rate in GDP, poverty and unemployment rate etc. The proportion of Foreign Direct Investment in total investment and GDP is quite satisfactory in China when compared with India. Though China is a communist country, it was able to attract huge level of foreign investment. It is obvious that the

China's participation in the global scene is significantly larger than that of India. The China's share in the US imports rose from 6 per cent in 1995 to 15 per cent in 2004. The OECD's Economic Survey of China predicts that it will overtake the USA to become the world's largest exporter by 2010. It is estimated that within a few years, China will outstrip USA in the number of households accessing internet in their home itself. China's share of the world demand for key base metal has risen from 5-7 per cent in the early 1990s to 20-25 per cent at present; it holds the world's largest currency reserves, amounting to US $ 670 billion. Hence, China is likely to become the world's largest economy by 2020. In parallel, India is playing an important role among the developing countries. In the first quarter of 2006, it is estimated that the economy of India is the fourth largest in the world as measured by Purchasing Power Parity (PPP), with a GDP of US $ 3.63 trillion. However, in the GDP per capita, India is ranked 122nd in the world. In IT sector, India closely follows USA. Bangalore in Karnataka has become the Indian Silicon Valley. India is also becoming one of the important players in the global scene. China and India perform better than USA in terms of their growth. This merely would not help them to become world superpowers and to outstrip USA. Though USA records a relatively lower growth rate in GDP when compared with China and India, the absolute GDP in USA is many folds larger than China and India. China and India are not self-sufficient in many grounds. China and India depend heavily on Western countries for their technological upgradation. These countries' scientific efforts are satisfactory; but not enough to overcome or compete with the Western countries. These countries' dependency on Western countries may continue even up to the end of 21st century. Even now, China and India have to address some fundamental socio and economic problems like extensive poverty and unemployment. Hence, definitely, China and India will not overcome USA within the 21st century. However, it can be safely concluded that by 2025–2030, the USA, China, India and possibly the Europe will constitute four substantial poles of power in architecture of global governance.

Should China and India attain the Superpower?

The history demonstrates the fact that concentration of power always gives birth to many inhuman activities. The USA is the practical example for that. It is criticized by many fronts that the present superpower USA acts as a global police with its strong economy and military power. It has global control and challenges the sovereignty of many developing countries in the world. Almost all the countries in the world directly or indirectly depend on the USA. The USA intervenes in the domestic affairs of many countries in the world in an unfair manner to maintain its superpower status. In the last 50 years, the USA has conducted more than 200 aggressive wars including Korean War (1950-53), Lebanon (1958), Cuba (1962), Vietnam War (1964-73), Cambodia (1970), Salvador (1981), Egypt (1983), Bolivia (1986), Gulf War (1987), Panama (1988), Kosovo (1993), Albania (1997), Sudan (1998), Afghanistan (2001) and Iraq (2003). USA is the only country in the world conducting large number of imperialistic aggressive wars. With its global influence, it has imposed economic ban on many countries and caused severe damages to the countries like Cuba, Angola, Nicaragua sometimes on India and Pakistan also. The USA is criticized for its imperialistic foreign policy and political conspiracy. It has caused collapse of governance in many countries and established the puppet government. With its intervention in the domestic affairs of many countries, it is said that USA is introducing new pattern of colonization and acts as a world-wide colonial ruler. Apart from these external evils caused by USA, the country itself has lots of unhealthy features. The USA declared itself as a strongest democracy in the world. So far, USA has justified all its aggressive wars in the name of democracy and acts as a global authority to maintain democracy and human rights. However, the country itself is not democratic even in the treatment of its own citizens. It treated the black people as slaves for a long period; even now the black people are fighting for their rights and equality. It is obvious that colour partiality is severe in USA. It was said that the relief measures taken by the government were very poor during hurricare Katrina; the main reason was that all the affected regions were black people's settlements; many anti-human and anti-social activities were also reported there. During the same period, India had a severe flood in Mumbai, the relief and rehabilitation works done by the Indian Government were highly appreciated by the international community.

Inter-personal relationship was also extremely good. It is obvious that the present American society has been beset by the social problems like increasing rates of murder, gun violence, drug and excessive alcohol abuse, family breakup, homelessness, wealth concentration, poverty, obesity and imprisonment etc. The crime rate is very high in USA. It ranks first in the number of prisoners in the world; it is more than 20 lakhs. The data base on crime incidence in the US is very poor. It appears that the US government deliberately hides the statistics on crime incidence in the country. Due to rapid modernization and urbanization, American life has become more materialized. The faith on marriage and family values have almost vanished. This has caused harmful demographic situations in the US. It is estimated that close to 60 per cent of first marriage end in divorce in America. Britney Spears is a popular pop singer in America. She got divorced just after 5 minutes of her marriage. It is noteworthy that about 40 per cent of American children are living with single parent family. The current American generation thinks that marriage inhibits personal liberation. This has caused fast spread of non-marriage culture in American society. The number couples having children out-of-wedlock goes on increasing in the US. Due to the social alienation and mechanization of life, the mental depression has become the common problem in American society. It is said that USA ranks first in the mentally sick population in the world. USA is the highly polluting country in the world. The US has caused severer environmental problems like high levels of air pollution and over depletion of non-renewable resources, etc. USA is accounted for only 5 per cent in the world population, but it causes more than 25 per cent of Carbon Dioxide emission in the world. The country's economic development is also criticized for, it has widened the economic disparity. It is noteworthy that the entire American economy is controlled by only a few hands. Silicon Valley in USA is the fastest wealth generating region in the country; however, the number of homeless people also goes on increasing in the same place. USA has this kind of developmental paradoxes in almost all the segment of its development. By understanding the negative consequences of American mode of development, China and India should not aim to become a superpower like USA. Instead, they should aim to attain economic development with human face consisting of socio-economic, ecological equality and balance and friendly diplomatic relations with the rest of the world.

Suggestions

The following measures are suggested for China and India to become the superpowers in the 21st century.

1. The abnormal population in these two countries causes lots of hurdles for the rapid economic expansion. Hence, China and India should take some serious measures to control and reduce its ever increasing population in order to obtain higher per capita income.
2. In the globalized and liberalized world environment, China and India should welcome the foreign investors to invest more in their countries. India should find some prospective avenues to attract foreign investors.
3. In the present market oriented development, China and India should take some serious efforts to enhance their competitiveness to become the global market leaders. These countries have got strong domestic market. If these countries could eliminate the role played by the external players in their domestic market then that would lead these countries to achieve still higher economic development.
4. To become superpowers, China and India should invest more on building infrastructures to the international standards, for they play an important role in the development of a country.
5. China and India should control their external debt for their healthy economic development. The external debt should be used only for the productive purposes.
6. In the present modernized world, technology plays a predominant role. Hence, to become superpower, China and India still have to pay greater attention for the scientific and technological development.
7. As China and India are in their take off stage, they should have a friendly diplomatic relation with the present superpower the US for their smooth economic development.

8. China and India should reduce their military expenses so that they can spend more on developmental projects.

CONCLUSION

In real terms, the superpower status of a country should mean the improved well-being of its citizens. The present superpower has experienced economic development with wider social disparity and injustices. It is noteworthy that richest country in the world has more than 12 per cent of its population below the poverty line; spread its negative externality to other countries and at the same time capsized the positive externalities of other countries. With the background of the evil experiences of USA, the concept of development should be seriously reviewed. The economic planning of a country should not aim merely to become the world superpower; instead it should aim at improving the well-being of its people with social justice and economic equality. China and India have the potential to become the superpower with their fast growing GDP. Yet, they have to address their fundamental problems like poverty, unemployment, etc. Hence, China and India should aim at development with human face.

References

Arvind Virmani (2005), "A Tripolar Century: USA, China and India", Working Paper No 160, *Indian Council for Research on International Economic Relations, New Delhi.*

Central Intelligence Agency (2006), "The World Fact Book—2006", USA.

Friedman, T.L., (2005), "The World is Flat—A Brief History of the Twenty-first Century", *Farrar, Straus and Girous, New York*

Institute for American Values (1995), "Marriage in America: A Report to Nation", New York, USA.

James Gustave Speth (2004), "Red Sky at Morning: America and the Crisis of the Global Environment", Yale University Press, USA.

Jimmy Carter (2005), "Our Endangered Values: America's Moral Crisis", *Simon & Schuster Adult Publishing Group*, New York, USA.

Kennedy, P. (1989), "The Rise and Fall of the Great Powers", Vintage Books, New York.

United Nations Office on Drugs and Crime (2004), "Seventh United Nations Survey of Crime Trends and Operations of Criminal Justice Systems, covering the period 1998-2000, *United Nations*, Washington DC, USA.

Internet Sources.

www.wikipedia.org

India and China : A Win-Win Game

Ashish Gupta

INTRODUCTION

In 1962, Dutch economist and Noble laureate Jan Tinbergen came out with the "gravity theory of trade" and immediately created ripples in the staid world of trade theorists. His theory that trade volumes between two countries were directly correlated to the combined size of their economies and inversely to the distance between them (smaller the distance, larger the trade) provided economists a fundamental tool to study trade patterns between any pair of countries. By his logic, India and China should have been one of the biggest trading blocs in the world by now.

Largest Trading Partners

Unfortunately, however, the two countries have yet to fulfil their enormous potential for trade. But don't write off the gravity theory. Or you'll repeat the mistake some members of a visiting Chinese delegation had made in 1997 when the bilateral trade was still far from the $ 1-billion mark. They brushed aside as a joke a report of the Federation of Indian Chamber of Commerce and Industry (FICCI) that said India-China trade would touch $ 10 billion by 2007. The trade between the two hit $ 18.7 billion in 2005—06, jumping 38% year-on-year. When Saroj Kumar Poddar, President of the same FICCI, told a Beijing audience that the two-way trade might hit $ 100 billion in the near future, nobody laughed. "If such a momentum is maintained, China will become India's largest trading partner in the next two or three years," says India's Commerce and Industry Minister Kamal Nath.

The composition of trade, however, is not much in India's favour. While imports from China are diversified and dominated by value-added products like electronic goods, India's sparse exports basket mostly contains low-cost inputs like iron ore, primary steel, plastics and minerals—with 15 products constituting 89% of the total. If trade is a slow starter, investment is a non-starter. In the last 13 years, for instance, the Indian government has cleared $ 67.15 billion of foreign direct investments (FDI). And the share of China in that was a minuscule 0.3% at $ 231.7 million. Again, during the same period, India granted 7,878 technical collaboration approvals to different countries with China's share being just 70. But then, these low numbers reflect the vast potential that exists for increasing trade and investments. "There is a huge potential for collaboration in various sectors like information technology, IT-enabled services, biotechnology, education, financial services, healthcare, tourism and energy," says Manoj Pant, Professor, School of International Studies, Jawaharlal Nehru University in New Delhi. "It's not only to feed each other's domestic market but also to export to third countries."

The potential is high but the will to fulfil that may be lacking. Call it distrust or fear, there is a strong resistance, particularly on the part of India, to go the whole hog in bilateral ties. "The Chinese will cooperate only in those areas where they have set specific goals to accelerate their development such as software development and energy independence," says Tom Masci, former corporate vice-president (Asia Pacific), Motorola.

Also, the lurking fear of being inundated by cheap goods from the "factory of the world" seems to be high in India Inc, which is opposed to a Free Trade Agreement (FTA) with China. "Unless there are internal reforms, especially those in the country's labour laws, the government should not consider entering into an FTA because there is no level playing field," Rahul Bajaj, Chairman and Managing Director, Bajaj Auto Ltd., told the recent CII annual conference.

"China is still transiting to a full-fledged market economy; the US and the European Union are still to grant China that status," reasons Amit Mitra, Secretary General, FICCI. What it means is that there is little transparency in the costing of products, capital subsidization and other subsidies, which makes Chinese goods unusually competitive in global markets. As a first step, India should go for a preferential trade agreement with China, feels the industry.

There may be some merit in this argument, but even in areas where there is an obvious synergy, the two neighbours have still to come together. The much-hyped marriage of Indian software and Chinese hardware hasn't quite happened. Instead, an element of competition has crept in with the Chinese staking their own claim to the global software pie and India waking-up to the possibility of becoming a low-cost hardware manufacturing hub. Thus both countries are stepping on each other's toes.

Combination of Manufacturing and Services

However, the fact remains that India and China complement each other's strengths. "Chinese manufacturing plus Indian services, Chinese hardware plus India software, will create an ideal win-win situation for both the countries," says Wang Jinzhen, Assistant Chairman of China Council for Promotion of International Trade (CCPIT). Kiran Karnik, President, Nasscom, feels embedded software is an ideal area for mutual collaboration. In China, Indian software players can offer solutions to improve the efficiency of Chinese user industries; they can use Chinese talent in chip design and telecommunication technology; and they can also leverage China as an offshore development center to serve the Japanese market, explains Karnik. Further, China's entry into the World

Trade Organisation (WTO) throws-up opportunities for Indian software providers in banking, securities, telecom, energy and utilites.

In fact, a clutch of Indian IT companies has already set up base in China, although for entirely different purposes. With their American and European clients setting up shops there to take advantage of the low-cost, facilities, the Indian software vendors had no choice but to follow suit. And they are scaling up. Wipro, for example, is looking to set-up a slew of development centers in China in a year or so. "The idea is to utilize the talented local pool for localization, customization as well as product and application testing services for our multinational clients," says Masaki Nagao, CEO, China and Japan Operations, Wipro Technologies.

Satyam Computer Services entered China in January 2002 to use it as an offshore base, but found itself servicing global majors there. It already has four centers—in Beijing, Shanghai, Dalian and Guangzhou—and is now scouting for a 1,000—seat campus in a Tier II city to cut costs. "Not just us, many companies are moving to Tier II or III cities to contain costs," says Virendra Aggarwal, Director and Senior Vice-President, Satyam Asia Pacific, hinting at the rising costs in the big coastal cities of China. Others like TCS, Infosys and Flextronics too are scaling up in China.

IT Education

Another area where Indians are doing well in China is IT education. NIIT was the first off the block, setting up a training center in Shanghai in 1996 in cooperation with Pudong Continuing Education Centre, the education arm of the Municipal Government of Shanghai. Today, NIIT covers over 20 Chinese Universities across 25 provinces and 100 locations. And it has over 25,000 students. "We realized that China was not only the gateway to the Far East, but it was home to a large number of multinationals who needed high quality support for their information, communications and technology requirements," says Prakash Menon, Head of NBIIT operations in China. "We were the first Indian IT training company to launch training curriculum in Mandarin," exults Menon.

Even for the Indian manufacturing players who live in constant fear of a "Chinese invasion", the big neighbour offers hope. "The best way India can emerge as an economic superpower is to learn to match Chinese prices and quality by locating India's manufacturing base in attractive countries outside India," says Vijay Govindarajan, Professor, Dartmouth's Tuck School of Business. Companies like Bajaj Electricals and Bharti have already taken the lead by making China a sourcing base for low-cost electrical appliances and telephone instruments. J.K. Tyres in using China as a base for exporting tyres to Southeast Asia and West Asia, while Videocon is manufacturing internet TV there.

Meanwhile, a number of Chinese companies like Haier, Bird and Huawei are looking to scale up their Indian operations. The government, however, is sitting on a couple of investment proposals including telecom equipment manufacturer Huawei's move to set-up a $ 100-million manufacturing center and Hutchison's proposal to invest in port infrastructure. "The government indecision has jeopardized the company's plan to make India the South Asian regional headquarter," says Wang Wei Jun, Chairman, Huawei Telecommunications (India).

Energy Security

One area China and India have identified for mutual cooperation is energy security. The two have been engaged in a dogfight for oil equity abroad. Last October, China National Overseas Oil Corporation Division (CNOOC) outbid Oil and Natural Gas Corporation (ONGC) in Angola. India also lost out to China in Kazakhstan and the Akpo field in Nigeria. "It's true that Indian enterprises have failed to beat their Chinese counterparts in grabbing energy equity, but the Chinese too had to pay a heavy price for the competition," points out Zheng Ruixiang, Senior Fellow, China Institute of International Studies, Beijing. Agrees Subir Raha, Chairman and Managing Director, ONGC: "We soon realized that unbridled rivalry was a disadvantage to both, regardless of who eventually won the bid because ultimately it was the seller who won":

> And wisdom soon prevailed on both ends. So when ONGC and CNOOC joined hands to bid for Petro-Canada's stakes

in the Al-Furat Petroleum Company in Syria, they won hands down because of their strong bargaining position. The cooperation between the two national oil companies covers the entire oil value chain, from upstream exploration and production to downstream activities such as refining and petrochemicals, marketing of petro products, transmission and city distribution of gas, laying of national and transnational energy pipelines, But all these would require the Indian security establishment to be less paranoid about the involvement of Chinese expertise in domestic energy locations.

Power of ONE

Another important area for India-China cooperation relates to the developmental objectives of the WTO and other international bodies such as IMF and UN. "China and India can offset each one's weaknesses with the other's strong points," says Jinzhen of CCPIT. Whenever the two speak with one voice, the world sits up and takes notice. This was in display during the multilateral trade talks in Doha 2001 where a paper submitted by India and co-sponsored by China ensured that the developed world's efforts to link investment with trade was taken out of the Doha Development Round. That's the power of India-China cooperation.

India-China Economic Ties : Develop a Different Paradigm

RAMGOPAL AGARWAL

INTRODUCTION

China's development performance during the last quarter of a century has been impressive and perhaps the most important event on the world economic stage. Impressive, especially because China has sustained over the last 25 years the highest growth rate of income achieved by any major economy. And it did so by relying on its own resources and with remarkable stability in inflation and growth rate. Significant also because it impacted the lives of 1.3 billion people—far more than that by the rise of all Western nations and many times that affected by the rise of Japan and the Asian Tigers.

China's Potential

Today, more than a few years back, there is a much better appreciation in India of the potential of China for trade and investment. Yet, by and large, the understanding of the ground reality of China remains shallow and there is a strong undercurrent of suspicion in India-China economic relations. This attitude does not serve us well for exploiting the opportunities presented by an economy that is likely to become the biggest market for goods and services within a decade, surpassing the US by a long chalk. It is about time, a different paradigm is developed.

One should first recognize that what is happening in India and China is a historical process that is shifting the centre of gravity of the world economy to Asia. This is the inevitable consequence of the working of global market forces, which are bringing about a process of facts price equalization between the East and the West.

However, though this will be a fulfillment of the Western principles of equality, democracy and markets, there is an understandable resistance to this historic change from those that occupy that privileged position now. China is fully aware of this tension and can be a strong partner of India in ensuring their rise.

Economic Equality Struggle

If one recognizes the reality of the joint struggle for economic equality, trade and investment relations with China can be seen in a different and more positive light. One would realize that the terms imposed on China for its accession to the World Trade Organisation were unfair. China was forced to give concessions in trade in goods and services which no other developing country did. In areas such as financial services and distribution, Beijing was forced to allow concessions more generous than those given even by developed countries, including the US.

Yet, China will not have market economy status until 2016, which means that a country importing from China does not have to follow the normal WTO rules in bringing anti-dumping action but can use a third-country price to justify such action. The Chinese are justly unhappy about the WTO agreement and in a relationship-based society such as China's this feeling of injustice is likely to affect ground-level implementation of the WTO agreement.

It is widely recognized that India is not yet well positioned to exploit the business opportunities in China. India's current exports to China are dominated by iron ore and other raw materials, which do not provide a basis for long-term sustained growth and are subject to fluctuation even in short and medium term. For India excellent opportunities should open up, particularly in the services sector, including finance, education, health, audit and accounting, legal practice and entertainment.

In addition, India can promote exports in a wide range of goods such as pharmaceuticals, auto and auto parts and engineering goods. But Indian businessmen complain of inadequate trade material available in English and non-transparent rules and regulations on trade and investment practices. The authorities seem to be preoccupied with controlling imports that promoting exports (the good old protectionist mindset).

If the paradigm of joint struggle for economic equality is accepted, the approach to trade relations will be entirely different. Three lines of action are suggested for the government, businesses and academic institutions.

Market Economy Status

First at the government level, unless there is clear evidence that Chinese exports to India or other developing countries are being deliberately under-priced for dumping, India should give market economy status to China. This status is not needed by China to promote its exports: It is doing quite well even with this unfair treatment. Its value is mainly symbolic. But this symbolic move by India will open the doors for other trade and investment negotiations.

Starting with this, India should initiate serious discussions with China for a Comprehensive Economic Partnership agreement along the lines of what has been done with Singapore keeping in mind the broader economic partnership mentioned above. As discussions proceeds, agreements can be signed on specific issues such as information-sharing mutual recognition of professional qualification, agreement on standards, etc.

The government should make a breakthrough in improving connectivity with China by air, sea and land. Over time, as trade in Asia increases, sea-lanes are going to get congested and land routes may provide the more cost-and time-effective alternative. New Delhi should be more supportive of road and rail links between India and China, including those through Nepal and Myanmar.

Need for Export Promotion

For the business world, time has come to recognize the need for export promotion, particularly to a country that is destined to be the largest market. In each of the areas in goods and services where India seems to have market potential in China, a mission should be fielded by the industry concerned to visit China and draw up an action plan for the short, medium and long-term. The vision of a shared economic struggle for peaceful rise of both China and India will help in making these missions more productive.

Last but not the least, the academic community in India should make a determined effort to help business-people learn the Chinese language by starting Chinese language and cultural courses in educational institutions. We are behind in this respect, even in comparison with such English-speaking countries as the US and the UK. With India's experience of relationship-based business operations, it should be realized that we can penetrate the Chinese markets, particularly in people-intensive service sectors, only if we are conversant with the language and culture of our customers.

China and India : The Asian Drivers

R. SESHASAYEE

INTRODUCTION

China and India have witnessed unprecedented economic growth in the last few years and are engaging with each other to cooperate across various sectors including collaboration in the third countries in the energy sector as well as bilateral exchange of scientific and technological research. The collaboration therefore very clearly goes beyond the growing trade flows and has matured in various areas of interest to both nations. Beijing and New Delhi realize the importance of building a strategic partnership for mutual benefit and growth.

Towards Inclusive Growth

The need for building stronger ties comes from the fact that both countries that are witnessing strong growth rates want to ensure inclusive growth for their people. The cross sector linkages between the two nations also make the relationship more stable and meaningful for both sides and reflect the importance of the two countries in the region and the world following sustained economic growth in the two economies for over a decade.

Growth Dynamics

China's economy grew at an average rate of 10% and India's at 6% per annum in the last decade. China's share in world trade increased from 1% in early 1990s to 6% in 2004 and that of India from 0.5% to 1% during the same period. The average annual growth in real GDP and real GDP per capita during 1990-2004 for China was 9.31 and 8.24 per cent, respectively and for India it was 5.71 and 3.90 per cent, respectively. The good macro-economic performance of both countries is expected to continue in the short and medium-terms and real GDP is expected to grow at 9.5 and 9.0 percent, respectively in China and at 7.3 and 7.0 percent, respectively in India during 2006 and 2007, according to the International Monetary Fund.

Building Bilateral Trade

Stronger economic linkages between India and China are evident if one looks at the trade figures in the last decade. Overall trade activity between China and India have gained momentum and bilateral trade between the two countries increased from US$ 1 billion to US $ 14 billion in 10 years. According to the statistics released by Beijing, Sino-Indian trade in first seven month of 2006 reached $ 13.6 billion, an increase of 27% over the same period last year. The trade target of US $ 20 billion by 2008 set by Dr. Manmohan Singh, Prime Minister of India and Mr. Wen Jiabao, Chinese Premier in 2005 may be achieved by the end of this year itself if the present growth momentum is maintained. The trade target of US $ 30 billion by 2010 would also be achieved much ahead of the deadline.

In recent years, to enhance bilateral trade and economic cooperation between the two countries, Confederation of Indian Industry has taken various initiatives like organizing "Made in India" shows (since 2003) in China, CEOs missions, seminars and conferences and interactions with counterpart organizations in China.

Sectors of export from India to China include products of high labour intensity and low capital intensity. Presently, iron ore constitutes majority of India's exports to China. Among the potential exports to China, marine products, oil seeds, salt, inorganic chemicals, plastic, rubber, optical and medical equipment and dairy products are the other important ones. In contrast, China exports almost all types of manufactured products. Value added items dominate Chinese exports to India, especially machinery, including electrical machinery, which together constitute about 40% of exports from that country to India. In view of the dynamic comparative advantage of India, services and knowledge trade between India and China have significant potential for growth in areas like biotechnology, IT and ITES, health, education, tourism and financial sector.

Every year, China and India exchange more than 100 business delegations to seek opportunities for investment. Indian enterprises, including Tatas, Ranbaxy, Bharat Forge, Sundaram Fastners, Mahindras, Infosys and others have already established presence in China. Chinese companies have also set up sub-companies, representative and project offices in India. In April 2006, China and India initiated the Bilateral Investment Promotion and Protection Agreement. It is expected that in the next two decades, the new Asian 'tigers' will be the driving force in global trade, with their combined exports expected to rise to 20% of world exports by 2010 and 30% by 2030.

Need for Greater Linkages

But recognizing the growth influence of India and China around the globe the two countries should build greater linkages across the spectrum. I have the following suggestions for the two countries during the current high-level visit from China:

1. Look at innovative ways of increasing bilateral trade flows by removing non-tariff barriers on all products and services and create a greater market for each other.
2. Build greater linkages between business in China and

India and create a strong platform for exchange of technologies and innovation in manufacturing.

3. Look at new opportunities for third country ventures in different areas.
4. Exchange best practice information on environment protection and conservation methods on both sides.

Finally, it is important to realize that the market potential of the two countries is yet to be fully tapped. Both countries need to promote bilateral trade and put more emphasis on their complementary economies and work together to expand their share of trade in the global markets.

It's time for Asia to Look Beyond the Dollar

Winner of the 2001 Nobel prize for economics, Joseph Stiglitz is a trenchant critic of the "market fundamentalism" of the International Monetary Fund. In an interview in New Delhi recently, he discusses some of the ideas in his latest book, *Making Globalisation Work* (Viking, 2006), including the need for an alternative to the dollar reserve system.

Can Asian countries push the debate by pricing trade, especially natural resources like oil, in currencies other than dollars? Would that provide the critical mass for us to move in the direction of a new system?

It's already happening. The U.S. would like to keep the dollar as the reserve currency, and all the seigniorage. But as it realises it is fighting a losing battle—that people are moving out of the dollar—it will not be able to keep the dollar as the sole reserve currency. So the U.S. may realise that it would benefit from the greater stability that a new system would bring.

Source : *The Hindu*, December 28, 2006.

Appendices

Appendices

Appendix 1

INDIA AND CHINA : MACRO GROWTH INDICATORS

	India	*China*
Growth Rate of GDP (%)	8.3	9.9
Avg. (5 Years) CAGR	6.66	8.92
Goods export growth (%)	27.9	28.4
Avg. (5 Years) CAGR	19.54	25.40
Goods import growth (%)	36.8	17.6
Avg. (5 Years) CAGR	20.38	24.78
Net inward FDI ($ bn)	4.4	60.3
Avg. (5 Years) CAGR	3.50	8.09
Gross forex reserves ($ bn)	137.2	818.9
Avg. (5 Years) CAGR	31.9	40.2

Source : Outlook, June 5, 2006.

Appendix 2

VITAL STATISTICS

	India	*China*
Global Exports (Share)	0.9%	7.2%
Literacy Levels	65%	95%
Life Expectancy	65 Yrs.	71 Yrs.
Global FDI Flows (Share)	0.9%	8.8%

Appendix 3

EXTERNAL ENVIRONMENT
(Annual per cent change unless otherwise noted)

			Projections	
	2003	2004	2005	2006
World output	4.0	5.1	4.3	4.3
Advanced Economies	1.9	3.3	2.5	2.7
United States	2.7	4.2	3.5	3.3
Euro Area	0.7	2.0	1.2	1.8
Japan	1.4	2.7	2.0	2.0
Other Advanced Economies	2.5	4.4	3.2	3.9
Newly Industrialised Asian Economies	3.1	5.6	4.0	4.7
Other Emerging Market and Developing Countries	6.5	7.3	6.4	6.1
Developing Asia	8.1	8.2	7.8	7.2
China	9.5	9.5	9.0	8.2
India	7.4	7.3	7.1	6.3
ASEAN-4*	5.4	5.8	4.9	5.4
Commonwealth of Independent States (CIS)	7.9	8.4	6.0	5.7
Russia	7.3	7.2	5.5	5.3
World Trade Volume (Goods & Services)	5.4	10.3	7.0	7.4
World Trade Prices (in US $ Terms)				
Manufactures	14.4	9.7	6.0	0.5
Oil	15.8	30.7	43.6	13.9
Non-fuel Primary Commodities	6.9	18.5	8.6	-2.1
Emerging Market and Developing Countries :				
Private Capital Flows (net) (in US $ billion)	158.2	232.0	132.9	53.8

* Includes Indonesia, Malaysia, Philippines and Thailand.

Source : World Economic Outlook; September 2005; The International Monetary Fund.

Appendix 4

INDIA'S CURRENT ACCOUNT DEFICIT VIS-A-VIS LEADING SOUTH EAST ASIAN ECONOMIES

The emergence of a widening deficit in India's current account has drawn attention to whether such a deficit is consistent with the BOP trends observed elsewhere in developing Asia. The table below shows the current account deficits, as per cent of GDP, for some select Asian economies:

Current Account Balances as per cent of GDP for Select Asian Economies

Country	*1990*	*1997*	*2005**
China	3.1	3.8	6.1
India	-2.5	-0.7	-1.8
Indonesia	-2.5	-1.6	-0.4
Japan	1.4	2.2	3.3
Korea	-0.8	-1.6	2.0
Malaysia	-2.1	-5.9	13.5
Philippines	-6.1	-5.2	2.1
Singapore	8.4	15.6	25.7
Thailand	-8.3	-2.1	-2.5
Vietnam	-4.0	-6.2	-4.7

Source : World Economic Outlook (WEO), Database, IMF.
*Estimates for 2005 are projections.

In their current accounts, China, Japan, and Singapore have had, not only consistent surpluses but also surpluses that were increasing over time. As far as the other economies are concerned, since the 1997 East Asian crisis, barring India and Thailand, current account balances have either turned positive (e.g. Korea, Malaysia and the Philippines) or in deficit, gone down as a proportion of GDP (e.g. Indonesia and Vietnam). Current account deficits have widened only in India and Thailand.

There is a major difference between the East Asian crisis affected countries pre-1997 and India in recent years. Pre-1997, the crisis-affected countries financed their large current account deficits by short-term debt capital. Under liberal capital account regimes, banks and financial institutions in these economies had mobilized large resources through short term portfolio flows and invested them in highrisk assets. These investments became non-performing after sharp drops in exchange rates and withdrawal of capital flows, triggering financial system collapses. The potential disruptive consequences of the sharp expansion in the capital account appear limited in the case of India because of the calibrated policy followed in liberalizing the capital account and the non-debt nature of the capital flows. Nevertheless, given the marked difference in the current account performance between India and most other economies in the region, there may be a continuing need to maintain a closewatch on the quality of the capital flows financing the current account deficit.

Source : *Economic Survey,* 2005-06, p. 103.

Appendix 5

EXPORT GROWTH AND SHARE IN WORLD EXPORTS OF SELECTED COUNTRIES

Country	*Percentage Growth Rate*				*Share in World Exports*				*Value (US $ billion)*
	1995-01	*2003*	*2004*	*2005**	*2001*	*2003*	*2004*	*2005**	*2004*
1. **China**	12.4	34.5	35.4	32.1	4.3	5.9	6.6	7.2	593.0
2. Hong Kong	3.6	11.9	15.6	11.4	3.1	3.0	2.9	2.8	259.0
3. Malaysia	6.6	6.5	26.5	12.1	1.4	1.3	1.4	1.4	125.7
4. Indonesia	5.7	5.1	11.2	44.6	0.9	0.9	0.8	0.8	71.3
5. Singapore	4.1	15.2	24.5	14.8	2.0	1.9	2.0	2.0	179.6
6. Thailand	5.9	17.1	20.0	12.0	1.1	11	1.1	1.1	96.0
7. **India**	8.5	15.8	25.7	21.0	0.7	0.6	0.8	0.8	71.8
8. Korea	7.4	19.3	30.9	18.1	2.5	2.6	2.8	2.8	254.0
9. Developing Countries	7.9	18.4	27.1	21.2	36.8	38.6	40.7	42.4	3685.1
10. World	5.5	15.9	21.2	14.9	100.0	100.0	190.0	100.0	9049.8

Source : IFS Statistics, IMF. * January-August, 2005.

Appendix 6

INDIA'S MAJOR TRADING PARTNERS, 2000-2005 (Percentage share in Total Trade (Exports+Imports)

Country	2000-01	2002-03	2003-04	2003-04	2004	2005
					April-October	
USA	13.0	13.4	11.6	10.3	11.1	10.0
UK	5.7	4.6	4.4	3.7	3.6	3.7
Belgium	4.6	4.7	4.1	3.7	3.7	3.4
Germany	3.9	4.0	3.8	3.5	3.5	3.6
Japan	3.8	3.2	3.1	2.7	2.6	2.4
Switzerland	3.8	2.4	2.6	3.3	3.2	3.3
Hong Kong	3.7	3.1	3.3	2.8	2.8	3.0
UAE	3.4	3.8	5.1	6.2	5.6	5.4
China	2.5	4.2	4.9	6.4	5.6	6.4
Singapore	2.5	2.5	3.0	3.4	3.3	3.7
Malaysia	1.9	1.9	2.1	1.7	1.9	1.4
Total (1 to 11)	48.6	47.9	48.1	48.0	46.8	46.4

Source : Economic Survey, 2005-2006, p. 114.

Appendix 7

INTERNATIONAL COMPARISON OF TOP TEN DEBTOR COUNTRIES—2003

Sl. No.	*Country*	*Total External Debt (US$ Billion)*	*International Classification*	*Debt Sustainability Indicators*			
				Debt to GNP	*Debt Service*	*Short term debt to total external debt*	*Concessional debt to total debt*
				(ratio as per cent)			
1.	Brazil	235.4	Severe	50	63.8	8.3	1.4
2.	**China**	193.6	Less	15	7.3	37.7	16.8
3.	Russian Feden Hion	175.3	Moderate	50	11.8	17.6	0.8
4.	Mexico	140	Less	23	20.9	6.6	0.9
5.	Argentina	166.2	Severe	104	37.9	13.8	0.8
6.	Indonesia	134.4	Severe	80	26	17	27.4
7.	Turkey	145.7	Severe	77	38.5	15.8	3.5
8.	**Indla***	113.51	Less	22	18.1	4.2	37.8
9.	Poland	95.2	Moderate	49	25.1	20.5	7.1
10.	Philippines	62.7	Moderate	77	22.1	9.9	22.6

*According to World Bank data.

Source : Global Development Finance 2005, The World Bank.

Appendix 8

INDIA'S GLOBAL POSITION IN TERMS OF SOCIO-DEMOGRAPHIC PARAMETERS

Country	*Life expectancy at birth ratio (per (years)*	*Under-five mortality rate (per 1,000 live births)*		*Infant mortality rate (per 1 ,000 live births)*		*Maternal mortality (per 100,000 live births)*
	2000-05	*1990*	*2003*	*1990*	*2003*	*2005*
China	71	49	37	38	30	56
India	63	123	87	80	63	540
Nepal	61	145	82	100	61	740
Pakistan	63	128	103	96	81	500
Sri Lanka	74	23	15	19	13	92
Bangladesh	63	144	69	96	46	380
South Asia	63	126	91	84	66	NA

NA: Not Available.

Source : UNDP, Human Development Report, 2005.

Appendix 9

TOP 15 COUNTRIES IN PCs IN-USE (YEAR-END 2005)

	In Use (mn.)	*Share (%)*
The US	230.4	25.49
Japan	73.66	8.15
China	63.52	7.03
Germany	50.42	5.58
The UK	38.62	4.27
France	32.4	3.58
South Korea	28.38	3.14
Italy	25.96	2.87
Canada	23.77	2.63
Russia	22.76	2.52
Brazil	22.4	2.46
India	16.98	1.88
Australia	14.62	1.62
Mexico	12.79	1.41
Spain	12.01	1.33
Top 15	668.6	73.96
World-wide total	903.9	100

Source : *The Hindu-Business Line*, October 31, 2006.

Appendix 10

TOP 15 COUNTRIES IN INTERNET USAGE (YEAR-END 2005)

	Users (mn.)	*Share (%)*
The US	197.8	18.3
Japan	119.5	11.1
China	86.3	8
Germany	50.6	4.7
The UK	46.3	4.3
France	35.8	3.3
South Korea	33.9	3.1
Italy	28.8	2.7
Canada	28.8	2.7
Russia	25.9	2.4
Brazil	23.7	2.2
India	21.9	2
Australia	18	1.7
Mexico	16.9	1.6
Spain	15.8	1.5
Top 15	750	69.4
World-wide total	1,081	100

Source : *The Hindu-Business Line*, October 31, 2006.

Appendix 11

THE CHINA : FACT FILE

With its 240-million-strong middle class, China accounts for 12% of global demand.

For richer....

- In 2004, purchases of luxury consumer goods exceeded $ 6 billion in China, according to investment banker Goldman Sachs.
- China is the world's third-largest consumer of luxury goods; it accounts for 12% of global demand.
- Chinese purchases of designer handbags, perfumes and watches will grow 25% a year; by 2015, China is widely expected to be the world's biggest consumer of luxury brands.
- China's "consumer (read middle) class" adds up to over 240 million people.
- For China's new-rich, consumption is shifting from a struggle to meet basic needs to a phase where high-end purchases are increasingly affordable.
- Young urban professionals pay big money for branded goods such as Louis Vuitton Bags, Christian Dior perfume and Cartier watches.
- In 2004, Cartier's had two boutiques in China; today, it has 11. By 2010, it will have 30.
- The Asian Development Bank reports that in 2004, urban incomes in China increased 7.7%, against 6.8% in its rural areas.

For poorer....

- The gap between the rich and the poor in China continues to widen.
- A survey by the China Academy of Social Sciences showed that in 2004, the richest 10% of the population earned 2.8 times more than the national average; at the same time, the poorest 10% earned less than a third the national average.

- According to the United Nations Development Programme, the richest 20% of China's population accounts for 50% of total consumption spending; the poorest 20% accounts for only 4.7%.
- China's rich, representing 24% of all urban households in the country, live along the southern Pearl River Delta, in eastern seaports, and in the Yangtze River Delta. In contrast, 76% of China's rural households that lack adequate food or shelter live in mountainous areas.
- The widening income disparity between rural and urban dwellers has led to thousands of public disturbances in China.

China remains a country of low consumption. The nation's consumption-to-gross domestic product ratio was 50% between 1996 and 2004, against the world average of 80%.

Source: *Outlook*, June 5, 2006.

Appendix 12

THE REFORMS SAGA: INDIA AND CHINA

CHINA

1978	:	Dismantled the People's Communes and allotted land to farmers.
1979	:	Set-up Special Economic Zones in Shenzen, Zhuhai, Shantoe and Xiamen to attract foreign direct investments.
1987	:	Contract system launched.
1988	:	Made Hainan island, a province and declared the whole island a SEZ.
1994	:	A single VAT of 17% introduced.
1995	:	Current account convertibility allowed, customs duty reduced.
1999	:	Recapitalisation of banks by creating four AMCs.
2000	:	Individuals allowed to tap the capital market.
2001	:	China becomes a WTO member.
2004	:	Hong Kong banks allowed to accept deposits in Yuan.
2005	:	China revalues its currency after over a decade.

INDIA

1991	:	New Industrial Policy announced; up to 51% foreign direct investment allowed in select industries.
1996	:	Minimum Alternate Tax introduced.
1997	:	Maximum income tax rate cut to 80% and corporate tax to 35%. New takeover code approved.
1999	:	IRDA Bill passed; FERA replaced by FEMA. Department of disinvestment created.
2000	:	SEZ created with 100% foreign equity. Quantitative restrictions on 714 items lifted in the small-scale sector.
2002	:	Full convertibility of deposit schemes for NRIs. Urban Initiative Fund set-up.
2003	:	SPV set up to finance core projects.
2006	:	National Rural Employment Guarantee Scheme launched. The Jawaharlal Nehru National Urban Renewal Mission established.

Appendix 13

GLOBAL GROWTH DYNAMICS
Contribution to Global Growth during 2006-2020 (in %)

China	*US*	*India*	*Brazil*	*Russia*	*Indonesia*	*UK*	*Germany*
26.7	15.9	12.2	2.4	2.3	2.3	1.9	1.9

Appendix 14

LARGEST ECONOMIES
($ billion at PPP)

Rank	*US* (1)	*UK* (6)	*Germany* (5)	*India* (4)	*China* (2)	*Japan* (3)
2005	12,457	1,962	2,426	3,718	8,200	4,008
2020	28,830	4,186	4,857	13,363	29,590	6,795

Source : Economist Intelligence Unit.

Appendix 15

BIG EMPLOYERS
Expected Vacancies in 2005-2020 (%)

India	*China*	*Rest of Asia*	*EU*	*US*	*Latin America*	*Others*
30.2	13.8	23.0	1.8	2.6	9.5	19.1

Appendix 16

INDIA : TRADE BOOM—2004-05

Major Exports to China	*$ Million*	*Share (%)*
Ores, Slag and Ash	2,782.18	52.10
Iron and Steel	617.10	11.50
Plastics and Articles	395.09	7.40
Organic Chemicals	348.32	6.50
Inorganic Chemicals	210.12	3.90

Major Imports from China	*$ Million*	*Share (%)*
Electrical Equipment	1,734.45	25.60
Nuclear Machinery	1,003.02	14.80
Mineral Oils	810.39	12.00
Organic Chemicals	790.21	11.70
Silk	289.11	4.30

Source : *Commerce Ministry*.

Appendix 17

TO SPEND IS GLORIOUS
Share in World Consumer Spending (%)

Year	*US*	*EU*	*Japan*	*China*	*India*
2005	32.5	27.2	9.8	3.3	1.9
2020	30.9	22.3	6.6	8.4	3.1

Source : IMF.

Appendix 18

CHINA ON TOP

	India	*China*
Starting Business	71 Days	48 Days
Registering Property	67 Days	32 Days
Arranging for Funds	90 Days	40 Days
Resolving Insolvency	10 Years	2.4 Years

Appendix 19

SWOT : THE BIG PICTURE

STRENGTH	India has a better regulatory environment and stronger financial system. India, with average age of 24 years against China's 32 years, is younger. India has better corporate governance and offers better returns on investments. India has a better pool of English-speaking workers. Strong services industry.
WEAKNESS	China's GDP per capita is now 2.2 times higher than India's in dollar terms. China has moved ahead of India in all social indicators. China's strong physical infrastructure gives it a substantial cost advantage over India. Infrastructure has made China a more attractive destination for investors.
OPPORTUNITIES	India is promoting private and foreign investments in more sectors. Given the high levels of foreign investments already, China is likely to see its investment ratio decline. India is more advanced in institutional infrastructure. India's financial market is strong, while Chinese banks are burdened with bad loans.
THREATS	The Chinese economy is much more integrated with the world economy through international trade and investment. Manufacturing sector's share in GDP in China is around 35% (India's 16%). China has a good number of "closet billionaires" who can bring much more to the already booming economy.

SWOT : TEXTILES

STRENGTH	India has 25% of the world spinning capacity. High availability of raw materials (in particular, man-made fibres). China heavily depends on imports. Lower labour cost when compared to China. Indian firms are focusing more on value addition, especially in the apparel manufacturing sector.
WEAKNESS	In 2005, the size of textile industry in China was $ 177 billion (66% was exported) and in India it was only $ 46 billion (35% was exported). China recognized the potential of the textile industry at least 20 years ahead of India. Spinning capacity in India is much lower and slower than that in China.
OPPORTUNITIES	Exports to the EU and US have increased 35% and 16% in the post-MFA era. Dereservation of knitting and woven garmenting sectors has made the textile sector more organized. Large investments are taking place in India—a conservative estimate of capital requirement is $ 30 billion or Rs. 140,000 crore.
THREATS	China has highly flexible labour laws compared to the rigid laws in India. Under-valuation of the yuan against dollar will help China to maintain a lead over competing suppliers like India who will be hit by a decline in dollar value. Strong competition from Bangladesh, Pakistan and Sri Lanka in garments.

SWOT : ENGINEERING

STRENGTH	Strong engineering and managerial skills available in the country. Locational advantage—a gateway to Asia. Lavish availability of raw materials. Legal and institutional framework to promote market—based growth. Strong entrepreneurial spirit of the country.
WEAKNESS	Inflexible labour laws put India at a disadvantage in labour-intensive industries. Certain sectors are reserved for SSIs. Lack of R&D in design, product innovation, advance process technology, etc. Poor supply chain. Scale of manufacturing, marketing and branding not impressive enough.
OPPORTUNITIES	Large domestic market-in several sectors India is the second largest market among low-cost countries. MNCs looking for low-cost manufacturing bases. India may emerge as one of the three top engineering goods exporters among low-cost off-shore manufacturers with a target of $ 250-300 billion exports by 2015.
THREATS	China has an advantage in the manufacturing sector. Its productivity is 1.6 times that of India. China has higher domestic consumption. China enjoys a 20-40% cost advantage over India. China has a larger base of engineers vis-a-vis India. Manufacturing rise and fall occur relatively quickly.

SWOT : LEATHER

STRENGTH	India has a strong domestic base for supply of raw leather, while China mostly depends on imports. Average wage level is lower in India ($ 60 a month) than China ($ 80). Average unit value realized by India per pair of footwear exported is $ 11 against China's $ 7 (global average is about $ 6).
WEAKNESS	China has the advantage of world-class infrastructure in especially economic zones with efficient linkage to major cities and ports. China has over 400 special zones to promote the sector against 11 in India. Speedier cargo clearance help China keep its transaction cost at 5-7% against India's 12-15%.
OPPORTUNITIES	The central government is taking initiatives for promoting leather industry and increasing leather exports. Rs. 290 crore sanctioned under Integrated Leather Development Programme for modernization. Some global footwear majors are looking to set up plants in India as China's cheap labour supply dries.
THREATS	China is already a big player in the global arena—it accounts for 22% of total global leather trade. India's leather industry is still small scale in nature and mostly unorganized—over 85% of the units are in the unorganized sector. China has lower import tariff on essential raw materials and inputs.

SWOT : IT & ITES

STRENGTH	India has maintained its cost leadership due to low labour cost—12% of average US hourly labour cost. (It is 19% in China) Largest base of English-speaking IT specialists. A 14-million pool of young university graduates, 1.5 times the size of China's. Conducive policies for BPO and off-shore IT.
WEAKNESS	Of the huge talent pool of English-speaking graduates India boasts of, only 10-20% possess the requisite capabilities expected by the big companies. In the IT hardware space, India scores lower in comparison to China. Comparatively weaker infrastructure in India can be a plus point for China.
OPPORTUNITIES	A McKinsey study shows that customers prefer India to China and Brazil due to superior vendor base even if cost of operations were to exceed 25% of its rivals. India is becoming a major force in complex, high-end and high-margin IT services. India's offshore IT and BPO industries may grow to $ 120-180 billion by 2015.
THREATS	Inadequate talent pool in the long run—only 4% of the graduates are engineers, compared with 20% in Germany and 33% in China. High employee turnover of 15-30% and pay hikes in the range of 12-15% is increasing the cost of labour. Growing competition from emerging markets as-well-as western IT biggies.

Source : *Outlook* June 5, 2006.

Appendix 20

HEALTH EXPENDITURE AND HEALTH INDICATORS IN SELECTED COUNTRIES

HDI Rank	*Country*	*Health expenditure as % of GDP (2001)*		*Per capita expenditure on health (PPP in $)*	*Out-of pocket expenditure as % of private expenditure (2001)*	*Life expectancy at birth (2001)*	*Infant mortality rate per 1000 live births (2001)*	*Per capita GDP ($) (2001)*
1	Norway	6.9	1.2	2,920	96.8	78.7	4	36974
7	The US	6.2	7.7	4887	26.5	76.9	7	34946
9	Japan	6.2	1.8	2,131	74.9	81.3	3	32540
13	The UK	6.2	1.4	1989	55.3	77.9	6	24186
52	Cuba	6.2	1	229	76.8	76.5	7	2234
58	Malaysia	2.1	1.8	345	92.8	72.8	8	3748
65	Brazil	3.2	4.4	573	64.1	67.8	31	2888
89	Azerbaijan	1.1	0.5	48	97.7	71.8	77	679
99	Sri Lanka	1.8	1.9	122	95	72.3	17	849
104	**China**	2	3.4	224	95.4	70.6	31	918
127	**India**	0.9	4.2	80	100	63.3	67	462
144	Pakistan	1	3	85	100	60.4	84	401
169	Ethiopia	14	2.1	14	84.7	45.7	116	93

Source : *The Hindu Business Line*, 2006.

Appendix 21

INDIAN, CHINESE FIRMS TOP "BRIBE PAYERS" INDEX

India and China top a list of 30 countries whose firms are most willing to pay brides to do business abroad, according to a survey by Transparency International (TI), an anti-corruption group. They are followed by Russia, Turkey and Taiwan—in that order. Britain is the sixth on the "Bribe Payers' Index," while the U.S. shares the ninth place with Belgium. French and Italian firms are among the "worst culprits" for paying bribes in low-income countries to gain business opportunities, the survey said. TI said its index was based on responses from more than 11,000 business people in 125 countries.

"The enforcement record on international anti-bribery laws makes for short and disheartening reading," said TI chief executive David Nussbaum. The countries whose firms were least prepared to pay bribes included Switzerland, Sweden, Australia, Austria, and Canada. TI said it focused on firms from the 30 biggest exporting nations, which among them accounted for more than 80 per cent of all world exports. "It is hypocritical that OECD-based companies continue to bribe across the globe, while their governments pay lip-service to enforcing the law," Mr. Nussbaum said.

Source : *The Hindu,* October 5, 2006.

Appendix 22

TRANSPARENCY INTERNATIONAL 2006 BRIBE PAYERS INDEX

Following is a table ranking exporting countries according to the likelihood of firms headquartered there to engage in bribery while doing business abroad. The higher the score, the less likely a company from that country will offer bribes or undocumented payments. Respondents answer on a scale of 1 to 7 where the former indicates bribes are common, to the latter where bribes never occur. Results are then converted to a score from 0 to 10.

S. No.	*Country*	*Average Score*	*S. No.*	*Country*	*Average Score*
1.	Switzerland	7.81	16.	Portugal	6.47
2.	Sweden	7.62	17.	Mexico	6.45
3.	Australia	7.59	18.	Hong Kong	6.01
4.	Austria	7.50	19.	Israel	6.01
5.	Canada	7.46	20.	Italy	5.94
6.	UK	7.39	21.	South Korea	5.83
7.	Germany	7.34	22.	Saudi Arabia	5.75
8.	Netherlands	7.28	23.	Brazil	5.65
9.	Belgium	7.22	24.	South Africa	5.61
10.	US	7.22	25.	Malaysia	5.59
11.	Japan	7.10	26.	Taiwan	5.41
12.	Singapore	6.78	27.	Turkey	5.23
13.	Spain	6.63	28.	Russia	5.16
14.	United Arab Emirates	6.62	29.	**China**	4.94
15.	France	6.50	30.	**India**	4.62

Source : *The Edge*, Singapore, October 9, 2006.

Appendix 23

INDIA LOSING BATTLE AGAINST HUNGER
India Ranks 3rd from Bottom of World List of Malnourished Kids

Yet another report confirms India's losing battle against hunger. In the Global Hunger Index, India ranks 117th for the prevalence of underweight children. Only Bangladesh and Nepal are worse-off. The proportion of children found underweight in India, according to the latest figures is 47.5 percent, which makes it worse than conflict-plagued, drought-stricken sub-Saharan Africa, where the figure is some 30 percent on average. India's figure is also worse than that of individual sub-Saharan countries.

These findings are from a report released by the Washington—based International Food Policy Research Institute (IFPRI). The Global Hunger Index combines three indicators: Child malnutrition, child mortality, and estimates of the proportion of people who are calorie-deficient. The index has been calculated for 1981, 1992, 1997, and 2003. The latest round ranks 119 countries, of which 97 are deemed "developing" and 22 "in transition."

Speaking to 'Express' on phone from Washington, the report's lead author Doris Wiesmann said the two major factors for India's low ranking were that per capita food availability did not increase from 1997 onward, and that child malnutrition rates remained at very high levels, with more than 46 percent of children under five years being underweight. India is a different story from Sub-Saharan Africa. A higher proportion of the population (33 percent) is calorie-deficient there than in India (21 percent) or South Asia as a whole (22 percent).

The sub-text to India's dismal showing is malnutrition in children under five. "Mothers, who are usually children's primary caretakers, and their education, nutritional knowledge, well-being and status in families and communities are particularly important in this respect," said Wiesmann. The results are a direct fallout of the low status of women in Indian society, several earlier studies have pointed out. "In India, women eat the 'last and the least, increasing the chances of anaemia", she explained.

This practice partly explain why 83 percent of women in India suffer from iron deficiency anaemia, as opposed to about 40 percent in sub-Saharan Africa. Not surprisingly, one-third of the babies born in India are born with low birth weight, compared to one-sixth in sub-Saharan Africa. "It has been observed that the women who have a say in the family, allocate more resources to their children's nutritional needs. Men have other priorities", she said.

There have been other studies that have explained India's presence as a hotspot despite its growing GDP. Lisa Smith, a IFPRI research fellow, and Usha Ramakrishnan, Associate Professor at Emory University, identified three factors contributing to the nutritional status gap between South Asia and sub-Saharan Africa in a recent study. The first, making by far the greatest contribution among the three, is women's status, followed by sanitation and urbanization.

Source : *The New Sunday Express*, October 15, 2006.

Appendix 24

INHERENT CHALLENGES IN CHINA

Should the State—Owned Town and Village Enterprises (TVEs) collapse, the entire social security net, and thus the social fabric of rural China would come under the threat of collapse. Critics of China's recent economic policies suggest that this collapse is inevitable. Again the ability of the state to sustain itself in the face of such a meltdown in the absence of democracy, or other institutions to mediate conflict, is questionable.

We can therefore expect two different and greatly divergent forms of pressure leading to a possible crisis in the Chinese political system. The first will come from the increasingly prosperous middle class, which wants greater freedom in personal and political choice. And the second may come from the rural majority, which could actually see its standard of living decline should the traditional system of rural industrialization, via the TVEs, so critical for employment and well-being in rural China, collapse. Inequality in China is already very high. Any dramatic economic change could hasten a rebellion from the poor.

The Chinese political system has to its credit consistently shown itself to be very competent in building infrastructure, both physical and social, attracting investment and achieving high rates of economic growth. Its ability to manage social conflict and changing societal demands, however, is less tested.

—Dhiraj Nayyar
Scholar in Economics at Trinity College, Cambridge.

Source : *The New Indian Express,* November 18, 2006.

Appendix 25

INDIA-CHINA TRADE CAN DOUBLE TO $ 30 BILLION BY 2009

Indo-China trade is poised for a major leap forward and has the potential to double from the current level of $ 15 billion to $ 30 billion by 2009. It could be achieved if vigorous efforts are made by both sides and new products are identified for trade, according to industry chamber FICCI.

In a paper on deepening the economic engagement between the two countries, it is highlighted that the key items of India's exports to China in 2004-05 included ores, slag and ash, iron and steel, plastics and articles thereof, organic and inorganic chemicals.

Further, India's exports to China are highly concentrated as top three export items accounted for 71 per cent of total exports and top five export items accounted for 81.4 per cent in 2004 – 3005, according to the paper.

On the other hand, India's imports from China present a balanced picture with both resources based and manufactured products listed in the top 10 imports. The key items of India's imports from China in 2004-05 included electrical machinery and equipment, nuclear reactors; mineral fuels and products; organic chemicals and silk.

Recommendations: *To grow the Indo-China trade further, the chamber recommends India to capitalize on the growing demand of construction industry in China for products like iron ore, slag, ash, plastic and linoleum. While the demand for specialty steel is strong in China, both due to the booming housing industry construction, China is also emerging as a big importer of aluminium, especially for its communication and transport infrastructure.*

The chamber also notes that the restructuring of China's textile sector could result in new opportunities for increasing exports of cotton yarn and fabrics to China. East China possesses the ability to complete in the market for international high quality textile garment and middle processing technology.

Source : *The Hindu Business Line*, November 13, 2006.

Appendix 26

CHINA'S EMPOWERED MIDDLE CLASS

The rising economy in China will lift hundreds of million of households out of poverty. Today 77 per cent of urban Chinese households live on les than 25,000 renminbi a year (100,000 renminbi is about $ 12,500). We estimate that by 2025 that figure will drop to 10 per cent. By then, urban households in China will make up one of the largest consumer markets in the world, spending about 20 trillion renminbi annually.

As this economic tide rises, we anticipate two phases of steep growth in the middle class. The first wave, in 2010, will be the lower middle class, defined as households with annual incomes of 25,001 to 40,000 renminbi. A decade later the upper middle class, with annual household incomes of 40,001 to 100,000 renminbi, will follow.

By around 2011 the lower middle class will number some 290 million people, representing the largest segment in urban China and accounting for about 44 per cent of the urban population, according to our model. Growth in this group should peak around 2015, with a total spending power of 4.8 trillion renminbi.

A second transition is projected to occur in the following decade, when hundreds of millions will join the upper middle class. By 2025 this segment will comprise a staggering 520 million people—with a combined total disposable income of 13.3 trillion renminbi.

The biggest opportunity for companies selling mass-consumer goods and services will be this newly empowered middle class. To serve these households successfully, companies will need to understand how the saving and spending patterns of consumers change as their incomes increase.

—Diana Farrell, Ulrich A. Gersch & Elizabeth Stephenson

Source : *The Hindu Business Line,* November 12, 2006.

Appendix 27

WORRIES ABOUT INDIA – CHINA ECONOMIC TIES

Trade between India and China is set to cross the $ 20 billion mark by the end of this year. But recent moves to subject Chinese investments to special security clearances have come as a dampener.

The overall positive assessment of the India-China relationship in the new century has largely been sustained by the booming bilateral trade. Bilateral trade is set to cross the $ 20 billion mark by the end of this year and steady streams of business delegations have begun to cross the border with an eye to investment. To some analysts this is proof that Bangalore and Shanghai rather than New Delhi and Beijing will shape the future of relations between two of the world's fastest growing economies.

But the continuing restrictions on Chinese investments and the proposal to make these restrictions official policy are testament to the limits of bilateral economic cooperation in the absence of a final boundary settlement. While burgeoning trade has helped provide momentum to the sweetening of relations on the political front, economic engagement can never be truly unfettered until full normalization of political ties is complete, including a boundary settlement.

—Pallavi Aiyar

Source : *The Hindu,* November 10, 2006.

Appendix 28

THREATS AND OPPORTUNITIES

Threat 1—Software/BPO

China can compete with India

- Attempts by China to increase its English-speaking population.
- Lower salaries in China, even as India's rising by 15-25% every year.
- Higher productivity among Chinese workers, willing to work longer hours.
- 40% of Indian software exports will be from bases in China.

Threat 2—Manufacturing

China's dominant global share in many areas

- China has scale; India has to opt for niche, but value-added products.
- Cheap inputs like manpower, energy in China give it a cost edge.
- China operates at several price points, from the lowest to the highest.

Threat 3—Bilateral Trade

China has a Surplus Balance

- India's exports basket is small; 5 commodities comprise 81.5%.
- China's exports basket consists of technology-based items.
- These include more value-added electrical/electronic products.
- FTA between the two will favour China more than India.

Threat 4—Energy

China's more Intent on Gobbling Overseas Fields

- China's state firms much bigger than ONGC Videsh in terms of financial resources.
- China has a first-mover advantage globally; it also uses its diplomatic clout in many deals.
- China's more aggressive in the bidding process; it links its cash deal with defence supplies.

In conclusion, let's not leave with a bad feeling that India can never compete on an equal footing. Our services sector may still hit back by climbing-up the value ladder, and re-outsourcing low-value work to China. The manufacturing segment may yet develop scale and skills to become global players in auto components and pharma. As she happened in the recent past, India may strike fresh domestic finds to fulfill energy needs. 'Made in India' products may still create a global buzz. Finally, India may just climb onto another futuristic bus, become the sort of knowledge economy that no one can be like. It's all in the realms of possibility.

—Arindam Mukherjee, Shuchi Srivastava & Alam Srinivas

Source: *Outlook*, November 27, 2006.

Appendix 29

INDIA AND CHINA: STRATEGY AND AGREEMENTS

Joint Declaration, November 21, 2006, New Delhi

The Ten Point Strategy

- Comprehensive development of bilateral ties.
- Strengthening institutional linkages and dialogue.
- Consolidating commercial and economic exchanges.
- Expanding all round mutually beneficial cooperation.
- Instilling mutual trust through defence cooperation.
- Seeking early settlement of Outstanding issues.
- Promoting trans-border connectivity.
- Boosting cooperation in science and technology.
- Revitalising cultural ties and people-to-people exchanges.
- Expanding cooperation on regional and international stage.

Agreements Signed

- Consulate General at Guangzhou and Kolkata.
- Cooperation between the MEAs of India and china.
- Shanghai Consulate General.
- Promotion and protection of Investments.
- Iron ore inspection.
- Phytosanitary requirement for rice export.
- Cooperation in agricultural research.
- Exchange programme in education.
- Commodity Futures Regulatory Cooperation.
- Cooperation between IIPA and Party School of the Central Committee of China.
- Forestry Cooperation.
- Conservation of Cultural Heritage.
- Prevention of theft and illegal import of cultural property.

Source : *The New Indian Express,* November 22, 2006.

Appendix 30

INDIA, CHIN CHIN

Progress can be achieved faster only by commanding the trend of history. Once it's understood that the Sino-India cooperation benefits rather than harms the two peoples, the two countries will speed up the process. India and China are two advanced and ancient civilizations. In the past century, though, they were both suppressed, inclined to harbouring suspicions in situations new to them. This isn't surprising for newly decolonised countries. But now it's time both India and China face each other with renewed confidence. Interaction between them, rather than distancing themselves from each other, will provide them with far more common interests to cooperate upon thana now. When 1.3 billion people can get along with 1 billion in Asia, the world is bound to be more peaceful—and also hopeful.

—Dingli Shen, Directo of the Center for American Studies at Fudan University, Shanghai

Source : *Outlook*, November 27, 2006.

Index